The People Choose
a President

Harold Mendelsohn
Garrett J. O'Keefe

The Praeger Special Studies program—utilizing the most modern and efficient book production techniques and a selective worldwide distribution network—makes available to the academic, government, and business communities significant, timely research in U.S. and international economic, social, and political development.

The People Choose a President

Influences on Voter Decision Making

PRAEGER SPECIAL STUDIES IN U.S. ECONOMIC, SOCIAL, AND POLITICAL ISSUES

Praeger Publishers   New York   Washington   London

Library of Congress Cataloging in Publication Data

Mendelsohn, Harold A
    The people choose a President.

    (Praeger special studies in U.S. economic, social, and political issues)
    Bibliography: p.
    1. Presidents—United States—Election—1972. 2. Voting—Summit Co., Ohio. 3. Public opinion—Ohio—Summit Co. I. O'Keefe, Garrett J., joint author. II. Title.
JK526 1972. M45   329'.023'730924   75-23983
ISBN 0-275-56110-0

PRAEGER PUBLISHERS
111 Fourth Avenue, New York, N.Y. 10003, U.S.A.

Published in the United States of America in 1976
by Praeger Publishers, Inc.

Printed in the United States of America

ACKNOWLEDGMENTS

Many persons and organizations proved indispensable in the conduct of the research reported here. First and foremost, the authors thank the Columbia Broadcasting System, Inc., and in particular its Office of Social Research, directed by Dr. Joseph T. Klapper, for the generous funding of this project. Special gratitude is expressed for the complete freedom given by the sponsor in the performance of all of the research under the grant. Moreover, Dr. Klapper and his associate, Helen Roberts, did a superlative job of smoothing the administrative and technical hurdles invariably involved in an undertaking such as this.

Marketing Research of Cleveland, Inc., served very capably as subcontractor for the mammoth and complex field data-gathering exercise required—including sampling, interviewing, and preliminary preparation of data recovered from the more than 7,000 interviews conducted. MRC's staff, under the professional and highly efficient supervision of Clark Zimmerman and Kay Strauss, performed their tasks with exceptional dispatch.

Special thanks for their assistance are due to Dr. Ira Cisin of George Washington University, who very helpfully consulted on sample-design problems, and Dr. Sidney Kraus of Cleveland State University, who aided in background research on the political environment of Summit County in 1972 and who assisted in fieldwork supervision.

The University of Denver Computing Center is thanked for its assistance and cooperation in data analysis. Project research assistant Jenny Liu did an outstanding job of supervising data analysis, and also made numerous substantive, as well as methodological, contributions to the study. We also thank Susan Lynn Mendelsohn for highly competent research assistance and tabular data preparation. Jane O'Keefe deserves special gratitude for the extensive, well-handled content analysis of open-ended interview data, and for the final preparation of this manuscript. Marcia Grad is thanked for an excellent job in expediting earlier reports of this research, assisted by Pat Reichert, Gwen Mooney, and Polly Rossie.

Finally, to the hundreds of Summit County, Ohio, residents who participated in this study, we are most grateful for their time and extraordinary cooperation.

CONTENTS

Chapter   Page

LIST OF TABLES

xi

LIST OF FIGURES

THE INFLUENCES
OF SOCIOLOGICAL,
PSYCHOLOGICAL, AND
POLITICAL DISPOSITIONS
ON VOTER DECISION-MAKING

Several kinds of influences are typically brought to bear on voter decision-making during election campaigns. This book attempts to delineate some of those influences and to describe their impacts on how voters chose candidates in the 1972 presidential contest between George McGovern and Richard Nixon. The first half of the book deals primarily with the sociological, psychological, and political dispositions voters brought with them into the campaign arena. These dispositions—including age, sex, race, income, education, occupation, party, and feelings about political issues—are described in terms of their apparent impacts on vote decisions. Whom did Summit County voters of diverse background characteristics end up choosing, McGovern or Nixon? When did they decide? And why did they choose as they did?

The second part of the book concerns how these diverse groups of voters used the 1972 campaign and reacted to it as an ongoing event. Specifically, how did the campaign, and in particular campaign communications media, influence vote choices?

If the research conducted over the past four decades has taught us anything, it is that the influences on vote decision-making are neither monomorphic nor readily discernible. Nor do social science theories regarding the alleged roles of such diverse phenomena as perception and learning, selective exposure, cognitive dissonance, two-step flow, or demographic and partisan attributes in determining voting choices explain in full the processes by which voters eventually make those choices. In the same vein, the speculative observations of journalists and political writers on the campaign trail who accord influential "conversion" weightings to this or that event remain nothing more than speculative observations. At best they may serve to generate a few hypotheses regarding what may or may not be influencing vote choices, but rarely do they point to empirically grounded cases of actual influence in terms of causing significant shifts of preferences from one candidate to the other.

Tracing the wide array of influences affecting vote decisions requires exploration of the vote decision process along with an examination of what is meant by "influence." It also demands isolating how variables relating to demography, political values and behaviors, mass media attitudes and habits, reactions to political issues, imagery, and events, and interpersonal communication patterns serve to affect vote decisions, either singly or, more importantly, in various combinations.

Consequently, we present our discussion of influence from several differing perspectives. We attempt to do this by offering two bodies of data: one a description of the voting behavior of Summit County's electorate, and the other a discussion of how those votes came about. Among the key findings are the following:

1. Demographic characteristics of voters were extremely weak predictors of vote choices overall, yet socioeconomics served to distinguish McGovern voters from Nixon voters across the board.
2. Voters' stands on political issues, together with their perceptions of images of candidates, predicted their candidate preferences. No dichotomy of issues versus images in predictive ability was found.
3. The better educated the voters were, the more interested they were in the 1972 campaign; and the more interested they were, the more likely they were to be exposed to campaign media and to become active participants in the campaign. This is in direct challenge to the "narcotizing dysfunction" concept.
4. Voters who anticipated being influenced by the media in their vote choices were more likely to report actually having been influenced during the campaign.
5. Voters more likely to report having been influenced during the campaign were those who more often anticipated being influenced, were more interested in the campaign, and had a more difficult time deciding upon a candidate. Attentiveness to the campaign and exposure to campaign media content were comparatively weak predictors of influence. In general, influence appears more determined by the gratifications for which voters depended upon campaign media than by simple exposure or attention to media. Of course, media exposure and attention remain as necessary conditions for influence to occur, and media content factors may well affect the direction and intensity of influence.

6. Selective exposure to campaign news and advertising media no longer seems to apply with regard to contemporary political contests. Democrats and Republicans were almost equally aware of each other's political communications. In the age of television there is no place to hide from the opposition.
7. Although large numbers of voters were aware of 1972's journalistic blockbusters—the Eagleton resignation and the Watergate break-in disclosures—only a handful reported that their vote decisions had been changed by either event. Two conclusions emerge: individual campaign "events" by themselves produce little change in vote decisions, and exposure is not equated with effect.
8. A persistent subset of up to 20 percent of the electorate indicated that their vote choices in 1972 had indeed been influenced by the media. A relatively small subset (less than 5 percent, mostly young, first-time voters) offered any evidence regarding the intervention of "personal influence" as a factor in their decision-making. Here we have a significant challenge to the "two-step flow" hypothesis.

THE SETTING: SUMMIT COUNTY, OHIO

Summit County stands joined to, yet apart from, the growing belt of industrialization wrapped around the south shores of the Great Lakes. The county's seat and urban center, Akron, straddles rolling hills some 40 miles south of Cleveland: too close to escape the mechanized, smoke-drenched climate of the Lake Erie docks, but far enough away to be a city unto itself. Between Akron and Cleveland, and indeed making up the bulk of the 413 square miles of Summit County, are open woodlands, lush green in summer and primitive in winter, punctuated by isolated houses and small communities like Fairlawn, Cuyahoga Falls, and Northfield. Interstate 80 bisects the northern half of the county; and interstate highways likewise link Akron with Cleveland and Canton to the south, and Youngstown to the east. The locale is readily accessible by regional trunk air services through the Akron-Canton Airport; and transcontinental flights are available through Cleveland's Hopkins Airport, less than an hour's drive away. Akron is regarded as a major industrial transportation area as well, being served by five railroads and nearly 200 motor carrier services.

The authors thank Dr. Sidney Kraus of Cleveland State University for assistance in the preparation of this section.

It is the commercial center for most of the county. Modern shopping centers dot the outskirts of the city; and the downtown district ("Main Street") is still relatively thriving, with its fair share of major department stores and specialty shops mixed in among the municipal and county offices, hotels, and the like. Summit County had a population of 575,290 in 1972, with over half of the residents living in Akron.

Tourist handbooks readily tell that Akron was founded in 1825; that the name comes from the Greek akros, or "high point"; and that it rapidly became a major manufacturing center thanks to the Ohio Canal, which ran through the town. The city lays claim to being the birthplace of the trucking industry, and more importantly to being the "Rubber Capital of the World." It houses such giants of the rubber manufacturing world as Firestone, General, Goodrich, Goodyear, Mohawk, and Seiberling, all of which pump more than $6 billion annually into the nation's economy. With four of these corporations—Firestone, General, Goodrich, and Goodyear—maintaining their international headquarters in Akron, the city gains not only a monumental economic asset but also more of the cultural amenities than are usually found in cities of under 300,000 population.

Apart from the usual movie houses, restaurants, community theater productions, and the like, cultural and entertainment activities in Akron typically include sports. Each year rather well-known sporting events take place in Akron, including the All-American Soap Box Derby, the American Golf Classic, the World Series of Golf, the CBS Golf Tournament, and the Firestone Tournament of Champions. These contests are well attended by local folk as well as by tourists and sports enthusiasts; they are heavily endorsed and supported by local industries.

Politically, the industrial center of Akron and its attendant Democratic sympathies clearly dominate the Republican minority who permeate the outer suburbs and rural tracts of the county. The pattern is not unlike that found in nearby Cleveland, which dominates Cuyahoga County with even greater strength and rigidity. Summit County has traditionally given a decisive edge to Democratic candidates in local and national elections. Since 1940, only in the Eisenhower landslide of 1956 and in President Nixon's crushing national victory in 1972 did Republican presidential candidates carry the county. Indeed, Nixon's 1972 win in Summit County was by a scant 51-49 percent margin, hardly approaching the 61 percent edge he attained nationally. The history of presidential voting is shown by Table 1.1.

Politics of the county also are influenced externally by state political organizations, and internally by the strong centering of labor unions in and around Akron. One important aspect of state influence can be traced to an election law that requires a man and a woman from

TABLE 1.1

Votes for Presidential Candidates in Summit County and Ohio, 1940-72

Year	Candidates	Summit County	Ohio
1940	Wendell Willkie (R)	63,405	1,586,773
	Franklin Roosevelt (D)	89,555	1,733,139
1944	Thomas E. Dewey (R)	64,696	1,582,293
	Franklin Roosevelt (D)	90,783	1,570,763
1948	Thomas E. Dewey (R)	60,174	1,445,684
	Harry S. Truman (D)	78,096	1,452,791
	Henry Wallace (Progressive)	2,796	37,596
1952	Dwight Eisenhower (R)	91,168	2,100,391
	Adlai Stevenson (D)	97,443	1,600,367
1956	Dwight Eisenhower (R)	102,872	2,262,610
	Adlai Stevenson (D)	93,378	1,439,655
1960	Richard M. Nixon (R)	109,066	2,217,611
	John F. Kennedy (D)	110,852	1,944,248
1964	Barry Goldwater (R)	68,000	1,470,865
	Lyndon B. Johnson (D)	142,319	2,498,331
1968	Richard M. Nixon (R)	82,649	1,791,014
	Hubert H. Humphrey (D)	100,068	1,700,586
	George Wallace (Am. Indep.)	26,157	467,495
1972	Richard M. Nixon (R)	111,812	2,454,324
	George S. McGovern (D)	108,263	1,523,716
	John Schmitz (Am. Indep.)	3,946	80,409

each congressional district to be elected directly in the primary to form the state Democratic and Republican committees. These elected members have not always been in accord with their party representatives on the county level. In fact, the relationship between the Democratic State Committee and the Democratic committees within the counties has become so strained over the years that the county chairmen formed a separate statewide group, the Democratic County Chairmen's Committee. Republicans in Ohio traditionally have been better organized and better financed than Democrats, at both state and local levels.

        Major unions within Summit County included the Akron Labor
Council of the AFL-CIO, the largest, with 35,000 members; the Teamsters Union; the United Auto Workers (UAW); the Allied Chemical
Union Local #1; and the American Federation of State, County, and
Municipal Employees (AFSCME). The Akron Labor Council did not
endorse any presidential candidate in 1972.
        The July 1972 edict by George Meany and the National Executive
Committee of the AFL-CIO withholding support from any presidential
candidate significantly decreased Summit County union activities in
the 1972 presidential race. Under Rule Four of the AFL-CIO bylaws,
all locals except the internationals are mandated to follow policies
set by the National Executive Committee. Frank King, president of
the AFL-CIO in Ohio, abided by Rule Four, as did Phil Leonard, the
Akron Labor Council's executive secretary and treasurer. Therefore,
the political action arm of the AFL-CIO, the Committee of Political
Education (COPE), which usually supports Democratic candidates with
substantial funding, manpower, and literature, was virtually inactive
in the county as far as the presidential contest was concerned.
        However, the AFL-CIO local chapter of the International Rubber
Union, not constrained by Rule Four, endorsed McGovern, as did the
UAW and AFSCME. The Teamsters supported Nixon.
        There can be little doubt that Meany's negative statement played
an important role in the political activity of the unions in the county.
Two instances of the effect of the Meany edict and Rule Four are
illustrative:

- Twenty percent of the Akron Labor Council (AFL-CIO) was
  made up of black members. When Kenneth A. Richards,
  chairman of the Black Political Awareness Coalition, sought
  support from the Council, certain conditions were set because
  PAC was endorsing McGovern. The Council paid for two
  printings of 60,000 pieces of literature and for rent and phones,
  with the understanding that PAC would not display presidential
  material in their offices or in their literature, and would not
  talk about presidential candidates over the phone. Leonard got
  assurances from PAC lawyers that they were abiding by
  these conditions.
- McGovern workers wanted to use the 35,000-name membership list of the Akron Labor Council, but Leonard would not
  allow it.

Most of the Democratic candidates seeking county and state offices
were supported by unions and were elected. Representative John
Seiberling, congressional candidate from the district including Summit
County and an incumbent Democrat of liberal cloth, won handily over

his Republican opponent. Of the several issues on the November ballot, by far the most publicized was State Issue No. 2, which would, in effect, have repealed the state income tax. The issue was not supported by the unions, and it was defeated in the county as well as in the state.

Other politically active special interest groups were the NAACP, which tacitly endorsed McGovern; the League of Women Voters, which was active and, as usual, nonpartisan; and various student groups, especially at the University of Akron, which were active for McGovern early in the campaign but whose support diminished toward the end.

Even in a campaign noted for its lackluster quality on both sides, Ohio kept up its tradition of volatile, or at least relatively active, election campaigns. Both presidential candidates paid major attention to the state, McGovern seeing it as one of the handful he must win if he was to have any hope of carrying the nation. Ohio was also one of the few states receiving a personal campaign appearance from President Nixon. Summit County was as closely attended to by the candidates as any other sector of Ohio, for political mythology has it that if one is to carry Ohio, one must win in Summit County.

McGovern "opened" his national campaign with the traditional Labor Day speech at a UAW picnic at Barberton, just southwest of Akron. In ensuing weeks, he returned to Cleveland and other nearby areas. Democratic vice-presidential nominee Sargent Shriver and Senator Edward Kennedy each made major speeches in Akron, focusing upon McGovern's commitments to labor. While no prominent Nixon "surrogates" made campaign appearances in Summit County itself, the President toured between Akron and Cleveland on October 28, stopping for occasional encounters with the scattered but enthusiastic crowds.

Residents of the county received most of the news about the 1972 presidential campaign from the daily evening newspaper, the Akron Beacon Journal, and from four network-affiliated television stations reaching Akron. The Beacon Journal, owned by the Knight chain but with considerable autonomy in editorial policy, averaged a circulation of 185,000. It presented its readers with quite adequate coverage of national political news, drawing much copy from the Washington Post-Los Angeles Times wire service, including the early Watergate revelations, which were given high play in the paper. Owner John Knight editorialized strong criticisms of the Eagleton matter and Nixon's handling of Watergate, and stated that he would not vote for either candidate; publisher Perry Morgan supported Nixon "reluctantly."

For television coverage Summit County residents relied primarily upon six stations located in Cleveland, including major American Broadcasting Company, Columbia Broadcasting System, and National Broadcasting Company affiliates. An ultrahigh frequency station, also an ABC affiliate located in Akron, provided most of the county with the clearest signal and also the greatest amount of community news coverage.

Four AM radio stations were situated in Akron; and numerous other radio signals were available from Cleveland, Canton, and other nearby cities.

It was in this setting that this investigation of influences on voter decision-making during the 1972 presidential election campaign was carried out.

THE 1972 SUMMIT COUNTY PRESIDENTIAL ELECTION STUDY

The basic research strategy for this study was to investigate the sociopsychological, interpersonal, and mass communications-related processes involved in voter decision-making during the campaign leading up to the 1972 presidential election. The basic research design involved a panel technique and called for initial interviews with a systematic random sample of 1,965 eligible voters in Summit County in late July 1972, followed by a series of monthly interviews with a subgroup of the larger pool before and immediately following the November election. All in all, members of the panel subgroup were interviewed five times: in late July, following the Democratic National Convention; in late August, following the Republican National Convention; in mid-September, as the "formal" campaigns were getting under way; in late October, during the heat of the race; and immediately after Election Day. A full description of sampling technique and a description of the panel and other subsamples appear in Appendix A.

This book focuses on only the 618 panel respondents interviewed in all five waves who actually voted for either George McGovern or Richard Nixon. While it was not a goal of this research to examine a sample validly generalizable to Summit County, there is no particular reason to believe that the subsample of 618 voters is atypical of Summit County voters.

The presentations of data that follow attempt to summarize key findings of the research. Extended tabular presentations of many of the results are available from the authors upon request. It should be noted that in some cases, percentage totals may not add to 100 due to rounding error. Also, where statistical levels of significance are reported, the intent is to describe more clearly the relative strength of relationships between variables, and not to test hypotheses. All

FIGURE 1.1

General Design of the Study

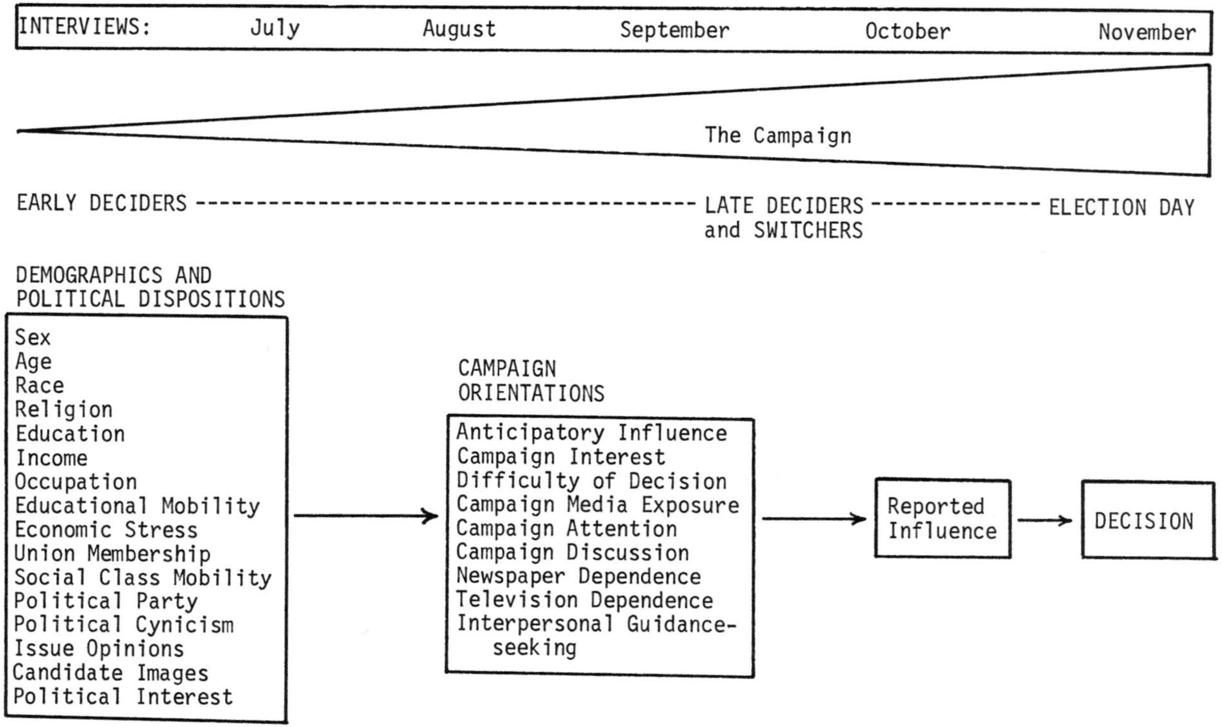

INTERVIEWS: July   August   September   October   November

The Campaign

EARLY DECIDERS -- LATE DECIDERS ------------- ELECTION DAY
                                                        and SWITCHERS

DEMOGRAPHICS AND
POLITICAL DISPOSITIONS

Sex
Age
Race
Religion
Education
Income
Occupation
Educational Mobility
Economic Stress
Union Membership
Social Class Mobility
Political Party
Political Cynicism
Issue Opinions
Candidate Images
Political Interest

CAMPAIGN
ORIENTATIONS

Anticipatory Influence
Campaign Interest
Difficulty of Decision
Campaign Media Exposure
Campaign Attention
Campaign Discussion
Newspaper Dependence
Television Dependence
Interpersonal Guidance-
     seeking

Reported
Influence

DECISION

11

measures and indices of variables described appear in Appendix B.

A schema outlining the study appears in Figure 1.

2

THE ELECTORATE:
A PROFILE

Political scientist John G. Stewart has observed:

> It is doubtful that a person's demographic characteristics
> (for example, age, income level, education, place of
> residence, etc.) are necessarily the key to his voting
> behavior in any given election, except as the issues or
> choice of candidates in the election relate directly to
> specific attributes or interests of that demographic
> group. . . . Otherwise, the individual's voting decision
> is likely to reflect a complicated web of concerns and
> interests, not all of which can be captured in demo-
> graphic terms.
>
> (Stewart 1974, p. 134)

This book addresses itself throughout to such a perspective. In
successive chapters, the influences of different kinds of "concerns
and interests" of citizens on how they decided to vote in the 1972
presidential election will be scrutinized.

Focus in Chapters 2-4 will be on the impact of demography,
socioeconomic factors, political dispositions, political issue positions,
and images of the candidates. In the final chapters attention turns to
the function of the presidential campaign, including mass-communi-
cations activity during it, in influencing voters. However, at the
beginning an overview is needed, including a description of who the
voters under study were, and which ones voted for George McGovern
and which for Richard Nixon.

In many ways the differences between Nixon and McGovern
voters boiled down to a classic split between the "haves" and "have-

nots" of American society, circa 1972. The Nixon voters were mainly "haves"—demographically (white, older, more educated, more "established"), socioeconomically (higher income, more upwardly mobile, better jobs), and politically (more interested, knowledgeable, and active, and less cynical). The McGovern voters were by and large quite the opposite demographically, socioeconomically, and politically. These differences are detailed below, with special emphasis also placed on the role of such important factors as party identification, the behavior of first-time voters, how black voters acted, the dilemma of blue-collar voters, the case of the Nixon Democrats, and how past histories of voters related to their decisions in 1972.

PARTY IDENTIFICATION AMONG VOTERS

A description of patterns of party identification within the Summit County panel provides a broad perspective on their political make-up. Half of the voters in the sample said they thought of themselves as Democrats, and over half of those thought of themselves as "strong" Democrats.* Twenty-nine percent of the sample were self-identified Independents, with 40 percent of the Independents indicating leanings toward the Democratic Party. Republicans made up 20 percent of the voting sample, with about a third of them proclaiming "strong" Republican attachments.

The associations found between key demographic variables and party identification in the sample of Summit County voters were not startling, given the pattern of such relationships expressed in similar research over the years.

Among the Democrats, women, whites, and blue-collar workers were in the majority. Approximately 40 percent of the Democrats occupied middle socioeconomic niches; percentages were roughly the same for upward social class mobility and for annual income under $10,000 (Tables 2.1 and 2.2).

Republicans, in contrast, had majorities among females, the educationally upwardly mobile, whites, Protestants, white-collar workers, individuals in the highest socioeconomic status bracket, and persons experiencing the least economic stress.† In comparing the

---

*The measures used for party identification and subsequent factors are presented in Appendix B.

†The female majorities among both Democrats and Republicans are reflections of their overrepresentation in the voter samples as a whole.

TABLE 2.1

Party Identification of Voters
and General Characteristics
(percentages)

	Democrats (N = 311)	Republicans (N = 130)	Independents (N = 177)
Sex			
Male	42	44	50
Female	58	56	50
Age			
18–24	15	8	23
25–34	21	24	29
35–49	32	32	25
50–64	23	23	19
65+	11	14	5
Education			
1–11 Years	33	14	14
12 Years	43	33	37
Some College	17	25	32
Completed College	8	29	18
Educational Mobility			
Upward	49	55	57
Downward	7	14	11
Nonmobile	44	32	32
Race			
White	79	99	91
Black	20	1	9
Religious Preference			
Catholic	35	14	29
Protestant	59	82	62

TABLE 2.2

Party Identification of Voters and
Socioeconomic Characteristics
(percentages)

	Democrats (N = 311)	Republicans (N = 130)	Independents (N = 177)
Occupation			
Blue-collar	51	24	43
White-collar	30	57	45
Union Membership	25	8	26
Union Belonged to Supported McGovern	7	2	4
Socioeconomic Status			
High	21	54	40
Middle	40	28	40
Low	39	19	21
Social Class Mobility			
Upward	45	49	54
Downward	37	40	31
Nonmobile	18	11	15
Economic Stress Index			
High	35	19	26
Moderate	33	28	38
Low	32	53	36
Annual Income			
Less than $10,000	44	26	37
$10,000-$14,999	35	34	40
$15,000 and over	21	40	23

demographic characteristics of Democrats vis-a-vis Republicans, the following are worth noting:

- Democrats were more likely to be young, less educated, educationally nonmobile, black, and Catholic. They were more apt to belong to unions, to occupy middle and low socio-economic statuses, to be nonmobile with regard to social class, to be experiencing high or moderate economic stress, and to be less affluent.
- Compared with Democrats, Republicans were more apt to be better educated, either upwardly or downwardly educationally mobile, white, Protestant, white-collar workers, in the highest socioeconomic status and income brackets, and undergoing the least degree of economic stress.
- Independents in the Summit County panel drew majorities from among the upwardly educationally mobile, whites (only 9 percent were black), Protestants, and the upwardly mobile with regard to social class.
- In comparison with either Democrats or Republicans, Independents were most likely to fall below the age of 35, to have had some college experience, to be educationally upwardly mobile, to belong to a union, to be upwardly mobile with regard to social class, to have been experiencing a moderate degree of economic stress, and to fall into the middle income bracket.

The Summit County data tend to substantiate other findings that suggest a significant cohort of "concerned independents" surfacing among the electorate in recent years (DeVries and Tarrance 1972), if indeed such a group has not been present to some extent all along (Key 1966; Flanigan 1972). That is, the demographics of the Independents, especially as they pertain to educational level, suggest the Independents to be rather a diversified group, perhaps more so than either the Democrat or Republican cohort. They are as likely as not to be relatively well-educated, and traverse all strata of occupational and income ranks. While certain Independents were likely to be apathetic enough about politics and public affairs in general not to vote, many others were highly involved with the 1972 campaign in a number of ways. The findings with respect to party identification and socioeconomics in general, then, buttress earlier propositions that Democrats, Independents, and Republicans are each likely to be heterogeneous groups, albeit with each group reflecting disproportionate demographic attributes.

The association between party identification and age deserves special mention here. Table 2.1 clearly indicates a growth in party affiliation with increased age between 35 and 49, and a corresponding decline in self-identification as "Independent" after 34. Indeed, among the 18-24-year-old first-time voters in the sample, there were proportionately more Independents than affiliated voters. Independents outnumbered Republicans by almost three to one. At first glance, such a pattern does not bode well for the future of party politics in the United States, particularly for Republicans. However, at least two interpretations are possible here. First, it may be that party affiliation and strength thereof are primarily a function of the political temper of the times that the individual has gone through in the formation of partisan disposition. That is, older voters may indicate greater party ties because they formed these ties in a more "politicized" era than younger voters have experienced. On the other hand, it may be that people form stronger and better-defined party links the longer they are affiliated with a party (or simply the longer they remain politically active). Available evidence from previous work gives somewhat greater weight to the second interpretation (Campbell et al. 1960). However, recent studies have suggested that aging among voters per se is specifically unrelated to Republican Party identification (Glenn and Hefner 1972), and that traditional relationships between party and social class in general have declined (Glenn 1973).

CANDIDATE PREFERENCE

Given this milieu of party identification and demographic and socioeconomic characteristics, how did George McGovern and Richard Nixon ultimately fare among these voters? Within the panel, the two contenders finished in a virtual dead heat, with Nixon garnering 51 percent of the vote and McGovern 49 percent. *

A number of demographic and socioeconomic factors were inserted into a regression analysis, with vote as the dependent variable, to attain a general view of the pattern of associations (Table 2.3). †

---

* As noted in Appendix A, these figures matched the actual vote tallies in preponderantly Democratic Summit County within 1 percent. Ten respondents who completed all waves of interviewing but voted for minor party candidates were not included in the panel.

†Multiple regression analysis was the most appropriate technique for depicting some of the multivariable relationships discussed here and in subsequent chapters. In effect, the method allows one to find out which of several independent factors are most closely asso-

TABLE 2.3

Regression Analysis of Vote,
by Key Characteristics
$(N = 618)^*$

	r	r^2 Added	Beta
Race	-.34	10%	-.32
Union Membership	-.24	06	-.20
Party	.21	02	.12
Income	.17	02	.09
Occupation	.19	01	.05
Education	.19	00	.04
Sex	-.01	00	.01
Age	-.01	00	.01
Class Mobility	.03	00	.00

Total variance explained $(R^2) = 20\%$

[*] Factors were scored such that voting for McGovern was correlated with being black, a Democrat, a union member, lower-income, blue-collar, less educated, female, younger, and having less class mobility.

---

ciated with one dependent factor. The ability of each of the independent factors to explain variation in the dependent factor is ascertained while controlling for the effects of the other independent factors. In this case, the ability of demographic and socioeconomic factors to explain presidential vote is examined. We see that race, union membership, political party, income, occupation, and education are each fairly well correlated with party identification (simple [r] correlation coefficients appear under the first column). However, when the association between each of those factors and vote is checked, controlling for all of the other factors, race and union membership emerge as the most explanatory or predictive of vote, explaining, respectively, 10 and 6 percent of the variance in vote.

The other factors each explain 2 percent or less of the variance in vote, and the total variance in vote explained by all of these factors combined is 20 percent. The standardized regression coefficients indicate the direction and weight of each independent factor in predicting vote, with all other factors controlled for. In sum, in this case race and union membership do better at explaining vote than any other factor.

Race was the primary predictor of vote. Union membership followed
in discriminating power, with party affiliation and income serving as
weak vote predictors. Falling considerably behind were occupation,
age, education, sex, and social class mobility. It should be noted
that black voters, regardless of their social status characteristics,
overwhelmingly supported McGovern.

The McGovern Cohort

    McGovern received nearly 75 percent of his votes from Demo-
crats, another quarter from Independents, and a negligible 2 percent
from Republicans (Table 2.4). Although whites accounted for three-
fourths of the McGovern vote, the Democratic challenger captured
practically all of the black voters, and these made up 24 percent of
his total voting bloc. Nearly all of these individuals were Democrats
to begin with, and they stayed within the fold.
    Six of every ten McGovern voters were Protestants. Yet, on a
proportionate basis, fewer McGovern voters than Nixon voters fell
into this subset. McGovern garnered proportionately more Catholic
votes than did his opponent. Females made up 55 percent of the
McGovern voting cohort and 56 percent of the Nixon subset. A majority
of the McGovern voters (51 percent) manifested upward educational
mobility, as did Nixon supporters (54 percent). Blue-collar workers
were in the majority within the McGovern subset (Table 2.5).
    Despite the McGovern "youth strategy," considerably less than
a fifth (17 percent) of his supporters were young, first-time voters.
One in ten McGovern partisans was aged 65 or over. Nixon's cohort
closely resembled McGovern's with regard to age distribution overall;
the largest proportion of each candidate's supporters, three in ten,
fell into the 35-49-year-old bracket.
    In terms of educational levels, a relatively substantial propor-
tion of McGovern supporters (one in three) had less than a full high
school education, while no more than one in every ten had completed
college. Almost a third of McGovern's voters were members of a
trade union household, yet only 8 percent held memberships in unions
that had endorsed him. Within the socioeconomic status category, the
bulk of McGovern support (40 percent) came from voters in the middle.
However, an almost equal proportion (37 percent) sprang from among
relatively low socioeconomic-level voters.
    Although slightly less than half (46 percent) of all socially
upwardly mobile voters supported McGovern, more than a third of
his vote cohort was composed of persons experiencing downward
cross-generational social class mobility. The Nixon cohort was
similar to that of McGovern on this one particular variable.

TABLE 2.4

General Characteristics of the Nixon and McGovern
Voting Cohorts
(percentages)

	Nixon Cohort (N = 312)	McGovern Cohort (N = 306)
Sex		
Male	44	45
Female	56	55
Age		
18–24	14	17
25–34	26	22
35–49	30	29
50–64	22	22
60+	10	10
Education		
1–11 Years	15	31
12 Years	41	37
Some College	24	22
Completed College	20	10
Educational Mobility		
Upward	54	51
Downward	12	8
Nonmobile	34	42
Race		
White	98	76
Black	2	24
Religious Preference		
Catholic	27	31
Protestant	70	60
Party Identification		
Democrat	27	74
Republican	40	2
Independent	33	24

TABLE 2.5

Socioeconomic Characteristics of the Nixon and
McGovern Voting Cohorts
(percentages)

	Nixon Cohort (N = 312)	McGovern Cohort (N = 306)
Occupation		
Blue-collar	35	51
White-collar	48	32
Union Membership	14	30
Union Belonged to		
Supported McGovern	1	8
Socioeconomic Status		
High	43	23
Middle	35	40
Low	22	37
Social Class Mobility		
Upward	51	46
Downward	36	37
Nonmobile	14	18
Economic Stress Index		
High	22	37
Moderate	34	32
Low	44	31
Annual Income		
Less than $10,000	31	46
$10,000-$14,999	37	35
$15,000 and over	32	19

With regard to economic stress, highly stressed individuals made up 37 percent of the McGovern cohort, and relatively unstressed voters made up 31 percent. As income levels increased, the likelihood of voting for McGovern decreased, so that the subset included 46 percent who earned less than $10,000 annually and a relatively small 19 percent who earned $15,000 and more.

The Nixon Cohort

The Nixon voting bloc proved more varied both politically and demographically (Table 2.4). Over one-quarter (27 percent) of the Republican incumbent's vote came from Democrats, and another third came from Independents; Republicans made up 40 percent of his cohort. However, Nixon gained only minuscule support from blacks: 98 percent of his coalition was white.

Protestants (70 percent), females (56 percent), and the upwardly mobile in terms of both education (54 percent) and social class (51 percent) contributed majorities to the Nixon cohort. Four in ten Nixon voters were high school graduates; however, on a proportionate basis, Nixon captured more votes from college graduates (20 percent) than he did from persons without a high school diploma (15 percent).

White-collar workers made up about half (48 percent) of the Nixon cohort, and blue-collar workers a third (Table 2.5). The higher his or her socioeconomic status, the more likely the voter was to choose Nixon. Consequently, four in ten Nixon adherents scored high in socioeconomic status, while a fifth scored low. A similar relationship was apparent in economic stress: the weaker the economic stress on Summit County voters, the more apt they were to fall into Nixon's cohort. Whereas 44 percent of the pro-Nixon voter group were undergoing relatively low economic stress, only 22 percent in that subset were experiencing severe economic pressures.

With regard to annual income, roughly a third in each economic bracket (low, middle, and high) cast their votes for Nixon.

McGovern Versus Nixon Voters

On a comparative basis, Nixon voters were proportionately more likely to be (1) college graduates, (2) whites, (3) Protestants, (4) Republicans and Independents, (5) white-collar workers, (6) of high socioeconomic status, (7) upwardly mobile in social class, (8) undergoing relatively low economic stress, and (9) located in the highest annual income bracket.

Relative to the Nixon cohort, McGovern voters were proportionately more likely to be (1) least well educated, (2) nonmobile with regard to cross-generational educational achievement, (3) blacks, (4) Democrats, (5) trade union members, (6) in the middle and lower socioeconomic status categories, (7) undergoing relatively severe economic stress, and (8) the least affluent.

All in all, McGovern appears to have gathered the large majority of his support from those segments of the population consistently identified with the traditional Democratic power sources: blacks, low-income and low-education voters, blue-collar workers, and the "have-nots." Nixon, on the other hand, captured very close to all of the Republicans, picked up sizable portions of Democrats and Independents, and overall attracted those subsets of the electorate that journalists are fond of referring to as representing "middle America."

Overall, then, votes for Nixon and McGovern modally distributed themselves along classic "top dog" versus "underdog" lines, with the better-off, conservative citizens of Summit County favoring the Republican incumbent and the socioeconomically depressed and politically disinterested voters casting their support to the Democratic hopeful. It appears that the antecedent socioeconomic positioning of Summit County voters would play as significant a role in determining vote choices as would such matters as political ideology, the issues raised in the campaign, and voters' perceptions of the candidates.

THE INFLUENCE OF DEMOGRAPHIC CHARACTERISTICS ON VOTE CHOICE

Sex

Sex of voters did not appear to influence preferences for either Nixon or McGovern; male and female voters distributed their votes between the two candidates in equal proportions.

Age: The Young First-Time Voters

First-time, youngest voters (18-24) favored McGovern (56 percent), while voters aged 25-34 favored Nixon (54 percent). Voters aged 35 and over distributed their votes equally between the two candidates. If the McGovern strategists counted on capturing the "youth vote" as such, they failed in Summit County. First-time voters in

TABLE 2.6

Modal Characteristics of First-Time Voters
(percentages)

	First-Time Voters (N = 95)	Total (N = 618)
Female	68	55
Completed High School	50	39
Downward Educational Mobility	19	10
White-collar Households	47	40
Middle Socioeconomic Status	46	37
Moderate Economic Stress	43	33
Annual Income Under $10,000	43	38
Independents	42	29
Republicans	11	21
Moderately Interested in Politics	58	52
Self-ascribed Political Knowledge Level Low	47	35
Actual Political Knowledge Level Low	55	40
Moderate Degree of Interest in 1972 Campaign	41	36
Active Participation in Campaign	48	32

the Summit County panel favored McGovern over Nixon by a relatively unimpressive overall margin of 56 percent to 44 percent.

Compared with the Summit County electorate as a whole, proportionately more first-time voters were female, were high school graduates, manifested downward educational mobility, came from white-collar and middle socioeconomic status households, manifested moderate economic stress, and were in the lowest income bracket (Table 2.6).

Politically, they were overrepresented in the Independent category and underrepresented in the Republican. Their interest in politics generally leaned toward the moderate side. Political knowledge levels, both self-ascribed and actual, tended to be relatively low, while interest in the 1972 campaign appeared to be moderate. Despite all this, the first-time voters in Summit County manifested a relatively high degree of active participation in the 1972 campaign.

First-Time Voters for Nixon

     First-time voters who cast their ballots for Nixon were more likely to be educationally downwardly mobile, white, and Protestant than were other young voters (Tables 2.7-2.9). In comparison with all other first-time voters, those in the Nixon corner were more likely to show symptoms of downward social class mobility, possibly due to their initial occupational experience. At the same time they were more often in the most affluent income bracket and, coincidentally, in the relatively low economic stress category—a reflection of the dominant older Nixon cohort's socioeconomic status.

     First-time voters who had decided for Nixon were twice as likely as the new electorate overall to consider themselves Republicans. Pro-Nixon first-time voters were more likely than first-time voters in toto to express a relatively high interest in politics in general, although their interest and active participation in the 1972 campaign were apt to be on the moderate side. Yet these young Nixon voters were more likely than the rest to report a relatively high degree of attentiveness to that campaign.

First-Time Voters for McGovern

     First-time voters for McGovern were more likely than the first-time voting cohort as a whole to be black and to be educationally upwardly mobile. Socioeconomically they were more apt to come from the least affluent and most economically stressed households, although they tended to manifest a disproportionate distribution within the middle socioeconomic category. Basically, young first-time voters who chose McGovern reflected the socioeconomic characteristics of the older McGovern supporters.

     Not unexpectedly, pro-McGovern first-time voters were more apt to identify themselves as Democrats. Although they were more likely than were all first-time voters to voice a relatively low interest in the 1972 campaign and to claim a relatively low level of political knowledge, first-timers who favored the Democratic nominee were more likely than the rest to have taken an active part in the 1972 campaign.

First-Time Voters Compared

     Substantial differentiations that separated first-time Nixon voters from those who supported McGovern occurred within the demographic categories of (1) education (high school and college graduates favored Nixon, as did the downwardly mobile and the static, while first-time voters who either had not graduated from high school or

TABLE 2.7

General Characteristics of First-Time Voters
for Nixon and McGovern
(percentages)

	All First-Time Voters (N = 95)	First-Time Voters for Nixon (N = 42)	First-Time Voters for McGovern (N = 53)
Sex			
Male	32	31	32
Female	68	69	68
Education			
1-11 Years	3	2	4
12 Years	50	52	47
Some College	34	29	38
Completed College	14	17	11
Educational Mobility			
Upward	55	48	60
Downward	19	24	15
Nonmobile	26	29	25
Race			
White	86	98	77
Black	13	2	21
Religious Preference			
Catholic	32	29	34
Protestant	53	64	43

had some college experience and the upwardly mobile preferred McGovern); (2) race (whites were more apt to vote for Nixon, blacks for McGovern); and (3) religious preference (Protestants favored Nixon, Catholics supported McGovern).

Within the socioeconomic categories, compared with first-time voters for McGovern, young Nixon supporters were more likely to exhibit high socioeconomic status attributes, to be downwardly mobile in terms of social class, to have experienced less severe economic pressure, and to be enjoying high family income.

Compared with their pro-Nixon counterparts, first-time voters who backed McGovern were more likely to hail from trade union households, to occupy a middle socioeconomic status, to be upwardly

TABLE 2.8

Socioeconomic Characteristics of First-Time Voters
for Nixon and McGovern
(percentages)

	All First-Time Voters (N = 95)	First-Time Voters for Nixon (N = 42)	First-Time Voters for McGovern (N = 53)
Occupation			
Blue-collar	44	45	43
White-collar	47	48	47
Union Membership	18	14	21
Socioeconomic Status			
High	35	38	32
Middle	46	41	51
Low	19	21	17
Social Class Mobility			
Upward	51	45	55
Downward	36	41	32
Nonmobile	14	14	13
Economic Stress Index			
High	25	17	32
Moderate	43	43	43
Low	32	41	25
Annual Income			
Less than $10,000	43	36	49
$10,000-$14,999	34	36	32
$15,000 and over	23	29	19

mobile with regard to social class, to have experienced relatively high
economic stress, and to show earnings of less than $10,000 annually.

With regard to political attributes, Republicans, first-time
voters with a high interest in politics generally, individuals who
believed themselves to be politically well informed (but who turned out
to be only moderately so), persons whose interest and participation in
the 1972 campaign was mild, and young voters who were highly attentive to the contest were proportionately more apt to favor Nixon.

TABLE 2.9

Political Attributes of First-Time Voters
for Nixon and McGovern
(percentages)

	All First-Time Voters (N = 95)	First-Time Voters for Nixon (N = 42)	First-Time Voters for McGovern (N = 53)
Party Identification			
Democrat	47	36	57
Republican	11	21	2
Independent	42	43	42
Interest in Politics Generally			
High	27	33	23
Moderate	58	52	62
Low	14	14	13
Self-ascribed Political Knowledge			
High	36	45	28
Moderate	17	14	19
Low	47	41	53
Actual Political Knowledge			
High	15	14	15
Moderate	31	33	28
Low	55	52	57
Campaign Interest			
High	35	36	34
Moderate	41	48	36
Low	24	17	30
Campaign Attention			
High	36	43	30
Moderate	50	48	51
Low	15	10	19
Campaign Participation			
High	48	38	57
Moderate	31	43	21
Low	21	19	23

In contrast, first-time voters who were Democrats, who were mildly interested in politics generally, who were less well informed about politics and knew it, whose interest in and attention to the 1972 campaign was low, but whose participation in it was nonetheless high, were likely to support McGovern.

It would appear from these profiles that first-time voters come to their initial election with no particular "youth" political ideology but, rather, with an ideological thrust that has developed within the milieu of their families' socialization patterns. * Given generally tepid political interest coupled with little political knowledge, many young first-time voters made up for their lack of political sophistication by participating actively in the campaign. Although they seemed to be open to "influence" from various sources (peers, the media, fellow campaign workers), they voted almost precisely as did the rest of the electorate.

Education

By a ratio of two to one, voters who had not completed high school chose McGovern (66 percent) over Nixon (34 percent); college graduates voted for Nixon over McGovern by the same ratio. Voters who either had completed high school or had some college experience favored Nixon (67 percent) over McGovern (33 percent). The assertion that the McGovern campaign was effective in its tilt toward "intellectuals" is not borne out by the findings in the Summit County study.

Voters whose attained educational level was below that of their parents (those manifesting downward educational mobility) were substantially more likely to vote for Nixon than for McGovern, by a margin of 61 percent to 39 percent. Upwardly educationally mobile voters also favored Nixon over McGovern, but by a considerably smaller margin: 52 percent to 48 percent. Voters who remained educationally static as far as mobility is concerned were likely to favor McGovern (55 percent) over Nixon (46 percent).

Race: The Black Voter

By an overwhelming margin of 94 percent to 6 percent, blacks voted for McGovern, while whites favored Nixon (57 percent) over

---

* For discussions of political socialization processes, and particularly the role of communication in those processes, the reader is referred to Chaffee, McLeod, and Wackman (1972), Jennings and Niemi (1968), Langton (1969), and McLeod and O'Keefe (1972).

TABLE 2.10

General Characteristics of Black Voters
(percentages)

	Total (N = 618)	Black Voters (N = 78)
Sex		
Male	45	42
Female	55	58
Age		
18–24	15	15
25–34	24	19
35–49	30	33
50–64	22	23
65+	10	9
Education		
1–11 Years	23	51
12 Years	39	33
Some College	23	14
Completed College	15	1
Educational Mobility		
Upward	52	41
Downward	10	5
Nonmobile	38	54
Religious Preference		
Catholic	29	5
Protestant	65	89

McGovern (43 percent). If anything characterized the black voters in
the Summit County panel, it was their relatively low socioeconomic
status. Socioeconomic lacks of every sort were in clear evidence
within the black voting subset, to the degree that if there was an
"underdog" in the 1972 election campaign, it was the black voter of
Summit County, Ohio.

Consider these facts: nearly six in ten black voters (58 percent)
were blue-collar workers; over half (54 percent) occupied the lowest
socioeconomic status. This was coupled with the facts that two-thirds
of the black voters sampled earned less than $10,000 per year and
that six in ten black voters scored high on the economic stress index
(in comparison with 29 percent for all voters studied (Tables 2.10–
2.12).

TABLE 2.11

Socioeconomic Characteristics of Black Voters
(percentages)

	Total (N = 618)	Black Voters (N = 78)
Occupation		
Blue-collar	43	58
White-collar	40	22
Union Membership	22	33
Union Belonged to		
Supported McGovern	5	12
Socioeconomic Status		
High	33	9
Middle	37	37
Low	29	54
Social Class Mobility		
Upward	48	36
Downward	36	41
Nonmobile	16	23
Economic Stress Index		
High	29	62
Moderate	33	19
Low	38	19
Annual Income		
Less than $10,000	38	65
$10,000-$14,999	36	22
$15,000 and over	25	13

Additionally, a majority (51 percent) of the Summit County black voters studied had less than a full high school education; 1 percent had completed college, 14 percent had some college education, and a third had graduated from high school. Moreover, 54 percent of the black voters, vis-a-vis 38 percent of all voters studied, showed no advancement over the educational levels of their parents.

More than three-fourths (78 percent) of the black voters studied considered themselves Democrats, and a fifth identified themselves as Independents. No more than 1 percent classified themselves as Republicans.

TABLE 2.12

Political Attributes of Black Voters
(percentages)

	Total (N = 618)	Black Voters (N = 78)
Party Identification		
Democrat	50	78
Republican	21	1
Independent	29	21
Interest in Politics Generally		
High	34	49
Moderate	52	32
Low	13	18
Self-ascribed Political Knowledge		
High	40	39
Moderate	25	30
Low	35	32
Actual Political Knowledge		
High	19	3
Moderate	42	26
Low	40	72
Campaign Interest		
High	44	41
Moderate	36	32
Low	20	27
Campaign Attention		
High	41	39
Moderate	46	45
Low	13	17
Campaign Participation		
High	32	46
Moderate	35	27
Low	33	27

Although blacks were considerably more likely than the electorate as a whole to proclaim a high interest in politics across the board (49 percent for blacks, 34 percent for all voters), they tended to be low scorers in terms of both interest in the 1972 campaign (blacks, 27 percent; all voters, 20 percent) and in actual political knowledge (72 percent for black voters and 40 percent for all voters). By a margin of 46 percent to 32 percent, black voters, compared with all voters in the Ohio panel, were more active participants in the 1972 campaign, relatively low interest in the campaign and relatively low political information levels notwithstanding.

All in all, black voters appear to have voted their interests— primarily social and economic in nature—by deciding almost unanimously to support George McGovern, practically at the moment he received the Democratic nomination (82 percent made their decision in July). In so doing, blacks removed themselves, for all intents and purposes, from the propaganda blandishments of the campaign, and found themselves engaging actively in the campaign rather than concerning themselves about the legitimacy of their personal decisions and the problem of seeking and finding suitable rationales to support those decisions.

Religious Preference

Catholics were slightly more likely to vote for McGovern (53 percent); Protestants favored Nixon by about the same margin (54 percent).

THE INFLUENCE OF SOCIOECONOMIC CHARACTERISTICS ON VOTE CHOICE

Occupation: The Blue-Collar Voter

Blue-collar workers were more apt to support McGovern (59 percent), and white-collar workers were more apt to back Nixon (61 percent), by substantial margins in each instance. Moreover, blue-collar voters were more likely to have decided early for McGovern (40 percent) than for Nixon (33 percent).

Blue-collar voters differed from all voters in the panel in many respects. With regard to age they were more likely to bunch up in the 35-49 bracket and, understandably, were nearly absent from the 65-plus "retirement" category. A higher proportion of high school

TABLE 2.13

Modal Characteristics of Blue-Collar Voters
(percentages)

	Total (N = 618)	Blue-Collar Voters (N = 265)
Age 35-49	35	30
Completed High School	46	39
Middle Socioeconomic Status	60	37
Low Socioeconomic Status	36	29
Nonmobile in Social Class	26	16
Annual Income $10,000-$14,999	42	36
Trade Union Member	35	22
Democrat	60	50
Self-ascribed Political Knowledge Low	40	35
Actual Political Knowledge Low	48	40

graduates was found among blue-collar voters, compared with all voters in the panel (Table 2.13).

Economic attributes, not unexpectedly, distinguished blue-collar voters from the rest in numerous ways. Compared with all the Ohio voters studied, blue-collar voters were more likely to occupy middle and lower socioeconomic statuses, to show little cross-generational social class mobility, to be in the middle income bracket, and to hold membership in a trade union. Worth noting is the fact that blue-collar voters did not differ from the panel as a whole with regard to experiencing economic stress.

Blue-collar voters were most likely to be Democrats. They were also most apt to score low on both self-ascribed and actual levels of political knowledge.

Blue-Collar Voters for Nixon

In relation to all blue-collar voters, blue-collar voters for Nixon were more likely to have completed high school, to show upward educational mobility, and to be white. In other words, these workers represented the managerial segments of the blue collar world: foremen, owners of service businesses, and so on (Tables 2.14-2.16).

Additionally, they were more likely to occupy a middle socioeconomic status and to have high annual income. Relative to all

TABLE 2.14

General Characteristics of Blue-Collar Voters
for Nixon and McGovern
(percentages)

	All Blue-Collar Voters (N = 265)	Blue-Collar Voters for Nixon (N = 110)	Blue-Collar Voters for McGovern (N = 155)
Sex			
Male	48	49	47
Female	53	51	54
Age			
18–24	16	17	15
25–34	27	27	27
35–49	35	34	36
50–64	22	21	23
65+	1	1	1
Education			
1–11 Years	29	19	37
12 Years	46	53	41
Some College	20	22	19
Completed College	5	6	3
Educational Mobility			
Upward	51	56	48
Downward	8	6	8
Nonmobile	42	38	44
Race			
White	83	97	72
Black	17	3	27
Religious Preference			
Catholic	31	32	30
Protestant	67	67	67
Total (N = 618)	100	42	58

TABLE 2.15

Socioeconomic Characteristics of Blue-Collar Voters
for Nixon and McGovern
(percentages)

	All Blue-Collar Voters (N = 265)	Blue-Collar Voters for Nixon (N = 110)	Blue-Collar Voters for McGovern (N = 155)
Union Membership	35	26	41
Union Belonged to Supported McGovern	9	6	12
Socioeconomic Status			
High	5	7	3
Middle	60	65	56
Low	36	28	42
Social Class Mobility			
Upward	47	49	45
Downward	28	27	27
Nonmobile	26	24	28
Economic Stress Index			
High	30	24	35
Moderate	34	39	30
Low	36	37	35
Annual Income			
Less than $10,000	37	24	38
$10,000-$14,999	42	42	41
$15,000 and over	22	35	21
Total (N = 618)	100	42	58

blue-collar voters, those who supported Nixon were more likely to be
either Republicans or Independents and were most likely to have voted
for Nixon in 1968 (64 percent). These blue-collar "managers" were
indistinguishable from their white-collar managerial counterparts
with regard to their political characteristics and actions.

Blue-collar voters for Nixon were more likely to have had a
moderate degree of interest in politics generally as well as to claim
a moderate level of political knowledge. Similarly, they were more
apt to report a moderate amount of attention paid to the 1972 campaign.

TABLE 2.16

Political Attributes of Blue-Collar Voters
for Nixon and McGovern
(percentages)

	All Blue-Collar Voters (N = 265)	Blue-Collar Voters for Nixon (N = 110)	Blue-Collar Voters for McGovern (N = 155)
Party Identification			
Democrat (N = 311)	60	37	76
Republican (N = 130)	12	26	1
Independent (N = 177)	29	36	23
Interest in Politics Generally			
High (N = 210)	30	24	35
Moderate (N = 323)	55	68	45
Low (N = 81)	14	7	19
Self-ascribed Political Knowledge			
High (N = 246)	37	34	39
Moderate (N = 154)	23	30	18
Low (N = 218)	40	36	43
Actual Political Knowledge			
High (N = 116)	15	14	16
Moderate (N = 259)	37	39	36
Low (N = 243)	48	47	49
Campaign Interest			
High (N = 269)	40	44	38
Moderate (N = 224)	36	39	34
Low (N = 125)	23	17	28
Campaign Attention			
High (N = 254)	39	39	38
Moderate (N = 286)	47	55	42
Low (N = 78)	13	6	20
Campaign Participation			
High (N = 195)	31	24	37
Moderate (N = 217)	37	41	34
Low (N = 206)	32	36	29
Total (N = 618)	100	42	58

Blue-Collar Voters for McGovern

Relative to all blue-collar voters, those who supported McGovern were less likely to have finished high school but more likely to be static with regard to cross-generational educational mobility, and more likely to be black. This subset occupied the manual worker and laborer slots of the blue-collar spectrum, and can be considered as genuinely "working class" in the classic sense.

On the matter of socioeconomics, McGovern blue-collar voters, compared with the rest, were more likely to be trade union members, occupants of the lowest socioeconomic status, and experiencing relatively high economic stress. They were more likely than blue-collar voters in toto to be Democrats and to have supported Hubert Humphrey in 1968 (78 percent). They were apt to be either highly interested or relatively disinterested in politics generally; however, their specific interest in the 1972 campaign was relatively low. This was accompanied by the relatively low attention blue-collar voters for McGovern displayed vis-a-vis all blue-collar electors. Still, blue-collar McGovern backers were more likely to be highly active participants in the 1972 campaign than were blue-collar voters as a whole.

The data on blue collar voters in Summit County once again point to the dangers inherent in the analysis of political behavior by demographics alone. In 1972 two distinct types of blue-collar voters were encountered: those who were virtually indistinguishable from the "middle class" Nixon voters, and a proletarian subset who supported McGovern. The differences between the two were fundamental, and the pathways through which the two blue-collar groups in the Summit County panel reached a final vote choice would be expected to differ in fundamental ways as well.

Income

Voters earning $10,000 or more annually (particularly those in the $15,000-plus bracket) were most likely to prefer Nixon (58 percent); the least affluent voters favored McGovern (59 percent).

Union Membership

Voters who belonged to a trade union household (67 percent), particularly if those unions had endorsed McGovern (75 percent), were most likely to choose the Democratic candidate.

Socioeconomic Status

By substantial margins, high socioeconomic status individuals were most inclined to vote for Nixon (65 percent) and low socioeconomic status individuals favored McGovern (62 percent). Voters in the middle socioeconomic status category were more apt to cast ballots for McGovern.

Social Class Mobility

Voters who were moving upward on the social class ladder were more inclined to favor Nixon (53 percent) than McGovern (47 percent). Surprisingly, the downwardly mobile voters split their votes exactly evenly between the two candidates. McGovern, however, received a major share of the nonmobiles' votes: 56 percent, compared with 44 percent for Nixon. The McGovern campaign appears to have had more success in attracting support from voters who were "locked into" their positions in the socioeconomic structure than from disaffected voters who were actually losing ground within the system.

Among voters who had supported Nixon in 1968, it was the upwardly mobile who were most apt to vote for him again in 1972 (47 percent). Interestingly, one in every ten 1968 Nixon voters who manifested upward social class mobility voted for McGovern in 1972. Although this appears somewhat as an erosion of support among Nixon's best "prospects," this defection was offset by the swing to Nixon among 9 percent of upwardly mobile former Humphrey voters. These data suggest that for small numbers of voters, changes in partisanship often accompany favorable changes in social class status.

Social class mobility affected the 1972 voting choices of the 1968 George Wallace partisans as well. Wallace voters who were upwardly mobile most often chose McGovern (26 percent) over Nixon (14 percent), while both the downwardly mobile and the nonmobile tended to split their votes between the two nominees.

Economic Stress

Inflation, plus the prospect of either imminent or eventual unemployment in 1972, put severe pressure on nearly three out of every ten (29 percent) voters in the Ohio panel. An additional third found themselves caught in moderate economic stress, while nearly four in ten Summit County voters (38 percent) were enjoying relatively low economic stress in 1972.

In particular, the oldest voters (68 percent), blacks (62 percent), those with less than a full high school education (56 percent), and those voters who were educationally nonmobile vis-a-vis their parents (40 percent) were most likely to have encountered severe economic stress. Voters aged 50-64 (53 percent), college graduates (43 percent), and those with upward educational mobility (45 percent) encountered the mildest degree of economic pressure.

Again we see a dichotomy in the Summit County electorate on the basis of financial well-being; and again we can expect that the more likely voters were to experience financial stress, the more likely they were to support George McGovern in 1972. A reversal of this pattern would be expected with regard to support for Richard Nixon, and the data support that expectation. Voters experiencing high economic stress were most likely to choose McGovern over Nixon by a substantial margin (62 percent to 38 percent). The reverse held true for voters who were undergoing relatively mild economic stress; among them Nixon votes outdistanced those for McGovern by a margin of 59 percent to 41 percent. Voters who felt a moderate degree of economic stress tended to favor Nixon (52 percent) over McGovern (48 percent).

THE INFLUENCE OF POLITICAL ATTRIBUTES ON VOTE CHOICE

1968 Vote Choices

Not surprising are the findings that 88 percent of the voters who cast their ballots for Nixon in 1968 did so again four years later, and that 80 percent of those who voted for Humphrey in 1968 chose McGovern in 1972. What merits attention is the fact that 57 percent of all of the 1968 Wallace voters in the Ohio panel cast their ballots for McGovern in 1972, while 43 percent demonstrated a preference for Nixon. Contrary to some journalistic interpretations, George Wallace's appeal was not monolithic.

1972 Pre-Convention Vote Preferences

Table 2.17 is interesting in that it shows a high degree of stead-fastness among Nixon partisans and, more importantly, points to

TABLE 2.17

Pre-Convention Choices of Nixon and McGovern Voters
(percentages)

Pre-Convention Choice	Nixon Voters	McGovern Voters
Nixon (N = 178)	94	6
Humphrey (N = 130)	25	75
McGovern (N = 88)	22	78
Wallace (N = 45)	56	44
Muskie (N = 43)	28	72
Kennedy (N = 31)	19	81
Total (N = 515)	51	49

some of the roots of the sizable defection of Democrats from the
McGovern candidacy.

It is revealing that Nixon garnered between a fifth and a quarter
each from among supporters of Edward Kennedy, Hubert Humphrey,
and Edmund Muskie in the spring of 1972. Not only did McGovern's
candidacy fail to unite Democrats, whose expectations were not ful-
filled by the Democratic National Convention; but, surprisingly, it
apparently disenchanted nearly a fourth of the voters who had preferred McGovern prior to his candidacy. This fact alone raises a
question regarding whether imagery of the 1972 candidates or their
stands on issues played the more important role in the Summit County
panel's vote decisions.

Finally, it is important to note that the majority of the voters
who preferred George Wallace in the spring of 1972 eventually voted
for Nixon over McGovern by a margin of 56 percent to 44 percent.
This represents a reversal of the 1972 vote distributions among individuals who claimed to have voted for Wallace in 1968, but does not
upset the notion that voters who supported Wallace in 1972 were far
from being of one and only one conservative political stripe. With
over four in ten 1972 Wallace supporters eventually choosing McGovern,
it is clear that the populist side of Wallace's appeal could be attractive
to many "liberal" voters as well.

Democrats Who Voted for Nixon

Reference group theory suggests that specific groups in society
often become dissatisfied with their stations in life and seek to identify

with groups that are more congenial to their aspirations. The clerk
who identifies with management may one day show up in the office
bedecked in elegant, conservative Brooks Brothers apparel; the
recently arrived suburban housewife who wants desperately to "fit in"
may seek out the local "tennis club" set; the small businessman who
experiences a modest windfall may suddenly contemplate sending his
pre-adolescent offspring to a posh boarding school.

In politics, voters often have the opportunity to show the world
that they differ from others sharing their characteristics by supporting
candidates who seem incongruent with their ostensible interests. Thus,
the urbanized liberal Jewish intellectual may consider voting for a
conservative candidate when he decides that "liberal" is no longer
politically chic. Or the conservative businessman may support a
liberal candidate because his business activities force him into relationships with "enlightened" business people who are successful. In
these cases, voters vote their aspirations more than their dispositions.

Democrats in the Summit County panel who voted for Nixon were
socially and economically on the move upward. For example, 49 percent of all the Democrats studied manifested upward educational
mobility, and 55 percent of the Democrats supporting Nixon showed
the same attribute (Table 2.18).

Fifty-two percent of the pro-Nixon Democrats, compared with
45 percent of all Democrats, were upward bound with regard to

TABLE 2.18

Modal Characteristics of Democrats Who Voted for Nixon
(percentages)

	Pro-Nixon Democrats (N = 83)	All Democrats (N = 311)
Educational Mobility Upward	55	49
Social Class Mobility Upward	52	45
Catholic	44	35
Annual Income $10,000–$14,999	43	35
White-collar Workers	34	30
Middle Socioeconomic Status	46	40
Moderate Economic Stress	39	33
Moderate General Interest in Politics	55	46
Moderate Attentiveness to 1972 Campaign	53	45

cross-generational social class mobility. Add to this the facts that
proportionately more Nixon-voting Democrats were Catholic, were
earning $10,000-$15,000 annually, were white-collar workers, occupied a middle socioeconomic status, and were experiencing only a
moderate degree of economic stress; these data yield a picture of the
Democratic defector as a social-economic striver who saw Richard
Nixon's emphasis on the payoff aspects of the "work ethic" as closely
reflecting his own experiences and wishes. Unlike the Nixon Republican voter who had already arrived, the Democratic Nixon supporter
saw himself starting on the way up, albeit in modest terms. For the
Republican Nixon voter, the President emerged as a protector and
defender of success-oriented goals already attained. To the Democrats who chose Nixon, he appeared to support strongly the climb
upward to success, and that support was somehow perceived as easing
the way significantly.

The Democratic defectors experienced relative ease in supporting
President Nixon in 1972. In this regard, 27 percent of all Democrats
encountered difficulty in vote decision-making, and 25 percent of the
Nixon-voting Democrats reported a similar experience. Moreover,
these particular voters seemed to be developing a habit of sorts with
regard to the Republican incumbent. Thirteen percent of all of the
Democrats in the Summit County panel supported Nixon in both 1968
and 1972. However, 34 percent of all Democrats who voted for Nixon
in 1972 had previously voted for him in 1968. Surprisingly, another
third of the Democrats who cast ballots for Nixon in 1972 had voted
for Humphrey in 1968. The inference here is that political ideology
per se played a relatively minor role in the 1972 defection of "Nixon
Democrats," while the personalities and issues of that campaign may
have played a major role.

Compared with all Democrats in the Summit County panel,
Nixon-voting Democrats manifested proportionately more moderate
interest in politics generally, as well as proportionately more moderate attentiveness to the 1972 campaign.

In brief, Democrats who voted for Nixon in 1972 were quite
unlike the voters who made up the "have-not" McGovern bloc. While
not quite situated within the Nixon "haves," they clearly were approaching that status at the time of the 1972 presidential campaign.

Political Cynicism

In all, four in ten Summit County voters scored high on political
cynicism, or lack of confidence in government. The one characteristic
that marked high political cynicism among voters in the panel was

TABLE 2.19

Degree of Political Cynicism, by Modal Socioeconomic
Attributes and Educational Characteristics
(percentages)

| | Degree of Political Cynicism | |
	High	Low
Low Socioeconomic Status (N = 181)	56	44
Annual Income Less Than $10,000		
(N = 237)	50	50
Social Class Mobility Downward		
(N = 223)	45	55
Social Class Mobility Upward		
(N = 299)	36	64
High Economic Stress (N = 181)	51	49
Education		
1-11 Years (N = 143)	57	43
12 Years (N = 241)	42	58
Some College (N = 141)	31	69
Completed College (N = 93)	24	76
Educational Mobility		
Upward (N = 324)	35	65
Downward (N = 59)	46	54
Nonmobile (N = 235)	46	54
Total (N = 618)	40	60

peripherality: the more detached, alienated, and remote the voters
were from the mainstreams of social, economic, and political activities, the more likely they were to express a high degree of cynicism
regarding politics in America. Here we note that low socioeconomic
status voters, the least affluent, the downwardly mobile with regard
to social class, and voters undergoing the greatest degree of economic
stress were most apt to score high on political cynicism (Table 2.19).

Additionally, as educational achievement increased, high political
cynicism diminished. The inverse relationship between educational
background and political cynicism in the Summit County panel was
further underlined by the overrepresentation of highly cynical voters
within the educationally downwardly mobile subset, as well as among
the educationally nonmobile. Upwardly bound voters most often
scored relatively low on the political cynicism index.

It is not surprising that low political involvement was cumulatively related to political cynicism among the Ohio panelists. In each

TABLE 2.20

Degree of Political Cynicism, by Political Attributes
(percentages)

	Degree of Political Cynicism	
	High	Low
Party Identification		
Democrat (N = 311)	48	52
Republican (N = 130)	29	71
Independent (N = 177)	36	64
Interest in Politics Generally		
High (N = 210)	33	68
Moderate (N = 323)	40	60
Low (N = 81)	59	41
Self-ascribed Political Knowledge		
High (N = 246)	36	64
Moderate (N = 154)	34	66
Low (N = 218)	50	50
Actual Political Knowledge		
High (N = 116)	30	70
Moderate (N = 259)	38	62
Low (N = 243)	48	53
Campaign Interest		
High (N = 269)	32	68
Moderate (N = 224)	42	59
Low (N = 125)	57	44
Campaign Attention		
High (N = 254)	35	65
Moderate (N = 286)	40	60
Low (N = 78)	59	41
Campaign Participation		
High (N = 195)	34	66
Moderate (N = 217)	42	58
Low (N = 206)	44	56
Total (N = 618)	40	60

TABLE 2.21

Voting for Nixon and McGovern by High Political Cynicism
(percentages)

	Voted for Nixon/McGovern		Early Deciders Nixon/McGovern		Late Deciders Nixon/McGovern		Switched to Nixon/McGovern	
	(N=312)	(N=306)	(N=256)	(N=206)	(N=31)	(N=50)	(N=22)	(N=38)
High Political Cynicism	34	46	33	43	36	49	50	66

instance, the lower the interest in politics generally and in the 1972 campaign specifically, the lower the level of political knowledge; and the lower the attentiveness to and active participation in the 1972 campaign, the greater the political cynicism (Table 2.20).

On a proportionate basis, Democrats were most apt to score high on political cynicism, while Republicans were most apt to score low. Of the voters who cast ballots for McGovern, 46 percent were highly cynical, but no more than 34 percent of those supporting Nixon could be so classified. Political cynicism affected early deciders and late deciders in both political camps in roughly the same ratios. It was among switchers that political cynicism seemed to play its most important role. Here, two-thirds of those who switched to McGovern from Nixon scored high on political cynicism; in contrast, no more than half of the voters who changed to Nixon from McGovern were intensely cynical about politics and politicians in general (Table 2.21).

Political Knowledge

When voters in the Summit County panel were tested on specific information levels pertaining to the 1972 political campaign in Ohio, 19 percent scored high and 39 percent scored low on levels of actual political knowledge; 42 percent scored in the middle range.

In gross demographic terms male voters (25 percent), college graduates (29 percent), and voters who manifested downward educational mobility (27 percent) were best informed.

On the other hand, females (45 percent), young first-time voters (55 percent), the least well educated (55 percent), the educationally nonmobile (46 percent), and blacks (72 percent) appeared to be the least well informed. In other words, the more socially advantaged the Summit County voters were, the greater their likelihood of manifesting a relatively high degree of political knowledge.

TABLE 2.22

Actual Political Knowledge Level, by Political Attributes
(percentages)

| | Actual Political Knowledge Level | | |
	High	Moderate	Low
Interest in Politics Generally			
High (N = 210)	29	41	30
Moderate (N = 323)	15	43	42
Low (N = 81)	9	41	51
Self-ascribed Political Knowledge			
High (N = 246)	30	44	26
Moderate (N = 154)	14	46	40
Low (N = 218)	9	37	54
Campaign Interest			
High (N = 269)	24	48	29
Moderate (N = 224)	18	40	42
Low (N = 125)	10	33	58
Campaign Attention			
High (N = 254)	25	48	26
Moderate (N = 286)	16	38	47
Low (N = 78)	9	36	55
Campaign Participation			
High (N = 195)	23	41	36
Moderate (N = 217)	22	44	34
Low (N = 206)	12	41	48
Total (N = 618)	19	42	39

A similar pattern emerged with regard to socioeconomic attributes. The better off the voters were in socioeconomic terms across
the board, the higher their levels of political knowledge. For example,
high socioeconomic status voters (27 percent), those earning $15,000
or more annually (25 percent), and voters experiencing the least economic stress (27 percent) were most apt to score high on political
knowledge.

Acting cumulatively on voters' levels of actual political knowledge
in Summit County were (1) interest in politics generally, (2) interest
specifically in the 1972 campaign, (3) attention to the campaign, and
(4) active campaign participation. A revealing finding is that as self-

ascribed political knowledge levels increased, so did actual political knowledge levels (Table 2.22).

Democrats in the Summit County panel were, on a proportionate basis, most likely to score low on actual political knowledge, while Republicans were most apt to score in the middle political knowledge range.

Levels of actual political knowledge per se did not substantially affect voting for Nixon or McGovern across the board. Nonetheless, two findings merit attention: highly knowledgeable voters favored Nixon over McGovern by a margin of 53 percent to 47 percent; and as levels of actual political knowledge decreased, the tendency to vote for McGovern increased. The reverse process occurred in the balloting for Nixon.

All in all, whether voters in the 1972 Summit County panel were politically knowledgeable or not was associated with how well educated they were; how economically well off they were; and how interested in, attentive to, and active in politics they were.

Interest in the 1972 Campaign

Voters who manifested the greatest interest in the 1972 presidential race favored Nixon over McGovern by a margin of 52 percent to 48 percent. Relatively disinterested voters preferred McGovern (54 percent) to Nixon (46 percent). Moderately interested voters, by 52 percent to 48 percent, tended to support Nixon over McGovern.

Attention Paid to the 1972 Campaign

The relatively inattentive voters supported McGovern more often than Nixon (65 percent to 35 percent). Voters who gave a moderate amount of attention to the campaign favored Nixon over McGovern by a margin of 55 percent to 45 percent. Highly attentive individuals distributed their votes evenly between the two candidates.

Active Participation in the 1972 Campaign

Active participation in the 1972 campaign was equally divided among the highly active voters in the panel (32 percent), the moderately active (35 percent), and those rather inactive (33 percent).

The highly active voters were 1.5 times as likely to vote for George McGovern (61 percent) as they were to support Richard Nixon (39 percent). Moderately active voters (57 percent) and those who were relatively inactive (55 percent) were more likely to favor Nixon. Clearly, McGovern voters were the predominant political activists in Summit County during the summer and fall of 1972. Whether voters would be highly active or relatively inactive in the campaign was determined, in the main, by four factors:

1. Age—Young first-time voters were highly active (48 percent); the oldest voters (50 percent) remained relatively inactive.
2. General interest in politics—The greater the voters' interest in politics, the more active their participation in the 1972 campaign. Among highly interested voters, 47 percent were highly active campaign participants, 33 percent were moderately active, and 21 percent were relatively inactive.
3. Interest in the 1972 campaign—Voters' participation in the 1972 campaign increased as their interest in the campaign rose. Among voters who expressed a great deal of interest in the campaign, 44 percent were highly active in it, 34 percent were moderately active, and 22 percent relatively inactive.
4. Attention paid to the 1972 campaign—Not unexpectedly, the more attention voters paid to the presidential race, the more active in the contest they were apt to be. Among voters giving high attention to the campaign, 45 percent were highly active in it, 36 percent were moderately active, and 19 percent were relatively inactive.

In brief, the more interested and attentive voters were with regard to the political happenings of 1972, the more likely they were to participate actively in the campaign.

Additionally, high active participation occurred with disproportionately high frequency among blacks (46 percent), members of unions that endorsed McGovern (50 percent), and voters claiming a high level of political knowledge (46 percent).

Although the media behaviors of voters in the Summit County panel will be treated in detail later, at this time it is important to note some specific aspects of media behavior as they affected active participation in the 1972 presidential campaign.

Overall, the greater voters' exposure to either general or campaign-related news media, the more apt they were to be highly active participants in the race (Table 2.23).

The more dependent the voters were on newspapers or television for political information, the more likely they were to be highly active

TABLE 2.23

Active Participation in 1972 Campaign,
by Media Attributes
(percentages)

	Active Participation in 1972 Campaign		
	High	Moderate	Low
General News Media Exposure			
High (N = 214)	41	36	23
Moderate (N = 192)	28	33	39
Low (N = 212)	26	35	39
Campaign Media Exposure			
High (N = 209)	36	43	21
Moderate (N = 203)	34	29	38
Low (N = 206)	25	34	42
Dependence on Newspapers for Political Information			
High (N = 258)	40	33	28
Moderate (N = 250)	26	37	36
Low (N = 110)	25	36	39
Dependence on Television for Political Information			
High (N = 164)	36	34	31
Moderate (N = 163)	36	35	29
Low (N = 291)	27	36	37
Anticipatory Influence			
High (N = 112)	36	38	27
Moderate (N = 281)	32	35	32
Low (N = 225)	28	34	38
Reported Influence			
High (N = 110)	41	36	24
Moderate (N = 255)	34	33	33
Low (N = 253	25	37	38
Total (N = 618)	32	35	33

participants in the campaign; also, reported high levels of media
influence on vote decisions (either anticipated or actual) were associated with highly active involvement in the 1972 race. These findings
on the relationship between high media dependency and highly active
participation bring up the question of the media's alleged effect, in
terms of voters' so-called passivity. Classically, the argument—
most clearly asserted in R. K. Merton and P. Lazarsfeld's "narcotizing dysfunction" hypothesis—suggests that high media exposure,
reliance, and influence render audiences immobilized to the extent
that their active participation in political affairs is either truncated
or, worse yet, nonexistent. The Summit County panel data seriously
challenge this interpretation. Rather than generating political passivity or apathy, high media exposure, dependence, and influence were
consistently correlated with highly active participation in an election
campaign. While 32 percent of all the voters in the Ohio panel scored
high as active campaign participants, (a) 41 percent of the voters
with the most frequent exposure to the news media, (b) 40 percent of
the voters who manifested the greatest dependence on newspapers for
political information, and (c) 41 percent of the voters who reported
the greatest degree of media influence on their vote decisions were
classified as being highly active participants in the 1972 presidential
race. Extensive discussion of political participation appears in
L. W. Milbrath (1965).

CONDITIONS OF VOTE DECISION-MAKING

Because a presidential election is the product of a dynamic,
multifaceted series of decisions by voters, it is important to go considerably beyond the final votes cast by the electorate in order to
understand some of the significant factors that influenced the outcome
of the 1972 presidential election. In order to proceed with the presentation, it will be necessary to examine three separate subsets of
voters:

1. The subset of Summit County early decider respondents who
   had decided for whom to vote as early as July 1972 (75 percent total) and who persisted in their initial choices
2. A cohort of Ohio voters (late deciders) who decided for Nixon
   or for McGovern sometime after the two nominating conventions were over (13 percent)
3. A relative minority of voters (switchers) who changed from
   a decision for one candidate to support of another at one

time during the course of the campaign (10 percent total).*

Early Deciders

Early deciders, as a subset, resembled all voters in the Summit County panel, with several noteworthy exceptions (Tables 2.24-2.26).

In comparison with all voters, early deciders were relatively less often Catholics, proportionately more apt to be in the high socioeconomic category, less apt to have experienced economic stress, more likely to be Republicans, and more active in the campaign.

As a subset, early deciders presented a profile of being rather economically secure and socially self-confident. It is a profile that projects an overall image of a voting group that makes up its mind very early in a campaign and sticks to its initial decisions rather dogmatically.

Late Deciders

In sharp contrast with all Summit County voters investigated, the late deciders emerged as quite a distinctive subset in the overall electorate. In terms of gross characteristics, proportionately more female voters, persons aged 50-64 years, individuals with some college education, the educationally upwardly mobile, whites, and Catholics were apt to be found among the late deciders in the Ohio panel.

Late deciders, compared with all Summit County voters on socioeconomic status characteristics, manifested considerable differentiation as well.

In contrast with all of the panel voters, late deciders were more likely to be trade union members, to occupy middle socioeconomic status, to be nonmobile in terms of social class vis-a-vis their parents, and to exhibit a moderate degree of economic stress.

---

*Fifteen cases, or 2 percent of the total, were classified as "vacillators," or voters who made more than one change in candidate choice in the course of the 1972 campaign. Because of the small number of cases, "vacillators" are excluded from this analysis and those following.

TABLE 2.24

General Characteristics of Early Deciders, Late Deciders, and Switchers
(percentages)

	Total (N = 618)	Early Deciders (N = 462)	Late Deciders (N = 81)	Switchers (N = 60)
Sex				
Male	45	46	41	48
Female	55	55	59	52
Age				
18–24	15	14	11	28
25–34	24	25	21	20
35–49	30	30	33	32
50–64	22	21	27	17
65+	10	10	7	3
Education				
1–11 Years	23	24	20	17
12 Years	39	39	40	42
Some College	23	21	28	27
Completed College	15	16	12	15
Educational Mobility				
Upward	52	50	62	62
Downward	10	11	4	10
Nonmobile	38	40	35	28
Race				
White	87	85	94	88
Black	13	14	6	12
Religious Preference				
Catholic	29	25	42	35
Protestant	65	68	48	62

TABLE 2.25

Socioeconomic Characteristics of Early Deciders,
Late Deciders, and Switchers
(percentages)

	Total (N = 618)	Early Deciders (N = 462)	Late Deciders (N = 81)	Switchers (N = 60)
Occupation				
Blue-collar	43	41	33	43
White-collar	40	42	49	47
Union Membership	22	20	27	25
Union Belonged to Supported McGovern	5	5	7	3
Socioeconomic Status				
High	33	36	27	28
Middle	37	35	47	45
Low	29	30	26	27
Social Class Mobility				
Upward	48	47	44	63
Downward	36	38	35	20
Nonmobile	16	15	21	17
Economic Stress Index				
High	29	28	28	40
Moderate	33	32	40	37
Low	38	41	32	23
Annual Income				
Less than $10,000	38	37	38	45
$10,000-$14,999	36	35	38	42
$15,000 and over	25	28	24	13

TABLE 2.26

Political Attributes of Early Deciders,
Late Deciders, and Switchers
(percentages)

	Total (N = 618)	Early Deciders (N = 462)	Late Deciders (N = 81)	Switchers (N = 60)
Party Identification				
Democrat	50	47	58	62
Republican	21	26	6	7
Independent	29	27	36	32
Interest in Politics Generally				
High	34	36	31	27
Moderate	52	52	49	55
Low	13	12	17	18
Self-ascribed Political Knowledge				
High	40	41	37	33
Moderate	25	26	19	27
Low	35	33	44	40
Actual Political Knowledge				
High	19	19	17	17
Moderate	42	42	43	43
Low	40	39	40	40
Campaign Interest				
High	41	42	36	30
Moderate	36	37	31	42
Low	20	18	31	23
Campaign Attention				
High	41	42	36	30
Moderate	46	46	44	57
Low	13	12	20	13
Campaign Participation				
High	32	35	16	22
Moderate	35	34	42	38
Low	33	31	42	40

With regard to their political attributes, late deciders differed from all voters in the Summit County panel in that they were most apt to be either Democrats or Independents and least likely to be Republicans. Whereas early deciders were more likely to have supported Nixon (51 percent) over Humphrey (41 percent) in 1968, late deciders were more apt to have chosen Humphrey (62 percent) over Nixon (19 percent). Overall, late deciders exhibited relatively low awareness, attention, interest, self-ascribed political knowledge, and participation levels vis-a-vis politics generally and the 1972 campaign specifically. Politically, they seemed to be peripheral at best, although in terms of actual political knowledge levels they did not differ from the electorate as a whole. In short, the late deciders' apparently lukewarm political approach seemed to stem more from a relative indifference to the 1972 campaign than from lack of knowledge.

Switchers

Switchers in the Summit County panel—those who made an early choice for one candidate but ultimately voted for another—differed markedly from all voters in the study as a whole. First, they differed with regard to such standard demographic characteristics as age, educational achievement and mobility, and religious preference. Compared with all voters in the panel, switchers were more apt to be young, first-time voters; they were more likely to be high school graduates; they tended to be upwardly educationally mobile; and they were more likely to be Protestants.

Relative to the panel as a whole, switchers were more likely to hold a middle socioeconomic status and to be upwardly mobile in terms of social class; either correlative with such upward class mobility or as a consequence of it, they found themselves undergoing relatively high economic stress. This, no doubt, was a function of their disproportionate representation in both the lowest (under $10,000) and middle ($10,000-$14,999) income brackets.

With regard to their political attributes, switchers were most likely of all voters in the panel to be Democrats. Their interest in politics generally, their self-ascribed political knowledge, and their participation in the 1972 campaign were all relatively low in comparison with all Ohio voters studied. These facts notwithstanding, switchers were more likely than the total voter cohort to show a moderate degree of interest in the 1972 campaign and to pay a moderate degree of attention to it. In these two latter instances, switchers differed markedly from both early and late deciders. On the matter of actual political knowledge, switchers were similar to the other voter types in the panel.

3

THE VOTING
PROCESS

Each national election in the United States is not one event, but represents a series of happenings over the time allotted to a presidential campaign. If the November election is seen as the third act of a major political drama, it is preceded (as is true of a Broadway play) by two acts and innumerable rehearsals. Caught up in the unfolding drama of a national election, the players (voters in this case) find themselves either taking their roles early and decisively or late and indecisively. Either they are prepared for their roles by virtue of background, inclination, and past experience, or they are not. Similarly, they either discover that they are comfortable with a role and persist in it, or they shift around, seeking a more compatible one. Finally, they either find that the call to perform is a relatively easy task, or they experience it as unduly challenging and difficult.

THE DILEMMAS OF DECISION-MAKING:
PSYCHOLOGICAL INFLUENCES

All too frequently empirical studies of vote decision-making perceive the act of voting as a simple, mechanical, behavioral response to campaign stimuli and leave it at that. Clearly, the act of voting is a far more complex behavioral manifestation. Think what voting entails in the matter of simple choice alone. Initially, one must decide whether to vote. If a decision to vote is made, then the citizen is faced with making a choice from among contending candidates. In turn, this calls for some knowledge of the candidates: at the very least, who they are and what they appear to stand for. Candidate choice then has to be legitimized, so that the prospective voter can defend that choice both to himself and to others. In order to do this, the prospective voter must arm himself or herself with ideas, images, information, opinions, and rationales that must be gathered from sources of all kinds, even though in many instances the voter's interest in politics may be low and his skill in obtaining political information may be wanting. For many voters, then, choosing a presidential candidate is not an easy task.

In coming to a final choice of candidate, the range of psychic stress that a voter may endure runs from early concern regarding who the winner will be, through undergoing considerable travail in reaching a vote decision, right to possible disappointment with the outcome of an election.

Early Concern Regarding Election Outcome

Let us first look into the matter of early concern among the Summit County panel regarding who the winner might be in the 1972 race. As early as July 1972, no less than 68 percent of all the voters in the panel expressed a high degree of concern regarding who the victor in the presidential contest might be. Twenty-three percent manifested a modicum of concern, while the remaining 9 percent felt little concern or were unsure about their feelings with regard to a potential winner. At the very least, then, national elections generate a certain degree of anxiety among the electorate—anxiety that may be heightened, diminished, or resolved through the various influences that come into play as presidential campaigns progress. In turn, the degree of early concern about candidates' chances of winning may influence voting choices.

In an election in which two-thirds of the voters expressed a high degree of concern regarding its outcome, it is not surprising to see reflections of the final vote outcome in those pre-election manifestations of concern. Frequent expressions of early concern regarding the eventual winner were dichotomized along the "haves" versus "have-nots" division that characterized Summit County's voters as a whole.

Within the "haves," early concern regarding a victor was disproportionately visible among the affluent (76 percent), those experiencing the least economic stress (73 percent), voters in the highest socioeconomic category (74 percent), college graduates (76 percent), white-collar workers (73 percent), and Republicans (83 percent).

Among the "have-nots," persons aged 50 and over (75 percent), voters who showed downward progress in both their educational (73 percent) and their social class mobility (73 percent), and blacks (72 percent) were most apt to express a high degree of early concern about the victor in the 1972 presidential race.

The highly concerned citizens of Summit County eventually voted for Nixon (54 percent) over McGovern (46 percent). Voters who were moderately concerned about who the winner might be, or who were relatively unconcerned, favored McGovern over Nixon by a margin of 54 percent to 47 percent in the first case, and by a margin of 64 percent to 36 percent in the second. In other words, McGovern supporters showed a relatively substantial degree of indifference regarding the likelihood of a Nixon defeat from the very beginning of the 1972 campaign. This rather lackadaisical orientation to McGovern early in the campaign ultimately translated itself into tepid commitment to the South Dakotan, indicating a certain inability of the McGovern campaign to spark enthusiasm, even among his supporters.

Eight in every ten concerned voters who backed Nixon were Republicans. Most often, concerned Nixon voters' actual knowledge of politics was high (46 percent), as were their interest in (45 percent) and attentiveness to (42 percent) the 1972 campaign.

Overall, highly concerned voters who ultimately chose Nixon resembled the "haves" in the Summit County panel, and the McGovern voters who manifested early concern about the outcome most closely resembled the "have-nots."

Half of the voters who showed early concern over the election outcome and supported McGovern were Democrats. Concerned McGovern voters most frequently manifested high interest in politics generally (48 percent) and in the 1972 campaign specifically (39 percent), claimed a high level of political knowledge (39 percent), and manifested high interest in (39 percent) and attentiveness to (39 percent) the 1972 race. They also showed a high level of active participation in the campaign (42 percent). In other words, their political characteristics were quite different from those of the McGovern cohort as a whole, and the one factor responsible for their difference was that they seemed genuinely to care about a McGovern win.

Three generalizations with regard to early concern about outcome are worth noting: (1) although three-fourths of a voter cohort may arrive at a fast and early decision for a particular candidate, fully two-thirds of the electorate can nevertheless express some uneasiness about their choice's actual ability to win; (2) early concern about the potential winning ability of one's choice seems primarily to center on self-interest, usually either in the hope of sustaining a desirable socioeconomic position or in the anticipation of ameliorating an undesirable one; and (3) early concern about an eventual winner in a particular presidential race appears to generate high overall voter involvement in that race.

Difficulty of Vote Decision-Making

In the Summit County panel overall, more than a fifth (22 percent) of the voters reported having experienced difficulty in making their final vote choice. Indeed, for 7 percent of the voters studied, making a final vote choice was "very difficult." Although 22 percent of all voters experienced difficulty in arriving at a final vote decision, disproportionate numbers of voters within given voter subsets were particularly likely to do so.* For example, Democrats (27 percent) were more likely than either Republicans (11 percent) or Independents (21 percent) to find voting in 1972 to be a difficult undertaking. As Table 3.1 shows, McGovern voters, compared with Nixon supporters, were twice as likely to experience travail in decision-making. Overall, and not surprisingly, switchers (55 percent) were 2.5 times more likely than all voters who encountered difficulty to find their decision-making arduous. Perhaps changing one's mind during a campaign is not so much a reflection of flippancy as an indicator of a painful attempt to resolve a true psychological conflict.

Early deciders, understandably, were least likely (14 percent), while late deciders (38 percent) were considerably more likely to encounter difficulty relative to all voters reporting such an experience.

Voting for McGovern, no matter when the decision was made, was more frequently difficult than was voting for Nixon; in particular, voters who switched to McGovern were far more likely to find it a hard decision (61 percent) than were those who switched to Nixon (46 percent).

Table 3.2 indicates two additional political facts that affected the difficulty in the vote decision-making process within the Summit County panel. First, voters who supported George Wallace in 1968 and found themselves choosing Richard Nixon in 1972 were highly troubled. Second, 1968 supporters of Hubert Humphrey who came to a 1972 decision for George McGovern also found great difficulty in casting their ballots.

Disappointment with the 1972 presidential candidate choices other than Nixon or McGovern appeared to affect McGovern voters more than it did those who voted for Nixon (Table 3.3). McGovern

---

*The concept of difficulty of decision-making among voters is more fully treated in Chapter 5.

TABLE 3.1

Difficulty of Vote Decision-Making, by Final Votes
(percentages)

	Experienced Difficulty in Making Vote Decision
Total (N = 618)	22
Voted for	
Nixon (N = 312)	15
McGovern (N = 306)	28
Early Deciders for	
Nixon (N = 256)	10
McGovern (N = 206)	19
Late Deciders for	
Nixon (N = 31)	36
McGovern (N = 50)	40
Switched to	
Nixon (N = 22)	46
McGovern (N = 38)	61

voters who had preferred either Muskie or Humphrey in the spring of
1972 were most likely to find their vote decisions difficult.

In particular, Muskie partisans were three times as likely to
report experiencing difficulty in casting ballots for McGovern rather
than for Nixon. That McGovern's candidacy was an unsettling one to
many voters in Summit County is evidenced by the somewhat surprising
fact that proportionately more of his own pre-convention partisans,
compared with all McGovern voters, reported experiencing difficulty
in deciding for the Democratic nominee on Election Day.

As might be expected, the experience of difficulty in coming to
a vote decision was affected by political disinterest and inactivity.
Voters whose interest in general politics was relatively low (28 percent), as well as voters whose interest (27 percent) and active participation (29 percent) in the 1972 presidential campaign were rather low,
were relatively more likely to have encountered difficulty in arriving
at a vote decision (high interest in politics, 23 percent; high interest
in the 1972 campaign, 21 percent; and high active participation in the
1972 campaign, 18 percent are the opposite figures).

For a substantial number of voters in Summit County, the 1972
campaign posed a peculiarly troublesome dilemma. Specifically,
Humphrey and Wallace partisans who were less than enthusiastic
about George McGovern, but nevertheless apparently felt compelled

TABLE 3.2

1968 Choices of Voters Who Experienced Difficulty
and Voted for Nixon or McGovern in 1972
(percentages)

		Experienced Difficulty in 1972	
	Total	Voted for Nixon	Voted for McGovern
In 1968 Voted for			
Nixon (N=201)	45	8	4
Humphrey (N=208)	46	7	23
Wallace (N=42)	9	22	17

TABLE 3.3

Difficulty of Making Final Vote Decision,
by Pre-Convention Choices
(percentages)

	Experienced Difficulty in Making Final Vote Decision	
	Voted for Nixon	Voted for McGovern
Pre-Convention Choice		
Nixon (N = 178)	8	2
Humphryy (N = 130)	10	20
McGovern (N = 88)	1	16
Wallace (N = 45)	9	18
Muskie (N = 43)	7	21
Kennedy (N = 31)	10	16
Total (N = 515)[*]	7	13

[*] Total of those who had a pre-convention choice.

to vote in 1972, were likely to find it an ordeal of sorts to support
either candidate, especially McGovern. Muskie partisans were similarly affected, being unable to make a choice early in the campaign
either through loyalty to Muskie or through lack of interest; these
voters were also relatively uninvolved in interpersonal networks of
political communication. They were pressed to seek political guidance and resolution of their difficulty from any available source,
including the media. To a substantial extent, the media were used to
overcome the decision dilemmas the 1972 campaign had posed for
these particular voters.

It appears from these data that one function served by early
vote decision-making is the avoidance of psychological stress resulting
from indecisiveness as an election campaign progresses. The longer
the prospective voter puts off his decision, the more unstable the
commitment and the more troublesome voting becomes. This seems
to be particularly true in cases where no prior commitments to the
contestants have been made.

The degree of early concern that one's favored candidate would
prove a winner had an inverse effect on the difficulty experienced by
Summit County voters in deciding for either contestant. Here, 17
percent of the voters who voiced high early concern about the election
outcome experienced difficulty in arriving at a final vote decision; in
comparison, 25 percent of those expressing moderate concern, and
47 percent of the voters who initially were relatively unconcerned had
undergone an arduous vote decision-making process.

One might conclude from these findings that as early concern
about the victor of a presidential campaign increases, it becomes
easier for voters to make an eventual decision on a particular candidate. Inversely, as voting time approaches for the initially unconcerned voter, the stress to make a decision begins to mount.

In order to generate commitment generally or specifically to
unfamiliar or incompatible candidates, the perplexed voter actively
sets out to find guidance; but political disinterest and inactivity—due
in some degree to the fact that his preferred candidates are hors de
combat—seriously constrain his systematic quest. For various reasons, especially fear of coming under fire from friends and relatives,
he shuns getting overly involved in interpersonal political discussions.
Nor does he necessarily turn to the media in an active quest for information; after all, exposure to conflicting points of view may exacerbate difficulty in vote decision-making. Rather, it appears that this
type of voter resigns himself simply to being subjected to whatever
help-giving balm the media may dish up during the campaign. In no
way is the lot of this voter subset a happy one. The rather substantial
presence of the perplexed voter in the electorate has been seriously
overlooked in the past. Uncovering its existence calls for a reexami-

nation of precisely what constitutes the voting act, as well as a reworking of orthodox models regarding exactly how that voting act comes into being among the rather diverse subsets that constitute the electorate as a whole.

Satisfaction with Election Outcome

Concern about a victor and difficulty in making vote decisions were not the only psychological stresses visited upon Summit County voters in the 1972 campaign. Undoubtedly a similar state of affairs has occurred in every previous election campaign and will be reflected in those to come. Regardless of talk relating to "landslides" and "mandates," not all voters come away from a national presidential election equally pleased with the results. Certainly, supporters of the losing candidate can be expected to be dissatisfied with the victor; but even partisans of the winner cannot all be expected to be equally satisfied.

In 1972 in Ohio, a full third of all the panel voters queried reported displeasure with Mr. Nixon's victory. Even though 51 percent had voted for the Republican candidate, no more than 38 percent of all the voters studied reported that they were "very pleased" with the incumbent's win, and 23 percent claimed to be merely "somewhat pleased." Four percent of the voters registered indifference.

As might be expected, McGovern voters showed disappointment twice as often as all voters who voiced displeasure with the results of the 1972 election (Table 3.4). Early McGovern deciders were especially prone to displeasure (75 percent). However, not all McGovern supporters were disappointed: one-fourth actually voiced some satisfaction with the Nixon victory, indicating that their commitment to the Democratic nominee was not altogether wholehearted. For this voter subset that, ostensibly, harbored ambivalent feelings about the candidacy of George McGovern throughout his campaign, the Nixon victory seemed to offer a sense of political release. They dutifully voted for McGovern; but in their hearts they apparently were unhappy with their choice, to some extent. When Nixon won, these voters were relieved in the knowledge that they had voted "right," but ended up with the choice they may have secretly or unconsciously preferred—a choice they could not, for various reasons, openly support. Note that half of the Democrats in the panel were pleased to some degree with the 1972 election outcome.

Three out of every four Nixon voters proclaimed their enthusiastic satisfaction with the President's 1972 victory, yet a full fourth registered only mild satisfaction. Most likely to show enthusiastic

TABLE 3.4

Reaction of Nixon and McGovern Voters
to 1972 Election Outcome
(percentages)

	Very Pleased	Somewhat Pleased	Not Pleased	Indifferent
Total (N=618)	38	23	34	4
Voted for				
Nixon (N=312)	73	25	1	1
McGovern (N=306)	3	22	69	6
Early Deciders for				
Nixon (N=256)	79	20	1	—
McGovern (N=206)	1	20	75	4
Late Deciders for				
Nixon (N=31)	45	48	—	7
McGovern (N=50)	2	28	56	14
Switched to				
Nixon (N=22)	50	46	5	—
McGovern (N=38)	11	26	55	8

reaction to the Nixon victory were those voters who decided early for
the Republican nominee and persisted in their initial choice (early
deciders for Nixon, 79 percent). Nearly half (48 percent) of the voters
who came to a decision for Nixon late in the campaign, and 46 percent
of the voters who had switched over to Nixon from McGovern during
the campaign, showed only a relatively mild degree of pleasure with
the Nixon win.

Despite the national landslide proportions of the Nixon victory
in 1972, his reelection was not met with unmitigated acceptance across
the board by the electorate of Summit County, Ohio. The fact that substantial numbers of voters in various walks of life viewed the prospect
of a second Nixon administration with displeasure would reflect itself
two and a half years later in a massive decline of national popular
support for a Chief Executive who would eventually be forced to resign.

Forty-seven percent of the first-time voters in the panel, 47
percent of the voters with less than a full high school education, and
76 percent of the blacks who were studied voiced disappointment with
the Nixon win. In terms of socioeconomic status, blue-collar workers
(43 percent), members of unions that supported McGovern (56 percent),
low socioeconomic status voters (43 percent), those experiencing high

economic stress (44 percent), and the least affluent (42 percent) were the most likely to be displeased with Nixon's defeat of McGovern.

Fifty-one percent of the Democrats, 3 percent of the Republicans, and 31 percent of the Independents felt displeasure with the results of the 1972 election. Again it is apparent that half of the Democrats in Summit County showed no remorse over the defeat of their own candidate.

CUMULATIVE GAINS IN VOTER SUPPORT
FOR MCGOVERN AND NIXON

Before we examine the development of choices for either 1972 presidential aspirant, let us look at the gross cumulative impacts of the Nixon and McGovern campaigns in Summit County from the perspective of vote gains for each candidate in the months between July and November.

Table 3.5 indicates that the gross cumulative gain in support for McGovern from July to November was just twice that which Nixon enjoyed. However, it is important to note that early voter support for McGovern in July lagged nearly 10 percent behind voter support for Nixon. In other words, on a net basis the cumulative gain in voter support for McGovern in Summit County over the campaign just about equaled that which Nixon garnered. It took McGovern more than two months to catch up to where Nixon began. Further, by October, just a month before Election Day, total voter support for McGovern was still behind what Nixon had attained in August.

Interestingly, the modal gain in Nixon support occurred early in the campaign, during the convention month of August. In contrast, McGovern voter support's modal gain occurred during October, the last month of campaigning. From a strategic point of view, Nixon campaigners in Summit County were confronted with the need to hold onto and expand, where possible, the considerable support the President enjoyed as he entered the fray. On the other hand, McGovern campaign strategists faced a difficult task of catching up before contemplating the possibility of pulling ahead. The gain trends indicate that while support for McGovern in Summit County increased as the 1972 presidential campaign progressed, the reverse applied to gains in voter support for Nixon.

All in all, the 1972 presidential campaign in Summit County resulted in no more than a 14 or 15 percent increase in voter support for either candidate. For more than seven out of ten voters in Summit County, the election campaign was effectively over in July 1972, at least as far as their psychological dispositions were concerned. For

TABLE 3.5

Candidate Support Trend: July–November
(percentages)

| | Support for | |
	Nixon	McGovern
Support in July (N = 438)	75.6	66.0
Gain in August (N = 464)	83.3	66.7
	(+8)	(+1)
Gain in September (N = 494)	88.8	70.9
	(+5)	(+4)
Gain in October (N = 526)	89.7	80.4
	(+1)	(+10)
Gain in November (Final) (N = 618)	100	100
	(+10)	(+20)
	(N=312)	(N=306)

the remainder, it is apparent that the campaign and perhaps the events
accompanying it may have played roles in their decision-making
processes—in some cases, important roles.

Early strong support for Nixon and its growth throughout the
campaign stemmed basically from the relative strength of commitments mustered by each of the candidates as the 1972 campaign
progressed.

Figure 3.1 shows that from the start, and during each month
that followed, net strength of commitment for Nixon outpaced that
for McGovern by substantial margins.[*] While strength of commitment to the incumbent President climbed steadily as each campaign
month passed, McGovern actually lost ground during September—
after the Eagleton affair had time to "sink in," and prior to the South
Dakotan's major policy address on Vietnam in October. It was during
this critical period, some five weeks prior to Election Day, that the
gap in strength of commitment between the two candidates was the
widest: Nixon enjoyed a 17 percent advantage over McGovern. By
the end of October, immediately before Election Day, Nixon's lead
in the contest for voters' commitment remained substantial, although

_____

[*] Net strength was derived by subtracting "not very strongly"
and "don't know" responses from "very strongly" and "fairly strongly"
responses to the question "Right now, how strongly do you feel about
your choice of (Candidate)?"

FIGURE 3.1

FIGURE 3.1

Trends in Net Commitments to Nixon and McGovern

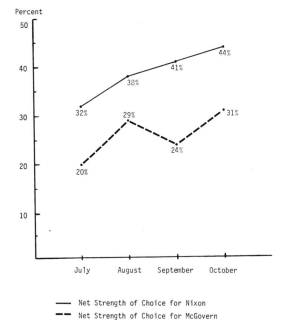

- Net Strength of Choice for Nixon
- - Net Strength of Choice for McGovern

FIGURE 3.2

Trends in Net Commitments to Nixon
Among Democrats and Republicans

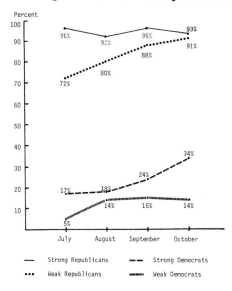

— Strong Republicans   - - Strong Democrats

••• Weak Republicans   ▬▬ Weak Democrats

it had been reduced to 13 percent. Clearly, as has been previously indicated, the candidacy of George McGovern was having difficulty from the start in sparking enough confidence to warrant strong partisan commitment, either to him or to his platform. It was a difficulty the Democratic candidate no doubt encountered among the national electorate, as well as among the Summit County voters, and one that he never managed to overcome.

Figure 3.2 shows that it was only in July 1972 that "weak" Republicans were not as fully committed to Nixon as were "strong" Republicans. However, weak Republicans fell into line as the campaign unfolded. Considerably more interesting is the steadily climbing trend in strength of commitment to President Nixon among "weak" Democrats. Here we see a substantial increase in commitment to Nixon among this subset during the critical September-October period. It is important to note that as overall commitment to McGovern dipped in September, those Democrats who bore their standard casually were increasing commitments to the opposition candidate. If these "weak" Democrats showed initial disenchantment with the McGovern candidacy, the South Dakotan's subsequent campaign appears to have cooled their lukewarm reaction to his race for the presidency.

Note that in Figure 3.2 commitment to Nixon ranged from 92 percent to 96 percent among highly partisan Republicans. Commitment to McGovern among strong Democrats, on the other hand, ranged between a low of 42 percent and a high of no more than 63 percent. Where commitment to Nixon among strong Republicans vacillated no more than 4 percent, commitment to McGovern ebbed and peaked throughout the campaign among the staunchest Democrats, rising to 58 percent in August from a low of 42 percent in July, then dropping to 50 percent in September, only to rise again to a high of 63 percent in October (Figure 3.3).

Until October 1972, casually affiliated Democrats gave only a slight edge to McGovern in their voting choice commitments. By the critical October period, weak Democrats' voting choice commitments favored Nixon over McGovern by a small margin. No matter how it may be viewed, McGovern's failure to wrest solid, steadfast commitment from the broad spectrum of Democrats contributed heavily to his defeat, both in Summit County and across the nation.

Not only did McGovern fail to garner strong support among Democrats, he also was unable to attract strong commitment among Independents, whom the McGovern strategists had considered essential to a victory. Figures 3.4 and 3.5 show that nonpartisan or "true" Independents' commitments to Nixon outpaced commitments to McGovern by ratios of eight to one in July, by three to one in August, by more than four to one in September, and by three to one in October.

FIGURE 3.3

Trends in Net Commitments to McGovern
Among Democrats

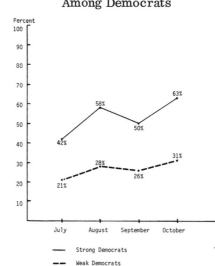

Note: There were too few Republicans to warrant analysis.

Democratic-leaning Independents showed proportionately more frequent commitment to McGovern at the start of the 1972 campaign and broadened that commitment by a substantial margin in August. However, the August high of 43 percent for McGovern dropped precipitously to 25 percent by September: 1 percent below the level of commitment to Nixon that was accorded by Independents sympathetic to the Democratic Party.

Although strength of commitment to Nixon among pro-Democratic Independents climbed as the campaign progressed, commitment to McGovern within this subset never again attained its August high point.

A similar trend can be noted among pro-Republican Independents' support of Nixon, where the peak of commitment to the incumbent President was also reached in August, at the time of his official nomination by the Republican Party. Commitment to Nixon among Republican-leaning Independents declined in each of the ensuing two months.

In terms of garnering voter commitment among Independents, McGovern was perhaps most effective in developing small but consistently increasing gains among Republican-minded Independents in the Summit County panel.

Because of the importance of economics in the 1972 national election, two economic variables, social class mobility and economic

FIGURE 3.4

Trends in Net Commitments to Nixon Among Independents

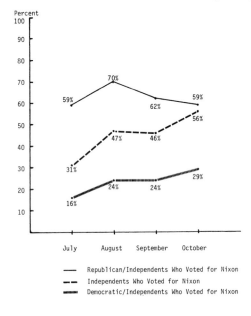

- —— Republican/Independents Who Voted for Nixon
- – – Independents Who Voted for Nixon
- ▬▬ Democratic/Independents Who Voted for Nixon

FIGURE 3.5

Trends in Net Commitments to McGovern Among Independents

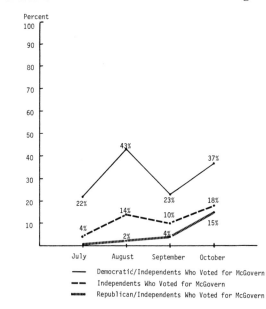

- —— Democratic/Independents Who Voted for McGovern
- – – Independents Who Voted for McGovern
- ▬▬ Republican/Independents Who Voted for McGovern

stress, and their influence on strength of voter candidate commitment
over the length of the campaign are plotted in Figures 3.6 and 3.7.
By a ratio of approximately two to one each month during the campaign, persons who were upwardly bound with regard to social class
showed strong support for Richard Nixon vis-a-vis George McGovern.
The two trend curves here were very similar in shape, with commitment to either candidate starting at a relatively low point in July,
ascending in August, declining in September, and peaking in October.

Among downwardly mobile voters, the trend patterns were
different from those of the upwardly mobile and for each candidate.
Commitment to Nixon among downwardly mobile Summit County panel
members showed a steady upward trend from July to September, with
a plateau in October. In each month other than September, commitment to Nixon among the downwardly mobile lagged considerably
behind that of the upwardly mobile; this was not so with regard to
McGovern. Commitment to the Democratic candidate was consistently
more frequent among the downwardly mobile than it was among the
upwardly moving voters. The trend of commitment to McGovern among
the downwardly mobile reflected that of their upward-bound counterparts: commitment to McGovern climbed in August from its initial low
in July, dropped in September, and rose to its peak in October.

Of interest are the similarities in the trend curves for candidate
choice commitment among voters who showed no cross-generational
social class mobility. Disparities between commitments to either
candidate within this subset were of a minor order; both pro-Nixon
and pro-McGovern nonmobiles indicated relatively small but steadily
increasing commitments to their particular choice each month.

Figure 3.7 indicates clearly that Nixon enjoyed consistently
increasing commitment from voters who were experiencing the least
economic stress in 1972. In contrast, the McGovern strategy of
attracting support from the underprivileged appears to have succeeded,
in that most of the Democrat's strength of commitment throughout the
campaign came from "have-not" voters who were undergoing severe
economic stress. Still, even among this subset, strong support for
the Senator was neither pervasive nor steadfast, and it never reached
the level of support that low-stress voters accorded Nixon.

Interesting to note is the relative strength of commitment to
Nixon that was evidenced among high-economic-stress voters, particularly in the latter months of the campaign. Lagging behind commitment to McGovern by only a scant fraction, the relatively high
levels of commitment to Nixon among highly economically stressed
voters indicated an apparent failure on McGovern's part to convince
substantial proportions of these panel members that his economic
policies, rather than those of Nixon, would substantially alleviate
their problems.

FIGURE 3.6

Social Class Mobility and Trends in Net Commitments
to Nixon and McGovern

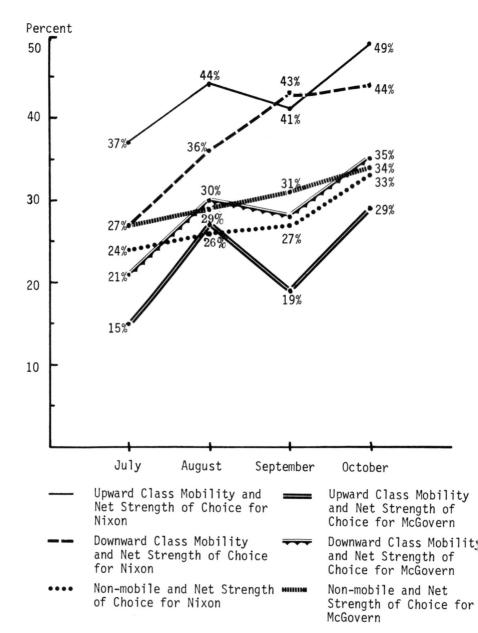

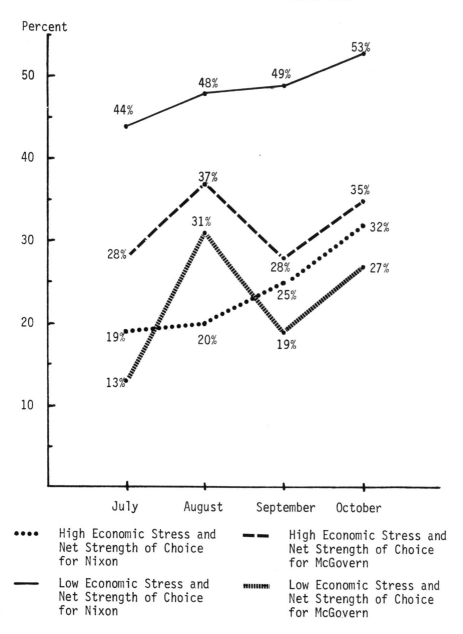

FIGURE 3.7

High and Low Economic Stress and Trends in
Net Commitments to Nixon and McGovern

•••• High Economic Stress and Net Strength of Choice for Nixon

— Low Economic Stress and Net Strength of Choice for Nixon

— — High Economic Stress and Net Strength of Choice for McGovern

⬛⬛⬛ Low Economic Stress and Net Strength of Choice for McGovern

THE STABILITY OF VOTE INTENTIONS

On the whole, commitment to Nixon was proportionately more
stable than was commitment to McGovern during the 1972 campaign.
There was a far greater likelihood of Republicans committing their
votes to the incumbent President early in his campaign (92 percent)
than of Democrats making early decisions to support McGovern (51
percent). In a similar vein, these Nixon voters were only half as
likely to encounter difficulty in making an early decision for the
President (10 percent) as were early-deciding McGovern voters (19
percent). That the great majority of the electorate has a general
idea of whom they might vote for very early in a presidential campaign is a cliche of voting behavior in America; the 1972 campaign
was no exception. Fully three-fourths of all the Summit County voters
interviewed in the July wave could readily specify a choice for either
George McGovern or Richard Nixon, favoring the latter by a margin
of 55 percent to 45 percent even before his official nomination.

As has been indicated, Republicans were far more often explicit
in their intention to vote for Nixon than were Democrats who declared
for McGovern in July. Similarly, Independents voiced considerably
more frequent early support for the incumbent President (45 percent)
than they did for the South Dakota Senator (26 percent). Moreover,
Republicans were most frequently determined with regard to supporting Nixon initially: whereas a fourth each in the Democratic and
Independent camps had not yet decided on a particular candidate in
July, barely one of every ten Republicans had no particular candidate
in mind at the time of the initial July interview.

Strength of voters' partisanship favored President Nixon compared with Senator McGovern (Table 3.6). Where better than nine in
ten "strong" Republicans announced their intention in July to vote for
Nixon, no more than two-thirds of the "strong" Democrats in the July
wave had similarly announced for McGovern.

It was evident as early as four months prior to Election Day
that McGovern would have difficulty in winning wide-ranging support,
not only from the electorate as a whole but even from among avowed
Democrats. Note the intentions expressed by voters of various leanings in July 1972. Overall, slightly more than a fifth of the July
sample claimed to be undecided about their vote intention; yet a third
of the voters who identified themselves as moderate Democrats
reported they still had to make up their minds. This is in sharp contrast with the 13 percent of the moderate Republicans surveyed in
July who voiced a similar lack of early crystallization. Further, by
a ratio of nine to one, more strong Democrats than strong Republicans remained undecided regarding their ultimate November choice.

TABLE 3.6

July Vote Intention, by Strength of Party Identification
(percentages)

	In July 1972 Favored		
	McGovern	Nixon	Undecided
Strong Democrats (N=159)	68	13	19
Moderate Democrats (N=152)	40	27	34
Democratic/Independents (N=75)	52	21	27
Independents (N=55)	15	49	36
Strong Republicans (N=45)	2	96	2
Moderate Republicans (N=85)	1	86	13
Republican/Independents (N=47)	11	77	13
Total (N=618)	36	42	22

Another early indication of the difficulties McGovern would encounter in the 1972 campaign appears in the July potential defection figures. Here 27 percent of the moderate Democrats reported their intention to vote for Nixon. In sharp contrast, no more than 1 percent of the moderate Republicans and 2 percent of the strong Republicans who were interviewed in July said they would cast ballots for McGovern in November.

Independents without specific political leanings indicated a preference for Nixon over McGovern by a margin of more than three to one in July 1972. Further, where 52 percent of the Democratic-leaning Independents registered an early preference for McGovern, fully three-quarters of the Independents who favored the Republicans voiced their determination to support Nixon.

Development of the Vote for Nixon

Early Deciders

In July 1972, among the 51 percent of the voters in the Summit County panel who eventually voted for Nixon, 9 percent were undecided and 41 percent voiced an intention to vote for the incumbent President. Apparently, the Nixon campaign and the events accompanying it were able to hold onto the major proportion of voters who proclaimed an

early commitment, and then managed to crystallize substantial numbers of voters who entered the campaign period indecisively.

Early deciders for Nixon were not unlike all Nixon voters in
their predominant characteristics and attributes (Tables 3.7-3.13).
Thus early Nixon deciders were most frequently represented among
Republican voters (92 percent), voters who had supported Nixon in
1968 (82 percent), voters who were moderately attentive to the 1972
campaign (67 percent), college graduates (60 percent), voters in the
high socioeconomic status category (57 percent), the downwardly
educationally mobile (56 percent), the most affluent voters (55 percent), whites (47 percent), and Protestants (47 percent).

Early Nixon deciders differed from all Nixon voters in proportionate terms as follows: they were more apt to be in the 25-34-year-
old group, to be Protestants, to be moderately attentive to the 1972
campaign, and to rely heavily on television for political information
(Tables 3.14-3.15). As we shall see, early Nixon deciders were more
likely to anticipate a moderate degree of media influence on their vote
decision, but they were less likely to report much actual influence in
this regard.

Nixon entered the 1972 campaign with the significant majority
of Summit County's Republican partisans already committed to him
as early as July. Indeed, early 1972 commitment to Nixon seems to
have been derived in most part from the carry-over support the
President had received from 1968 partisans, particularly those who
could be classified as genuine WASPs.

Two additional observations are in order: first, on the basis of
early intention, it was apparent that Nixon could count on support
from a little less than half of Summit County's Independents; and
second, a sizable defection factor of at least a fifth of the Democrats—
away from McGovern and toward Nixon—was evidently in the making
as early as July 1972.

How the Summit County panelists voted in 1968 played an
important role in early intentions to vote for Nixon. Eight in ten of
the President's former supporters announced their commitment to
him early in the 1972 campaign. In short, in the very beginnings of
the 1972 campaign the Republican candidate was assured a solid base
of partisan support as a carry-over from 1968. Strategically, it was
important to maintain that base and expand it to the highest degree
possible (only 11 percent to cover the totality); simultaneously to
crystallize the undecideds; and to win and hold onto early support for
Nixon among first-time voters and those who were not strictly Nixon
partisans.

In Summit County, Nixon made substantial inroads into first-time
voters (31 percent), and into 1968 Wallace supporters (29 percent), as
far as attracting early commitments from these subsets goes. He did

TABLE 3.7

General Characteristics of Nixon and McGovern
Early and Late Deciders
(percentages)

	Early Deciders		Late Deciders	
	for Nixon	for McGovern	for Nixon	for McGovern
Sex				
Male (N=277)	42	34	4	8
Female (N=341)	41	33	6	9
Age				
18-24 (N=95)	31	39	3	6
25-34 (N=147)	46	33	6	5
35-49 (N=183)	43	32	5	9
50-64 (N=133)	41	34	6	11
65+ (N=60)	45	35	3	7
Education				
1-11 Years (N=143)	27	50	3	8
12 Years (N=241)	42	32	6	7
Some College (N=141)	42	28	6	11
Completed College (N=93)	60	19	4	7
Educational Mobility				
Upward (N=324)	42	29	6	10
Downward (N=59)	56	27	—	5
Nonmobile (N=235)	37	40	5	7
Race				
White (N=537)	47	26	6	9
Black (N=78)	1	82	1	5
Religious Preference				
Catholic (N=178)	34	32	7	12
Protestant (N=401)	47	32	4	6
Total (N=618)	41	33	5	8

TABLE 3.8

General Characteristics of Nixon and McGovern
Switchers and All Voters
(percentages)

	Switchers		All Voters	
	for Nixon	for McGovern	for Nixon	for McGovern
Sex				
Male (N=277)	4	7	50	50
Female (N=341)	4	6	51	49
Age				
18-24 (N= 95)	10	8	44	56
25-34 (N=147)	3	5	54	46
35-49 (N=183)	3	8	51	49
50-64 (N= 60)	—	3	50	50
65+ (N= 60)	—	3	50	50
Education				
1-11 Years (N=143)	3	4	34	66
12 Years (N=241)	4	6	53	47
Some College (N=141)	4	7	53	47
Completed College (N=93)	2	8	67	33
Educational Mobility				
Upward (N=324)	4	7	52	48
Downward (N=59)	3	7	61	39
Nonmobile (N=235)	3	5	46	55
Race				
White (N=537)	4	6	57	43
Black (N=78)	4	5	6	94
Religious Preference				
Catholic (N=178)	5	7	47	53
Protestant (N=401)	3	6	54	46
Total (N=618)	4	6	51	49

TABLE 3.9

Socioeconomic Characteristics of Nixon and McGovern
Early and Late Deciders
(percentages)

	Early Deciders		Late Deciders	
	for Nixon	for McGovern	for Nixon	for McGovern
Occupation				
Blue-collar (N=265)	33	4	5	10
White-collar (N=247)	51	26	6	5
Union Membership (N=135)	23	47	5	11
Union Belonged to				
Supported McGovern (N=32)	9	63	9	9
Socioeconomic Status				
High (N=206)	57	23	6	5
Middle (N=231)	36	34	6	10
Low (N=181)	32	44	3	9
Social Class Mobility				
Upward (N=299)	43	29	5	7
Downward (N=233)	44	36	4	9
Nonmobile (N=96)	31	41	7	10
Economic Stress Index				
High (N=181)	28	42	4	8
Moderate (N=204)	41	31	7	9
Low (N=233)	52	29	4	7
Annual Income				
Less than $10,000 (N=237)	31	41	5	8
$10,000-$14,999 (N=224)	43	30	6	8
$15,000 and over (N=157)	55	27	5	8
Total (N=618)	41	33	5	8

TABLE 3.10

Socioeconomic Characteristics of Nixon and McGovern
Switchers and All Voters
(percentages)

	Switchers		All Voters	
	for Nixon	for McGovern	for Nixon	for McGovern
Occupation				
Blue-collar (N=265)	4	6	42	59
White-collar (N=247)	4	7	61	39
Union Membership (N=135)	4	7	33	67
Union Belonged to				
Supported McGovern (N=32)	—	—	25	75
Socioeconomic Status				
High (N=206)	2	6	66	35
Middle (N=231)	5	7	47	53
Low (N=181)	3	6	38	62
Social Class Mobility				
Upward (N=299)	4	8	53	47
Downward (N=233)	2	4	50	50
Nonmobile (N=96)	5	5	44	56
Economic Stress Index				
High (N=181)	5	8	38	62
Moderate (N=204)	4	7	52	48
Low (N=233)	2	4	59	41
Annual Income				
Less than $10,000 (N=237)	5	7	41	59
$10,000-$14,999 (N=224)	3	9	52	48
$15,000 and over (N=157)	3	2	63	37
Total (N=618)	4	6	51	49

TABLE 3.11

Political Attributes of Nixon and McGovern
Early and Late Deciders
(percentages)

| | Early Deciders | | Late Deciders | |
	for Nixon	for McGovern	for Nixon	for McGovern
Party Identification				
Democrat (N=311)	19	51	3	2
Republican (N=130)	92	—	3	1
Independent (N=177)	45	26	10	7
Interest in Politics Generally				
High (N=210)	34	44	6	6
Moderate (N=323)	48	27	4	8
Low (N=81)	33	33	4	14
Self-ascribed Political Knowledge				
High (N=246)	39	38	6	7
Moderate (N=154)	53	25	3	7
Low (N=218)	36	34	6	11
Actual Political Knowledge				
High (N=116)	45	32	4	8
Moderate (N=259)	43	32	5	9
Low (N=243)	39	36	5	8
Campaign Interest				
High (N=269)	43	35	5	6
Moderate (N=224)	43	32	4	7
Low (N=125)	35	31	6	14
Campaign Attention				
High (N=254)	42	35	5	7
Moderate (N=286)	67	43	8	10
Low (N=78)	10	16	1	6
Campaign Participation				
High (N=195)	34	49	1	6
Moderate (N=217)	45	27	7	8
Low (N=206)	44	26	6	10
Total (N=618)	41	33	5	8

TABLE 3.12

Political Attributes of Nixon and McGovern
Switchers and All Voters
(percentages)

| | Switchers | | All Voters | |
	for Nixon	for McGovern	for Nixon	for McGovern
Party Identification				
Democrat (N=311)	5	7	28	73
Republican (N=130)	1	2	96	4
Independent (N=177)	4	7	59	41
Interest in Politics Generally				
High (N=210)	4	3	45	55
Moderate (N=323)	3	7	56	44
Low (N=81)	3	11	42	58
Self-ascribed Political Knowledge				
High (N=246)	4	4	49	51
Moderate (N=154)	1	9	58	42
Low (N=218)	5	6	47	53
Actual Political Knowledge				
High (N=116)	4	4	53	47
Moderate (N=259)	3	7	51	49
Low (N=243)	4	6	49	51
Campaign Interest				
High (N=269)	3	5	52	48
Moderate (N=224)	4	7	52	48
Low (N=215)	2	9	46	54
Campaign Attention				
High (N=254)	3	4	50	50
Moderate (N=286)	6	12	55	45
Low (N=78)	1	1	35	65
Campaign Participation				
High (N=195)	3	4	39	61
Moderate (N=217)	4	7	57	43
Low (N=206)	3	8	55	45
Total (N=618)	4	6	51	49

TABLE 3.13

1968 Vote Choices of Nixon and McGovern Voters
(percentages)

| | In 1968 Voted for | | | |
	Nixon (N=201)	Humphrey (N=208)	Wallace (N=42)	Total (N=618)
1972 Early Deciders				
For Nixon	82	13	29	41
For McGovern	8	57	33	33
1972 Late Deciders				
For Nixon	3	4	12	5
For McGovern	2	12	12	8
1972 Switchers				
For Nixon	2	3	2	4
For McGovern	3	8	10	6
1972, All Voters				
For Nixon	88	20	43	51
For McGovern	12	80	57	49

not do nearly as well among voters who had supported Humphrey in
1968 (13 percent). Yet even this relatively small proportion of
Humphrey voters shifting into the Nixon camp early in 1972 demonstrated the President's apparent ability to nibble away at potential
McGovern partisans in a bits-and-pieces manner that, on the national
scene, ultimately coalesced into the Nixon "landslide." Contrary to
1972 political folklore proclaiming the demise of the historic Democratic coalition, the Republican victory of 1972 appears to have been
made up of substantial fragments of that coalition being chipped away,
rather than the entire structure collapsing into dust. As far as
Summit County was concerned, no new "conservative majority" had
emerged as of 1972; the data on ticket-splitting support this observation.

Late Deciders

As Tables 3.7-3.13 show, voters who arrived at a decision to
support Nixon relatively late in the 1972 campaign were most apt to
be found among Wallace supporters from both 1968 (12 percent) and
1972 (11 percent), among Independents (10 percent), and among
members of unions that had endorsed McGovern (9 percent).

TABLE 3.14

Mass Media Attributes of Nixon and McGovern
Early and Late Deciders
(percentages)

	Early Deciders		Late Deciders	
	for Nixon	for McGovern	for Nixon	for McGovern
General News Media Exposure				
High (N=214)	40	36	6	6
Moderate (N=192)	44	30	6	8
Low (N=212)	41	34	4	10
Campaign Media Exposure				
High (N=209)	43	34	7	4
Moderate (N=203)	45	33	4	8
Low (N=206)	37	34	4	13
Dependence on Newspapers for Political Information				
High (N=258)	42	34	4	6
Moderate (N=250)	43	33	6	7
Low (N=110)	36	33	6	10
Dependence on Television for Political Information				
High (N=164)	48	34	4	3
Moderate (N=163)	35	37	7	9
Low (N=291)	42	31	5	10
Anticipatory Influence				
High (N=112)	36	40	7	5
Moderate (N=281)	47	26	3	8
Low (N=225)	37	39	6	10
Reported Influence				
High (N=110)	26	34	6	11
Moderate (N=255)	40	34	5	9
Low (N=253)	49	33	4	6
Total (N=618)	41	33	5	8

TABLE 3.15

Mass Media Attributes of Nixon and McGovern
Switchers and All Voters
(percentages)

| | Switchers | | All Voters | |
	for Nixon	for McGovern	for Nixon	for McGovern
General News Media Exposure				
High (N=214)	3	6	49	51
Moderate (N=192)	3	8	53	47
Low (N=212)	5	5	50	50
Campaign Media Exposure				
High (N=209)	3	5	53	47
Moderate (N=203)	3	6	51	49
Low (N=206)	5	7	47	53
Dependence on Newspapers for Political Information				
High (N=258)	4	6	52	48
Moderate (N=250)	3	6	52	48
Low (N=110)	3	6	44	46
Dependence on Television for Political Information				
High (N=164)	2	6	54	46
Moderate (N=163)	3	5	48	52
Low (N=291)	3	7	50	50
Anticipatory Influence				
High (N=112)	4	8	46	54
Moderate (N=281)	5	7	56	44
Low (N=225)	2	4	46	54
Reported Influence				
High (N=110)	12	7	45	56
Moderate (N=255)	2	8	48	52
Low (N=253)	1	4	55	45
Total (N=618)	4	6	51	49

In part, then, Nixon's 1972 campaign in Summit County seems to have been effective in attracting support from a relatively small but important subgroup of politically unsophisticated, white, blue-collar voters who were unaligned in the traditional two-party sense; who found their preferred choice, George Wallace, hors de combat; and who may have resented their local unions' endorsement of McGovern. We find among the late deciders who voted for Nixon an important subset of working people who had already manifested disenchantment with the orthodox partisan political setup and apparently viewed their unions' attempts to jockey them into McGovern's corner as unsuitable to their political interests and inclinations.

Switchers

Voters who had first decided to support McGovern and then changed to Nixon during the course of the 1972 campaign[*] reflected three modal characteristics and attributes: they were most likely to be among voters who had indicated a pre-convention preference for Senator Edward Kennedy (13 percent); they were most apt to report a relatively high degree of media influence on their vote decisions (12 percent); and switchers to Nixon were most often encountered among young first-time voters (10 percent).

The picture here is one of a minuscule subset of unsophisticated young voters who, in their disappointment with the withdrawal of their favorite as the Democratic choice, initially turned to the "Kennedy surrogate"—George McGovern. Disappointed with McGovern's performance during the campaign and open to mass media influence as a substitute for political experience, this handful of voters ultimately switched to the Nixon camp.

Development of the Vote for McGovern

Early Deciders

As previously noted, 49 percent of the panelists in the Summit County study voted for George McGovern. Of all those who cast ballots for the South Dakotan in November 1972, 14 percent indicated that they had no idea in July about whom they might support. McGovern's overall crystallization problem in Summit County appeared to be

---

[*]In all, 22 voters (3.5 percent of all the voters in the panel) switched to Nixon.

somewhat more difficult than that facing Nixon as the 1972 campaign got under way.

That McGovern was indeed confronted with a serious initial problem of crystallizing support for his candidacy was underlined by the fact that in July 1972 nearly a fifth (17 percent) of the Democrats who finally did cast their ballots for him were undecided about whom to support. In contrast, no more than a twelfth of Nixon's Republican voters were undecided about their votes in early summer.

Early McGovern deciders reflected the predominant distributions of characteristics and attributes that were evident among the overall McGovern cohort (Tables 3.7-3.13). Consequently, early deciders for the 1972 Democratic presidential candidate were heavily distributed among blacks (82 percent), members of unions that had endorsed McGovern (63 percent), 1968 Humphrey voters (57 percent), Democrats (51 percent), and voters with less than a twelfth-grade education (50 percent). In other words, Roosevelt-like Democratic "underdog" voters who were 1968 Humphrey partisans were among the very first to climb aboard the McGovern bandwagon.

In contrast with the pattern for all McGovern voters, proportionately more early McGovern deciders were among those with a high level of self-ascribed political knowledge and among voters manifesting moderate attentiveness to the 1972 campaign. Missing from the McGovern camp as the presidential campaign calliope was tuning up were the substantial chunks of the middle-class that had already been preempted by the incumbent President.

Whereas Nixon started off in 1972 with the initial support of nine in ten of Summit County's Republicans solidly behind him, McGovern's prospects among Democrats were barely over 50 percent in July. Before McGovern strategists could contemplate winning support from voters in the opposition camp, they were faced with a serious problem of wooing substantial numbers of defecting and wavering Democrats back into the fold. This they never quite succeeded in doing; for example, even though McGovern managed ultimately to land eight out of ten 1968 Humphrey voters, in July he started off with fewer than six in ten. Right from the beginning, then, McGovern was faced with the necessity of playing a game of catch-up among his best prospects.

Perhaps one of the most surprising facts emerging from the Summit County study is the indication that the majority (57 percent) of voters in the panel who had supported George Wallace in 1968 voted for McGovern four years later. In fact, McGovern enjoyed a considerable edge over Nixon among both types of Wallace voters: those who had made up their minds very early in the campaign, and those who did so later.

Much of the political folklore swirling about the 1972 election had it that the 1968 Wallace voter had no other place to go but to Nixon.

The Summit County data offer a significant contradiction. What appears to have happened, at least among the Summit County panel, is that there were at least two types of voters who had been attracted to the Alabaman's banner in 1968: those who empathized with his overall ultra-conservative ideology, and those who viewed him as fundamentally a populist who was particularly sensitive to the needs and interests of the "little guy," the ordinary workingman. In Summit County it appears that the Wallace ideologists ultimately switched their support to Nixon, while voters seeking a candidate who ostensibly showed a principal concern for the lot of America's economic and social underdogs ultimately turned to McGovern.

In turn, early McGovern deciders reflected the classic model of the "Roosevelt Democrats." As a bloc, the Democratic coalition of yesteryear remained intact and loyal to George McGovern in Summit County. However, there was sufficient defection in each component of that coalition to place McGovern's candidacy in serious jeopardy right from the start. The fact that half of the declared Democrats in the panel shied away from his candidacy early in the campaign was a warning sign of the lack of enthusiasm that would dog the South Dakotan throughout the race.

McGovern appears to have succeeded in crystallizing substantial segments of voters who, by virtue of their attributes and political postures, classically would have been identified as Democratic partisans. Yet the initial hesitancy and lack of consensual early support for the Democratic nominee among substantial subsets of these voters no doubt called for a considerable strategic effort to contain the threat of massive defections from the Democratic camp. It seems that in the summer of 1972 Nixon was contemplating a classic campaign of reinforcing the major bulk of his Republican partisans and then converting elements of the opposition; at the same time, McGovern's campaign dilemma focused primarily on the need to reconvert disaffected Democratic partisans, while secondarily reinforcing a relatively more stable core of partisans. It was apparent that pro-McGovern conversions from the opposition camp would be extremely difficult, if not impossible.

Late Deciders

In terms of their predominant characteristics and attributes, late McGovern deciders were most likely to be among reluctant voters whose first choice for president in 1972 was George Wallace (16 percent), those in the low general political interest group (14 percent), voters with a relatively weak interest in the 1972 campaign (14 percent), voters whose exposure to campaign news and informational media was relatively low (13 percent), voters whose discussions of

TABLE 3.16

Interpersonal Communication Attributes
of Nixon and McGovern Voters
(percentages)

| | Early Deciders | | Late Deciders | |
	for Nixon	for McGovern	for Nixon	for McGovern
Campaign Discussion				
High (N=156)	49	37	4	2
Moderate (N=260)	43	30	4	8
Low (N=202)	34	35	7	13
Interpersonal Cross-Pressure				
High (N=169)	45	32	1	7
Moderate (N=226)	45	32	6	6
Low (N=223)	35	36	7	12
Total (N=618)	41	33	5	8

| | Switchers | | All Voters | |
	for Nixon	for McGovern	for Nixon	for McGovern
Campaign Discussion				
High (N=156)	3	2	56	44
Moderate (N=260)	4	8	52	48
Low (N=202)	3	7	44	56
Interpersonal Cross-Pressure				
High (N=169)	5	6	51	49
Moderate (N=226)	2	6	54	47
Low (N=223)	4	5	47	53
Total (N=618)	4	6	51	49

the campaign were relatively infrequent (13 percent), Catholics (12 percent), Democrats (12 percent), individuals who had voted for either Humphrey (12 percent) or Wallace (12 percent) in 1968, voters whose 1972 pre-convention choices were either Muskie (12 percent) or Humphrey (11 percent), and voters who apparently had been experiencing a limited amount of interpersonal cross-pressure (12 percent) (Table 3.16).

Late deciders who eventually supported McGovern were the
"alienated" voters on whom the McGovern strategists had pinned their
hopes as the cornerstone of a Democratic victory. Yet because
"alienated" voters are by definition the most difficult to reach by a
political campaign, yeoman efforts are necessary to activate their
support. It is apparent that McGovern's attempts to reach this subset
did pay off in a minimal fashion late in the 1972 campaign, but they
did so by forfeiting the more socially integrated elements of the Summit County electorate. This trade-off undoubtedly contributed substantially to the South Dakotan's defeat nationally, as well as in Ohio.

Switchers

Switchers to McGovern from Nixon were most likely to be overly
represented among voters who would have preferred Ted Kennedy as
the Democratic candidate (13 percent), who gave a moderate amount
of attention to the 1972 campaign (12 percent), who manifested a relatively low degree of interest in politics generally (11 percent), and
who had cast their ballots for George Wallace in 1968 (10 percent).

It appears that disappointment over the failure of favorites to
receive the Democratic presidential nomination in 1972 affected voters'
decisions to switch to McGovern, as it did in change-overs to Nixon.
Here we see a dynamic wherein tiny numbers of voters who were
denied the opportunity to support either Senator Kennedy or Governor
Wallace vented their frustration by first throwing their support to
Nixon then then indifferently deciding for McGovern, perhaps as a
final, weak gesture of partisan loyalty. *

THE INFLUENCE OF PRE-CONVENTION CHOICES
ON VOTERS

Voters in the Summit County panel were asked about their
preferences for various presidential hopefuls prior to the national
nominating conventions. Coming out of the 1972 primaries and prior
to his actual nomination, Richard Nixon had the support of one of
every three voters in Summit County who claimed a preference for
a major presidential hopeful. †

_____

*A total of 38 voters (6 percent of all 618 voters studied)
switched to McGovern.

†Eighty-three percent (515 of the 618 voters in the panel) named
a major contender as their pre-convention favorite.

McGovern's pre-convention position with Summit County voters was considerably more precarious. Ranking third after Nixon and Humphrey in favored position prior to the Democratic nominating convention, George McGovern had been acceptable to not more than 17 percent of the panel in the spring of 1972. Contending with McGovern on the Democratic side for voters' favor were Hubert Humphrey (preferred by 25 percent of all the voters), George Wallace (9 percent), Edmund Muskie (8 percent), and Edward Kennedy (6 percent). One in every ten Summit County voters who preferred Nixon in the spring of 1972 was a Democrat, indicating very early in the race that Democratic defection away from any of the party's nominees (other than Humphrey or Kennedy) might become substantial. Both Humphrey (80 percent) and Kennedy (77 percent) had the support of the largest majorities of Summit County Democrats prior to the 1972 nominating convention. One can surmise that had either of them emerged as the Democratic nominee, the serious partisan defections occurring when McGovern was nominated might not have taken place.

The sources of pre-convention partisan support for both McGovern and Wallace are interesting. Wallace actually drew proportionately more support (67 percent) from Democrats prior to the nominating conventions of 1972 than did McGovern (61 percent). At the same time, McGovern's pre-convention support tended to come from a larger proportion of Independents (34 percent) than did Wallace's among that particular subset (29 percent).

On a proportionate basis, Muskie's pre-convention support was most likely to stem from Summit County voters who identified themselves as Democrats (51 percent) and secondarily to come from Independents (44 percent).

Both Nixon and McGovern were faced, following their nominations, with the strategically formidable task of building a majority from among voters who had not been previously disposed to their candidacy. The pool from which each was forced to draw were voters who had supported any Democrat in the spring of 1972. Nixon succeeded, but McGovern did not.

Nixon managed to hold onto more than nine of every ten voters who had favored him prior to the Republican convention; McGovern had lost a fourth of his own pre-convention partisans to his opponent by Election Day 1972. Further, Nixon managed to capture the majority of pre-convention Wallace votes, along with substantial votes, ranging between 19 percent and 28 percent, from each of the pre-convention hopefuls' early supporters. In simple fact, McGovern failed to unite pre-convention Summit County supporters of Democratic hopefuls solidly behind him in his challenge to the Republican incumbent. Particularly, he suffered serious defections from within two key voter subsets: the partisans of Humphrey and of Muskie.

Table 3.3 shows that McGovern's candidacy was an especially
bitter pill for pre-convention supporters of Humphrey and Muskie to
swallow; voters who found it difficult to cast their ballots for George
McGovern were most likely to have preferred either Muskie or
Humphrey prior to the South Dakotan's nomination. Additionally,
those who had favored Wallace in the spring of 1972 found it particularly difficult to support McGovern in the fall of that year.

THE INFLUENCE OF UNION ENDORSEMENTS
ON VOTERS

Reflecting the highly industrialized character of Summit County,
fully 96 percent of the voters in the panel were aware of the nonendorsement policy that was adopted by the national AFL-CIO early
in the 1972 presidential race. Approval for the policy of nonendorsement was equally divided among voters in the panel, where four in
every ten either favored the policy or registered disapproval; only
15 percent of the voters studied had no opinion on the matter.

That the policy of nonendorsement adopted by the AFL-CIO was
not altogether a popular one among blue-collar workers in Summit
County was evidenced by the fact that it won approval among only 36
percent of the union members in the panel, and among 38 percent of
those panelists belonging to a union that eventually endorsed McGovern.
In actuality, more union voters in the panel disapproved of the nonendorsement policy than approved (48 percent of the union members
and 56 percent of those in McGovern-supporting unions were unhappy
with the decision). The reverse was true of nonunion panelists, where
42 percent approved and 40 percent disapproved. Voters who approved
the AFL-CIO stand and those who had no opinion on the matter favored
Nixon over McGovern by a margin of 59 percent to 41 percent in the
first instance and by 54 percent to 46 percent in the second. In contrast, McGovern was favored over Nixon by voters who opposed the
AFL-CIO policy (59 percent to 41 percent) and by those who had been
unaware of it (63 percent to 37 percent).

Whether the AFL-CIO policy of nonendorsement hurt McGovern's
chances seriously remains open, in light of these findings. Had the
national unions endorsed the South Dakotan, such support undoubtedly
would have helped his candidacy; but whether such help would have
been critical to his victory remains questionable, given the sizable
disaffection with local endorsements of the Democratic nominee that
has been noted.

TICKET-SPLITTING

Data gathered from the panel on their votes for Ohio state offices indicated that the sizable Democratic defection from the candidacy of McGovern reflected more a temporary dissatisfaction with an ostensibly unappealing candidate than it did a permanent retreat from the party. Table 3.17 shows that seven in ten Summit County Democrats voting in the 1972 presidential election supported Democrats in the Ohio State Legislature races. Whereas 28 percent of the Democrats had crossed over to Nixon in the presidential race, no more than 16 percent supported a Republican for the Ohio State Legislature in the same general election. At the same time, Republicans crossed party lines with regard to the legislature races in the same proportion (around 4 percent) as they had in their presidential balloting.

Nixon voters in the Summit County panel were far more likely to split their tickets with regard to statewide races than were McGovern partisans (Table 3.18). Whereas 53 percent of the Nixon supporters in the panel voted for either an Ohio House or Ohio Senate Republican candidate, 88 percent of the McGovern voters cast ballots for Democrats who ran for seats in either house of the Ohio Legislature. Roughly three in ten Nixon supporters voted Republican in both state races, but nearly three-fourths of McGovern's backers voted for Democratic candidates for both branches of the Ohio Legislature.

Four in ten Nixon voters split their tickets by voting for at least one Democratic nominee to either branch of the Ohio Legislature, and more than a fifth actually voted for the two Democrats who ran for seats in each of Ohio's two legislative branches. In comparison, only one in ten McGovern supporters voted for one Republican candidate for a seat in either house of the Ohio Legislature, and a minuscule 2 percent voted the Republican ticket for both Senate and House.

Totally, 11 percent of the Summit County Democratic voters cast ballots fro President Nixon in 1972, and in the very same election voted Democratic for each of the two Ohio Legislature races. This is one more indication that 1972 support for Nixon in Summit County did not necessarily reflect support across the board for Republican ideology, but that support stemmed significantly from voters' assessments of the presidential candidates.

In Summit County, Nixon defection occurred most frequently among Democrats who had noted for Nixon in 1968 (54 percent), Catholics (18 percent), voters in the $10,000-$14,999 annual income

TABLE 3.17

Ticket–Splitting Among Democrats, Republicans, and Independents
(percentages)

	Democrats	Republicans	Independents
Voting for Ohio State Representative			
Republican (N=158)	16	56	29
Democratic (N=347)	70	5	25
Voting for Ohio State Senator			
Republican (N=141)	11	57	32
Democratic (N=341)	73	4	23

TABLE 3.18

Ticket–Splitting Among Nixon and McGovern Voters
(percentages)

	Voted for Nixon	Voted for McGovern
Voted Republican in either Ohio State Legislature contest	53	10
Voted Republican in both Ohio State Legislature contests	31	2
Voted Democratic in either Ohio State Legislature contest	41	88
Voted Democratic in both Ohio State Legislature contests	22	72
Total (N=618)	51	49

bracket (16 percent), voters who were relatively disinterested in politics generally (16 percent), and voters whose interest in the 1972 campaign was moderate (15 percent).

The finding regarding the return to the Democratic fold on the 1972 local scene by the majority of the Democratic defectors from McGovern is of major importance. Again, this gives testimony to the observation that McGovern's candidacy itself, rather than disenchantment with the Democratic Party per se or its ideological stance, lost the presidential race for the Senator from South Dakota.

CHAPTER
4

**ISSUES, IMAGES,
AND VOTE DECISIONS**

The presidential election drama of 1972 has been reviewed, up until now, primarily in terms of describing the outward roles of the cast of voters and their behavior in electoral decision-making. As in attempting to understand any major drama, however, a closer inspection must be made of the values underlying the behavior of the principal characters.

The demographic and related political characteristics discussed earlier can be seen as setting the structural environment for political decision-making and action. Voters constrained by differing aspects of this environment are likewise apt to differ in their motivations, their values, and their beliefs as to what political options will give them the greatest benefit. At some point environmental and psychological characteristics interact to affect a voting decision. In this chapter the impact upon electoral decision-making of two value-related factors will be explored: voters' orientation toward politically relevant issues, and voters' perceptions of the personal attributes of the presidential candidates. The association among voters' issue positions, their candidate image perceptions, and actual votes will be traced through the early and late decision stages of the campaign.

CAMPAIGN ISSUES AND VOTE DECISIONS

Research on American voting behavior over the years has indicated that people generally vote for candidates whom they see as being like themselves in the positions they hold on salient political issues (see, for example, Berelson, Lazarsfeld, and McPhee 1954;

Campbell, Converse, Miller, and Stokes 1960; Miller, Miller, Raine, and Brown 1973). Recent evidence suggests that in presidential elections with high party defection rates (as in 1964 and 1972), voters' positions on issues may be better predictors of vote than party identifications and demographic characteristics (Shulman and Pomper 1975). The ensuing discussion focuses on salience of issues for Summit County voters in 1972, their own positions on issues, and their perceptions of candidates' positions on issues, as related to their final vote decisions.

Salience of Issues and Vote Decisions

Studies of opinions held on substantive political issues by the American electorate have traditionally shown much greater citizen concern with issues involving domestic (particularly economic) policy than with those relating to foreign policy (Key 1966; Flanigan 1972). However, this pattern of issue concern is likely to shift in times of grave crisis in foreign policy, particularly in times of war, when the effects of the conflict are deeply felt domestically. The concern of Americans over U.S. military involvement in Southeast Asia had risen steadily since 1964, when between one-third and one-half of respondents in national opinion polls said they had no opinion with respect to the Vietnam issue. Since 1968 the topic had been in the forefront of citizens' minds as a critical national policy question, as the war began making its impact felt in communities across the United States.

Voters in Summit County paralleled the general U.S. electorate in declaring the Vietnam war to be a political issue of major concern to them in September 1972. Over two-thirds of the Summit County respondents listed the war as one of the three campaign issues about which they were personally most concerned (Table 4.1). Welfare, taxes, and the economy were each named by over a quarter of the voters.* Furthermore, the voters were most likely to perceive McGovern and Nixon as disagreeing the most on these issues, particularly the war (Table 4.2). Far down the lists, both of personally

---

* Issue salience is emerging as a concept of considerable viability in light of recent research on the agenda-setting function of the media (McCombs and Shaw 1972). The definition of issue salience used thus far here is akin to M. McCombs and D. Shaw's, following W. Lippman (1922), in that it reflects an intrapersonal psychological construct of the relative importance of issues (see McLeod, Becker, and Byrnes 1974).

TABLE 4.1

Campaign Issues of Most Concern to Voters
(N = 618)
(percentages)

	Mentioned
Issue*	
War in Southeast Asia	68
Welfare	29
Taxes	26
Economy	25

*Item: "Which three issues that have come up in this year's presidential campaign are you most personally concerned about right now?" (September)

TABLE 4.2

Voters' Perception of Issues McGovern and Nixon
Disagreed About Most
(N = 618)
(percentages)

	Mentioned
Issue*	
War in Southeast Asia	69
Welfare	38
Taxes	25
Busing	23
Economy	19

*Item: "As you personally see it, which three major issues do McGovern and Nixon disagree about most?" (August)

TABLE 4.3

Issues Most Taken into Account in Voting Decision
(N = 618)
(percentages)

	Mentioned
Issue*	
War in Southeast Asia	71
Welfare	22
Economy	22
Taxes	17
Unemployment	14

*Item: "Which three issues in this year's presidential campaign did you most take into account in deciding which presidential candidate to vote for?" (November)

important issues and of issues candidates were perceived as disagreeing on the most, were some of the topics more popularly construed by many commentators as being close to the heart of voter decision-making in 1972. The mythical "three A's"—abortion, acid (or general drug abuse), and amnesty—which purportedly caused sizable numbers of voters to look askance at McGovern, were each mentioned as important issues by no more than 3 percent of the respondents.

Similarly, minuscule weights were accorded the matter of Thomas Eagleton, the prisoner of war issue, pollution, and Watergate. The only real anomaly between ranking the issues of personal voter concern and ranking the candidates' issue disagreement involved busing school children to achieve racial integration. While a substantial 23 percent listed busing as a point of conflict between the candidates, only 10 percent voiced personal concern over it.

Not surprisingly, in November the voters saw this same constellation of issues as being the ones they most took into account in voting for either McGovern or Nixon (Table 4.3).*

*One exception was that unemployment rose rather markedly in salience in November, garnering mention by 14 percent of the voters. No parallel in terms of significantly rising unemployment rolls in Summit County was found to help account for this, albeit some concern over unemployment at the national level was a consistent campaign topic.

TABLE 4.4

Issues Most Taken into Account, by Vote Decision
(percentages)

	Early Deciders		Late Deciders		All Voters	
	Nixon	McGovern	Nixon	McGovern	Nixon	McGovern
War in South-east Asia						
Total Mentioned (N = 439)[*]	42	32	10	13	53	47
Welfare						
Total Mentioned (N = 130)	47	32	7	10	55	45
Economy						
Total Mentioned (N = 129)	47	32	7	12	53	47
Taxes						
Total Mentioned (N = 107)	35	39	8	15	44	56
Unemployment						
Total Mentioned (N = 86)	17	61	6	15	23	77

[*] N's based upon all voters.

To what extend did the McGovern and Nixon cohorts differ in
their evaluations of relative importance of these issues in making their
vote decisions? In a word, markedly. Nixon voters showed consistently greater concern with war, welfare, and the economy, while
McGovern partisans more often mentioned taxes and unemployment
(Table 4.4). The differences on war, welfare, and the economy were
slightly more pronounced among early deciders, and slightly reversed
for those voters who made their decisions later in the campaign. In
other words, Nixon voters appeared more likely than McGovern partisans to have taken the war, welfare, and the economy into account in
making their voting decision, while McGovern voters were more likely
than Nixon supporters to have considered taxes and unemployment.
These findings square extremely well with inferences presented earlier.
The war, welfare, and the general economy, while capital in the minds
of most citizens, might have been of even more concern among the
white, "comfortable," middle-class Nixon cohort, while burdensome

taxes and the threat of unemployment, again of widespread concern, were of even greater importance to most of the economically pressured factions within McGovern's camp.

Position on Issues and Voting Behavior

The voters in the Summit County panel not only perceived the issues of the war, welfare, and the economy as most important in making up their minds for whom to vote, but their subjective positions on these issues were closely allied with their choice of candidates.

In July, respondents were given a list of 17 statements indicating positions on various issues considered relevant to voters at the time of the 1972 campaign.[*] Responses to the statements were factor-analyzed in order to determine whether an underlying pattern of relationships would evolve clearly enough to allow some reduction of the data. An orthogonal varimax rotation yielded five factors that appeared conceptually valid, in that they described cohesive issue factors that were descriptive in terms of previous knowledge of voter issue areas. Items loading above .35 on their respective common factors were extracted to serve as approximate indices representing each of the factors.

The indices were labeled social welfare, economics, war, crime, and morality. The social welfare index included the specific issues of government welfare spending, busing, guaranteed minimum income, and low-cost housing. The economics index was represented by the issues of price control, government attention to the working-man's needs, and government action on unemployment. Withdrawal of forces from Vietnam and isolationism constituted the war index, while the death penalty and protection of rights of lawbreakers made up the crime index. The morality index was composed of the abortion and marijuana issues.

The two issue indices that most strongly differentiated voters for McGovern from voters for Nixon were war and social welfare. The McGovernites clearly preferred immediate withdrawal of U.S. forces from Vietnam and less American foreign involvement in general, and they typically agreed more with pro-social welfare programs than did Nixon voters. Voters' positions on issues centering on the economy were the next most effective in separating the two voting camps. Following distantly behind were voters' positions on morality

---

[*] The issue statements appear in Appendix B.

TABLE 4.5

Regression Analysis of Issue Indices and Vote Preferences

	Early Deciders			Late Deciders			Actual Vote		
	r	r² Added	Beta	r	r² Added	Beta	r	r² Added	Beta
War	-.35	5.6%	-.23	-.23	4.7%	-.18	-.34	10.6%	-.24
Social Welfare	-.40	16.1	-.27	-.14	2.4	-.11	-.33	6.3	-.22
Economics	-.30	3.3	-.19	-.19	1.7	-.14	-.28	3.6	-.18
Morality	.08	0.8	.05	-.07	1.3	-.10	-.07	0.7	-.07
Crime	.08	0.1	.05	.04	0.2	.02	.08	0.2	.06
Total variance explained (R²)	25.9% (N=462)			10.3% (N=141)			21.4% (N=618)		

Note: This analysis and succeeding ones were based on scoring a preference for Nixon = 1 and a preference for McGovern = 2. A low score on the war issue index indicated greater anti-war sentiment; a low score on the social welfare index indicated more pro-welfare views; a low score on the economic index indicated favor of more government action in the economic sector, as in price controls and alleviation of unemployment; a low score on the morality index indicated a more "liberal" viewpoint; and a low score on the crime index indicated favor of more stringent anti-crime measures.

and crime. Indeed, voters' stances on morality and crime essentially failed to discriminate candidate preference at all.

This pattern is quite clearly depicted in Table 4.5. Voters' positions on the issue indices of war and social welfare correlate most highly at the zero-order level with actual vote (-.34 and -.33, respectively), followed by economics, morality, and crime. Introducing a multiple linear regression analysis of these variables did little to change the order or relative strength of impact of each of the issue indices upon final vote; that is, the association between each issue index and final vote did not essentially change when the impact of the other issue indices upon vote was controlled for. The analysis indicated that 21 percent of the variance in vote could be explained by the voters' positions on issue indices.

What emerges is a broadly painted picture of McGovern supporters being generally in favor of U.S. troop withdrawals from Vietnam and against related foreign involvements, in favor of increased welfare-related programs at home, and in favor of greater government attention to economic problems confronting the country. Nixon supporters in general could be characterized by their opposing viewpoints. Moreover, the above three issue clusters closely parallel the issues discussed above that rated as most salient in the voters' minds.

Nixon and McGovern voters seemed in high agreement on the remaining issue clusters centering upon crime and morality. These were related somewhat differently with earlier voting intentions than they were with actual vote (Table 4.5). Voters who had decided whom to vote for in July exhibited nearly the same tendencies as all November voters taken as a group, in terms of the association between issue stance and vote intention, except that social welfare outpulled the war as the ranking issue in discriminating vote choice. *

However, those undecided in July showed somewhat different patterns between their positions on issues and those whom they eventually voted for. For these respondents the best predictor of vote was clearly the candidates' positions on the war; the second most effective predictor was the social welfare issue, closely followed by economics and morality.

---

* Early deciders here included voters who had made up their minds for a presidential candidate in August, and stuck with their decisions. Late deciders included those voters who reached their final choices after August, that is, early undecideds and switchers as well. No substantial differences in issue positions (or image perceptions of the candidates) were found between them, the early undecideds, and the switchers.

TABLE 4.6

Issue Index Standard Scores, by Vote Preference

| | Early Deciders | | Late Deciders | | All Voters | |
	Nixon (N=256)	McGovern (N=206)	Nixon (N=53)	McGovern (N=88)	Nixon (N=312)	McGovern (N=306)
Issue						
Welfare	.36	-.46	.17	-.09	.32	-.33
Economy	.30	-.32	.13	-.24	.28	-.29
War	.36	-.34	.19	-.28	.33	-.34
Crime	-.13	.03	.12	.19	-.08	.09
Morality	.05	-.10	.18	.04	.07	-.07

Hence, the late deciders (primarily a working-class, middle-education, and middle-income grouping) not only saw the war as a relatively more salient issue than did early deciders, but the importance of the war issue to them was reflected more in their voting decisions. To a lesser extent, the same can be said for the morality issue.

Late deciders for Nixon, as opposed to those for McGovern, were more "hawkish" with respect to the war and less concerned with working-class economic issues. It is interesting that among late deciders as a group, issue positions overall explained substantially less of the variance in candidate choice ($R^2 = .09$) than they did among early deciders ($R^2 = .25$).

An inspection of the relative scores of each group of voters on the five issue indices elaborates these points (Table 4.6). The greatest differences in standard scores between McGovern and Nixon voters occur on the indices reflecting stands on the war and welfare, followed by economics. When early versus late deciding cohorts are compared, more interesting differences arise, as is shown by the following examples.

Early deciders for Nixon had higher "anti-economic" and "anti-welfare" scores, they expressed fewer negative feelings about the war, and they were more in favor of strong crime-prevention measures. On the other hand, McGovern early deciders were the most decidedly "pro-economic" and "pro-welfare," and they held stronger anti-war positions; but they were rather neutral with regard to crime prevention.

Late deciders for Nixon were the most substantially "pro-morality" but tended to be fairly neutral on other issues. Late deciders for McGovern scored as the least disposed toward rigorous crime-prevention programs and felt rather strongly against the war (though to a lesser extent than did early deciders for McGovern); on other issues, they also tended toward the middle ground.

While it may hold that late deciders are among the least politically interested of the electorate, they did indicate definite stands on the issues of relevance to them, and these stands were quite indicative of their voting decisions.

Taken another way, these findings imply that one way either McGovern or Nixon could have approached the undecided vote with some hope of success would have been to focus upon the economy and possibly on "law and order" as principal issues. Senator McGovern's positions on the economy never emerged meaningfully from behind the rhetoric on the war and social welfare-related arguments.

While President Nixon, early in his campaign planning, vowed to focus on the economy and foreign policy (White 1973), the rather stiff financial downtrends of 1972 did not really allow a credible Nixon attack on that issue.

Thus neither candidate seized the economic issue as a primary campaign topic. Neither did they make political capital of crime: one perhaps saw it as a phenomenon that had to be rooted out through more subtle social action programs, and the other feared backlash due to the soaring crime rates during his own administration and to the rising legal problems among his own appointees.

On the other hand, in looking at the voting bloc as a whole, it is interesting that such comparatively little concern over crime and morality, and so few voting choices related to these issues, were in evidence. This may not indicate that substantial numbers of citizens considered lawlessness, drugs, abortion, and attendant crucial community concerns (many with racial overtones) to be insignificant issues. It does imply, however, that neither the salience of these issues nor positions with respect to them underlay voting behavior in the 1972 presidential election. Voting appeared more meaningfully related to traditional national problems, about which voters may have perceived the presidential candidates actually could do more. International relations and federally sponsored welfare programs may be viewed as an area over which the executive branch can attempt moderate influence, albeit with sporadic success. The President, however, may be seen as much less effective in establishing adequate local crime control methods, and least effective in resolving moral dilemmas.

What differences in positions on issues were found between Democrats for Nixon versus Democratic loyalists, and between Independents for McGovern versus those for Nixon? First, the two Democratic factions were most clearly divided in feelings about welfare, with Democratic Nixon backers being substantially anti-welfare and

TABLE 4.7

Issue Index Standard Scores, by Vote Preference, by Party

Issue	Democrats Nixon (N=83)	Democrats McGovern (N=228)	Independents Nixon (N=104)	Independents McGovern (N=73)	Republicans Nixon (N=125)	Republicans *
Welfare	.35	-.37	.20	-.21	.41	—
Economy	.05	-.29	.19	-.27	.51	—
War	.23	-.38	.33	-.19	.40	—
Crime	.00	.06	-.16	.21	-.07	—
Morality	.23	.00	-.04	-.31	.05	—

*Scores not computed for McGovern Republican voters due to small N (N = 5).

TABLE 4.8

Correlations (r) Between Issue Indices and Voter
Demographic Characteristics
(N = 618)

Issue Index	Age	Education	Income	Occupation	Race
Welfare	.07	.18	.26	.09	-.31
Economy	-.04	.27	.19	.21	-.11
War	.02	.21	.12	.12	-.14
Crime	.04	.00	-.07	-.03	.02
Morality	-.23	-.21	-.10	-.16	.03

McGovern voters being just as strongly in favor of it (Table 4.7). The McGovern faction was also strongly behind governmental economic action, while the defecting group was more toward the middle. The McGovern supporters were definitely anti-war, while the Democratic defectors tended toward the opposite end of the spectrum (though not nearly as much as Republican and Independent Nixon voters). Interestingly, the Democrats for Nixon were highly conservative on the morality dimension, while the McGovern loyalists tended toward neutrality. Hence, at least in terms of issues, Nixon picked up a segment of Democrats who took a strong stand against welfare, were fairly conservative on the war and morality, and were "middle of the road" on economics and law and order.

Independents voting for Nixon differed most from those who favored McGovern in their position on the war. Those supporting Nixon were also notably more opposed to welfare and government economic strictures. The two groups of Independents differed substantially on the crime issue, with the Nixon voters forming the strongest anti-crime group of all compared, and McGovern Independents being the least so. The McGovern backers were highly liberal on morality, while Nixon voters were equivocal on that issue.

Demographic associations with the issue dimensions followed predictable patterns (Table 4.8). Voters in upper status categories of income, education, and occupation tended to be more strongly opposed to welfare and governmental economic measures, somewhat more positive toward the war, and more conservative on morality. Black voters tended in the opposite direction on the above points, no doubt much as a function of socioeconomic status. Age was basically unrelated to issue stances, except that younger voters were notably more liberal on morality.

Perceived Agreement on Issues and Voting Behavior

The relationships between panel respondents' stands on issues and their choices for President serve primarily to describe who voted for whom in terms of issues. A more meaningful interpretation in terms of voting decision processes may be gleaned from examining not only voters' stands on issues alone, but voters' perceptions of how closely each presidential candidate's issue position matched the voters' own. For a preliminary examination of this, simple absolute value-difference scores (D-scores) were computed between each respondent's score on each issue index and each respondent's perception of both George McGovern's position on the issue index and

TABLE 4.9

Regression Analysis of Respondent-Candidate Issue Perceived Agreement on Vote Decision

	Early Deciders			Late Deciders			Actual Vote		
	r	r² Added	Beta	r	r² Added	Beta	r	r² Added	Beta
Nixon/Economics	.42	18.2%	.31	.15	1.0%	.08	.34	12.1%	.26
McGovern/Welfare	-.40	11.6	-.24	-.11	0.2	-.04	-.34	10.1	-.20
McGovern/Economics	-.35	6.7	-.24	-.14	1.3	-.12	-.30	5.6	-.22
McGovern/War	-.27	1.2	-.09	-.23	4.5	-.15	-.28	2.1	-.12
Nixon/Welfare	.25	1.6	.11	.02	0.3	-.02	.20	1.0	.10
Nixon/War	.28	2.0	.08	.22	2.8	.15	.26	0.8	.08
Nixon/Morality	.21	0.2	.07	.04	0.6	.04	.17	0.1	.07
McGovern/Morality	-.20	0.1	-.07	-.07	0.0	-.04	-.16	0.1	-.06
McGovern/Crime	-.07	0.0	-.02	.01	0.0	.03	-.08	0.0	-.02
Nixon/Crime	.07	0.0	.02	.06	0.0	.00	.06	0.0	.01
Total variance explained (R^2)	41.8%			10.9%			32.1%		
	(N=462)			(N=141)			(N=618)		

Note: The analysis is based on scoring a preference for Nixon = 1, and a preference for McGovern = 2. On the issue perception D-scores, a low score indicated greater agreement with the respective candidate.

Richard Nixon's position.* This resulted in one D-score representing each respondent's perceived agreement with McGovern on each issue index, and one D-score representing each respondent's perceived agreement with Nixon on each index. These D-scores were then compared with respondents' vote decisions.†

Table 4.9 presents the fruits of this analysis in regression analysis form, with vote decisions again being the focal variables. The main predictor of actual vote, in terms of variance explained, was degree of perceived agreement between respondents' position and Nixon's position on the economic issue; put another way, the more voters saw themselves as agreeing with Nixon on economics, the more likely they were to vote for him. Conversely, the more voters saw themselves disagreeing with Nixon's economic position, the more likely they were to vote for George McGovern.

The next best predictor was perceived agreement between voters' own stand and McGovern's perceived stand on social welfare, immediately followed by perceived agreement with McGovern's positions on economics and the war, Nixon's position on welfare, and Nixon's stand on the war. Perceived agreement on both candidates' positions on crime was the least effective predictor of vote.

Data presented earlier suggested that among voters' own issue positions, their stances on the war, welfare, and economics, in that order, were the main predictors of vote. However, in terms of voters' perceived agreement with candidates' positions, it appears that voters were more likely to have voted parallel to both candidates' perceived agreement with them on economics and to perceived agreement with McGovern's position on welfare. Hence, the war issue does not appear quite as important a predictor when viewed in terms of voters' perceptions of candidates' positions. Voters may not have thought McGovern and Nixon to be as widely divided on the war issue as on economics. It should also be noted that voters' perceptions of McGovern's, rather than Nixon's, positions on welfare and the war were the more predictive of direction of vote.

In comparing early versus late deciders with respect to perceived agreement and vote, the overall variance in vote explained by perceived

---

*Respondents were not only asked their own opinions on the 17 issue statements but were also asked to respond to each issue statement as they thought McGovern and Nixon would respond. Each candidate's perceived positions on the issue indices were then computed for each respondent in the same way as respondents' scores on the indices were computed.

†These measures in no way describe the accuracy with which respondents perceived candidates' positions on issues.

agreement is considerably lower among late deciders ($R^2 = .41$). In
other words, early deciders cast votes more in line with perceived
issue agreement with candidates. Moreover, early deciders differed
from late deciders in the relative predictive power with respect to
specific issues. Most noticeably, perceived agreement with McGovern's
and Nixon's positions on the war issue was markedly higher in predictive power among late deciders than among early deciders.

Curiously, early deciders' perceived agreement with Nixon's
stand on welfare resulted in a vote prediction opposite that found among
late deciders. Early deciders who saw themselves more in agreement
with Nixon's welfare stand were more likely to vote for Nixon; late
deciders, likewise seeing themselves agreeing more with Nixon on
welfare, tended to vote for McGovern.

These tentative analyses do not go far in explaining the specific
nature of interactions between perceived issue agreement and vote, yet
they raise some provocative possibilities. For example, it could be
that late deciders for McGovern agreed more with Nixon's welfare
position but saw other decision-making attributes as more salient; or
it could be argued that late deciders for Nixon disagreed more with
Nixon on welfare but again were more concerned with other attributes.
More likely, it is a combination of the above. In any case, more
detailed analysis of direction of vote, perceived agreement on issues,
and related decision-making attributes in political campaigns is certainly called for.

CANDIDATE IMAGES AND VOTE DECISIONS

They want him to be larger than life, a living legend,
and yet quintessentially human; someone to be held up
to their children as a model; and someone to be cher-
ished by themselves as a revered member of the family.

Thus did the author of the best-seller The Selling of the President 1968 characterize the American political quest for the ideal
President. To meet the ideal, it has been assumed and well-
documented that presidential candidates, and indeed most candidates
for major offices, rely to some extent upon accentuating the positive
attributes associated with their image and downplaying the negative.
The business of "image projection," notably through the mass media
and especially through television, has received much exploration in
recent years (McGinness 1969; Nimmo 1970; Mendelsohn and Crespi
1970; Hiebert et al. 1971). Unfortunately, relatively little effort has
been expended in attempting to determine image perceptions of the

TABLE 4.10

Personal Qualities Most Associated with McGovern and Nixon, [*]
by Vote Decision
(N = 618)
(percentages)

	McGovern		Nixon	
	Voted for McGovern	Voted for Nixon	Voted for McGovern	Voted for Nixon
Trustworthiness/ Nontrustworthiness	25	26	27	27
Effectiveness/ Noneffectiveness	9	10	13	18
Strength/Weakness	5	12	4	12
Friendliness/Unfriendliness	10	3	6	8

[*] Item: "If you had to describe the main qualities and characteristics of (George McGovern/Richard Nixon) in five or six words and
phrases, which five or six words and phrases would you use?"
(October)

intended audiences: the voters. What work has been reported typically
focuses upon the conceptual and operational difficulties inherent in
such analysis (Carter 1962; Tannenbaum, Greenberg, and Silverman
1962).

The measurement of image perceptions in our sample was relatively simplistic, based upon extrapolation from earlier studies and
image dimensions typically associated with political candidates.

Respondents in July were presented six pairs of image attribute
opposites (warm, friendly-cold, unfriendly; strong-weak; smart-dumb;
can be trusted-cannot be trusted; safe-dangerous; and effective-not
effective), and were asked to report which word or set of words in
each pair most closely described how they felt about George McGovern
and Richard Nixon.

In October respondents were asked to list the six personal qualities they most closely associated with McGovern and with Nixon. This
served as a general indicator of salience of images. Table 4.10 de-
picts the response frequency of the most mentioned personal qualities
associated with each candidate. The qualities listed most often were

TABLE 4.11

Regression Analysis of Image Attributes and Vote Orientations

	Early Deciders			Late Deciders			Actual Vote		
	r	r² Added	Beta	r	r² Added	Beta	r	r² Added	Beta
Nixon/Trust	.68	46.2%	.35	.17	0.2%	.03	.57	31.6%	.32
McGovern/Safe–Dangerous	-.41	1.2	-.11	.07	0.3	-.04	-.31	6.1	-.15
Nixon/Effective	.57	8.5	.24	.10	0.0	.00	.47	3.6	.20
Nixon/Safe–Dangerous	.62	1.5	.18	.09	0.1	-.04	.50	1.2	.13
McGovern/Effective	-.35	1.1	-.07	.16	0.4	.08	-.24	0.9	-.06
Nixon/Warm–Cold	.41	0.6	.04	.17	2.1	.17	.35	0.5	.06
McGovern/Trust	-.35	4.5	-.10	.21	3.8	.20	-.21	0.4	-.06
McGovern/Warm–Cold	-.22	0.1	-.02	.07	0.3	-.07	-.15	0.1	-.03
Nixon/Smart–Dumb	.22	0.0	-.05	.14	0.5	.11	.21	0.1	-.02
McGovern/Smart–Dumb	-.20	0.0	-.04	.08	0.2	-.07	-.11	0.1	-.02
McGovern/Strong–Weak	-.31	0.0	-.05	.16	0.9	.08	-.19	0.0	-.01
Nixon/Strong–Weak	.40	0.0	.03	.03	0.9	-.07	.32	0.0	.00
Total variance explained (R²)		63.8% (N=462)			9.9% (N=141)			44.6% (N=618)	

easily assimilated into the fixed-response categories described, and
are so presented. Trustworthiness (positive or negative) was foremost
in the voters' consideration as a quality to be associated with both
candidates. On the other hand, Nixon was somewhat more likely to be
described as effective than was McGovern, particularly among Nixon
voters. He was also more likely to be pictured in terms of strong
versus weak by both cohorts of voters. Association of friendliness
with the candidates appeared to depend very much on whom one voted
for; McGovern partisans were more likely to describe McGovern as
friendly, while Nixon voters were more likely to describe their candidate as such.

Similarly, the fixed-response image attribute that best discrim-
inated between Nixon voters and McGovern voters centered upon those
voters' feelings as to whether or not Richard Nixon could be trusted
(Table 4.11). Nixon voters rather decisively indicated feelings that
the President was trustworthy, while McGovern partisans just as
decisively said they felt he was not. Interestingly, following trust in
discriminating power among voters were perceptions of McGovern on
the safe-dangerous dimension, with McGovern supporters naturally
seeing him as safer than did Nixon backers. Perception of Nixon's
effectiveness was next in discriminating import, succeeded closely by
perceptions of Nixon on the safe-dangerous attribute. Nixon voters
were likely to see Nixon as somewhat more safe than backers of
McGovern saw their candidate. Other ranking attributes in this regard
were McGovern's effectiveness, Nixon's "warm-cold" image, and
trust in McGovern. The "strong-weak" attribute of both candidates
ranked last. *

---

*
  Of course, Nixon's trust and effectiveness dimensions were
highly correlated (r = .51 for the sample as a whole). Yet a major
question deserving close scrutiny is to what extent trust can be sepa-
rated from effectiveness in public perception of political figures. An
effective person who lacks trustworthiness may be quite welcome
under many circumstances, but typically not in situations where that
person is perceived by others as having significant power over them.
Classic explication of the phenomenon of credibility has suggested that
at least two dimensions of the concept warrant investigation: those of
trustworthiness and expertise (Hovland and Weiss 1951). In terms of
the credibility of political figures, expertise may be translated into
effectiveness. The bulk of research on political credibility thus far
has focused on the trustworthiness dimension; no doubt the expertise,
or effectiveness, dimension deserves much further exploration. Post-
1972 election opinion poll results appear in some instances to suggest
that even citizens who may not have perceived President Nixon as

TABLE 4.12

Image Attribute Mean Scores, by Vote Preference

Attributes*	Early Deciders		Late Deciders		Actual Vote	
	Nixon (N=257)	McGovern (N=222)	Nixon (N=56)	McGovern (N=83)	Nixon (N=312)	McGovern (N=306)
Warm-Cold						
Nixon	1.38	2.12	1.55	1.86	1.41	2.04
McGovern	1.54	1.23	1.40	1.51	1.53	1.31
Strong-Weak						
Nixon	1.13	1.75	1.43	1.48	1.18	1.68
McGovern	1.89	1.36	1.60	1.89	1.85	1.51
Smart-Dumb						
Nixon	1.05	1.27	1.19	1.36	1.07	1.29
McGovern	1.29	1.08	1.25	1.34	1.28	1.16
Trustworthiness						
Nixon	1.17	2.40	1.68	1.09	1.25	2.28
McGovern	1.93	1.36	1.55	1.89	1.87	1.53
Safe-Dangerous						
Nixon	1.10	2.17	1.58	1.75	1.18	2.05
McGovern	2.07	1.36	1.66	1.77	2.01	1.48
Effectiveness						
Nixon	1.13	2.14	1.66	1.85	1.22	2.06
McGovern	2.01	1.43	1.64	1.89	1.96	1.57

*Attribute scoring: Positive direction = 1.
                  Negative direction = 3.

Among late deciders, perceptions of McGovern's trustworthiness explained the most variance in vote. Perceptions of the candidates as strong versus weak likewise rose in predictive power among the late deciders. The most striking factor among late deciders is certainly that image perceptions of McGovern explained much greater variance

trustworthy in his handling of the Watergate matter and attendant scandals were still willing to forgive any alleged trespasses he may have committed in that realm and continued to support him as a credible "expert" in effectively carrying out the duties of his office.

TABLE 4.13

Image Attribute Mean Scores, by Vote Preference, by Party

Attributes	Democrats for		Republicans for		Independents for	
	McGovern (N=228)	Nixon (N=83)	McGovern (N=5)	Nixon (N=125)	McGovern (N=73)	Nixon (N=104)
Warm-Cold						
Nixon	2.08	1.52	—	1.28	1.93	1.48
McGovern	1.30	1.65	—	1.50	1.37	1.47
Strong-Weak						
Nixon	1.76	1.41	—	1.08	1.74	1.13
McGovern	1.52	1.92	—	1.94	1.49	1.68
Smart-Dumb						
Nixon	1.31	1.16	—	1.03	1.26	1.06
McGovern	1.17	1.36	—	1.23	1.12	1.26
Trustworthiness						
Nixon	2.33	1.52	—	1.08	2.12	1.25
McGovern	1.51	1.86	—	1.94	1.52	1.79
Safe-Dangerous						
Nixon	2.02	1.37	—	1.07	2.12	1.15
McGovern	1.46	2.05	—	2.10	1.53	1.88
Effectiveness						
Nixon	2.08	1.45	—	1.10	1.99	1.1
McGovern	1.55	2.02	—	2.02	1.60	1.82

than image perceptions of Nixon, as happened among early deciders.
The events of the campaign cannot help but have played a role in these
perceptions of late deciders. It is especially interesting that lack of
trust in McGovern was associated with voting for him among late
deciders, but not among early deciders.

It is noteworthy that on all of the image dimensions save one,
Nixon voters saw their candidate as more "positive" (more trustworthy,
more effective, and so on) than McGovern voters saw their candidate
(Table 4.12). The one dimension on which this was not found was
"warm-cold." On the contrary, McGovern voters saw Nixon as relatively more negative than Nixon voters saw McGovern on every dimension save "strong-weak." McGovern thus appeared to have been seen

as more "neutral," or perhaps simply more ambiguous, than the
incumbent President. At any rate, McGovern does not seem to have
aroused the intensity of image perceptions that Nixon did.

Late deciders also scored the candidate they eventually voted
for as considerably less positive on each attribute than did early
deciders.

Finally, when comparing the responses of Nixon voters with
those of the McGovern supporters, Nixon was seen by far as being the
stronger, safer, and more effective candidate. He was also seen as
being slightly smarter than McGovern, but slightly less trustworthy.
McGovern was perceived as decidedly more friendly than Nixon.

Democrats who cast their votes for Richard Nixon differed from
Republican Nixon partisans in their more "neutral" image perceptions
of both the President and George McGovern (Table 4.13). Independents, in like manner, were less likely to perceive marked image dis-
tinctions between the candidates than were party loyalists, regardless
of whom they voted for.

ISSUES, IMAGES, AND VOTE DECISIONS

Were voting decisions more reflective of voters' perceptions of
the images of the presidential candidates, or of voters' perceptions of
how closely the candidates agreed with them on issues? Table 4.14
presents a preliminary examination of this question in the form of a
regression analysis combining both image and issue position perceptions of voters as predictors of vote decisions. The results indicate
that the answer to the question is mixed. Among all voters, perceptions of Nixon's trustworthiness, McGovern's safe-dangerous image,
and Nixon's effectiveness appear as the main predictors of vote; but
voters' perceived agreement with McGovern on the economic issue
follows closely. Ranked directly under the above were perceived
agreement with Nixon's economic position and with McGovern's welfare
stand, and perception of Nixon's safe-dangerous image. While the
main image perceptions are more efficient predictors of vote, issue-
related perceptions play no small role here; and a more explicit
detailing of these relationships must await a more extensive investigation of interactions between these variables. In the previous analysis,
image perceptions alone accounted for 44 percent of the variance in
vote, while perceived agreement on issues accounted for 32 percent.
Taken together in the above analysis, the two groups of variables
combined to account for 49 percent of the variance. This indicates
rather strong interaction effects that merit closer scrutiny.

TABLE 4.14

Regression Analysis of Vote Preference, by Image
and Candidate-Respondent Issue Agreement

	Early Deciders			Late Deciders			Actual Vote		
	r	r^2 Added	Beta	r	r^2 Added	Beta	r	r^2 Added	Beta
Nixon/Trust	.68	46.1%	.32	.17	0.0%	.02	.57	31.5%	.25
McGovern/Safe-Dangerous	-.41	1.4	-.09	.07	0.1	-.05	-.31	5.5	-.12
Nixon/Effective	.57	7.6	.23	.10	0.1	-.05	.47	3.6	.15
McGovern/Economics	-.35	0.3	-.07	-.14	0.0	.02	-.30	2.2	-.12
Nixon/Economics	.42	1.2	.12	.15	0.1	.08	.35	2.1	.10
McGovern/Welfare	-.40	0.2	.05	-.11	0.2	.07	-.34	1.5	-.09
Nixon/Safe-Dangerous	.62	2.3	.19	.09	0.0	-.02	.50	1.4	.09
Nixon/Welfare	.25	0.0	-.02	.02	1.1	-.13	.20	1.0	.06
McGovern/War	-.27	0.1	.04	-.23	0.1	-.06	-.28	0.6	-.06
Nixon/Warm-Cold	.41	0.0	.02	.17	2.3	.18	.35	0.6	.07
McGovern/Effective	-.35	1.2	-.06	.16	0.9	.10	-.24	0.2	-.04
Nixon/Morality	.21	0.0	.00	.04	0.8	-.06	.17	0.0	.03
Nixon/War	.28	0.1	-.06	.22	0.1	-.04	.26	0.0	.03
McGovern/Crime	-.07	0.1	-.05	.01	0.0	.00	-.08	0.0	-.03
McGovern/Morality	-.20	0.6	.04	-.07	1.3	.14	-.16	0.1	-.03
McGovern/Trust	-.35	4.5	-.09	.21	3.6	.20	-.21	0.0	-.03
McGovern/Smart-Dumb	-.20	0.1	-.05	.08	0.1	-.04	-.11	0.0	-.02
Nixon/Smart-Dumb	.22	0.1	-.04	.14	1.0	.10	.21	0.0	-.01
McGovern/Strong-Weak	-.31	0.2	-.05	.16	0.1	.07	-.19	0.0	-.01
McGovern/Warm-Cold	-.22	0.0	-.01	.07	0.6	-.09	-.15	0.0	-.01
Nixon/Crime	.07	0.0	.02	.06	0.7	-.11	.06	0.0	.01
Nixon/Strong-Weak	.40	0.0	.00	.03	0.1	-.06	.32	0.0	.00
Total variance explained (R^2)		66.1%			14.6%			50.3%	
		(N=462)			(N=141)			(N=618)	

At this point it appears that in terms of images and issues, vote decisions most closely parallel voters' perceptions of trust vis-a-vis the incumbent Nixon, coupled with perceived agreement or disagreement with the economic policies of both candidates. McGovern's image does not appear to have entered into the decision-making process nearly as much as his positions on selected issues, or at least voters' perceptions of those positions. For Nixon, the reverse appears to hold true. Voters' perceptions of his image were more predictive of vote than his perceived issue positions and were, in fact, the most salient predictors of vote overall.

When early and late deciders are compared, the ranking of variables differs considerably. As expected from the previous analyses, trust in McGovern was a decidedly greater factor among late deciders than early, as were perceptions of Nixon on the warm-cold dimension. All image and issue-agreement perceptions combined yielded considerably less explained variance in vote among late deciders ($R^2 = .14$) than among early deciders ($R^2 = .66$), and issues explained very little variance among late deciders when combined with images. In sum, late deciders voted less consistently according to image and issue-agreement perceptions; and where these were related to vote, the pattern of association was substantially different from that of early deciders. Late deciders' perceptions of McGovern's image appear more closely related to vote than do those of early deciders, for whom Nixon's image and both candidates' issue positions appeared more important.

Numerous relationships within this analysis look immensely appealing in terms of more accurately delineating voting proclivities as related to images and issues. The temptation to probe further into this uncharted territory without more exact analytic tools and introspection will be abandoned at this time, however.

Self-Perceived Decision Attributes of Voters

It was of some interest to ascertain which attributes voters perceived themselves as taking into account in deciding for whom to vote. Following the election, the respondents were asked which of three

TABLE 4.15

Perceived Decision Attributes, by Vote Preference
(percentages)

Attribute	Early Deciders		Late Deciders		Actual Vote	
	Nixon	McGovern	Nixon	McGovern	Nixon	McGovern
Party (N = 57)	9	54	5	28	14	86
Personal Qualities (N = 184)	47	34	9	8	57	44
Issue Position (N = 350)	45	31	9	13	54	46
Don't Know (N = 27)	30	19	7	41	41	59
Total (N = 618)	41	33	9	14	50	49

Note: Percents based on total responses in each set.

TABLE 4.16

Regression Analysis of Issue and Image Perceptions, Demographic
Characteristics, and Party, by Vote Preference

	Early Deciders			Late Deciders			Actual Vote		
	r	r² Added	Beta	r	r² Added	Beta	r	r² Added	Beta
Nixon/Trust	.68	46.0%	.29	.17	0.1%	.04	.57	31.5%	.23
McGovern/Safe-Dangerous	-.41	1.2	-.07	.07	0.0	.01	-.31	5.5	-.11
Nixon/Effective	.57	8.4	.21	.10	0.6	-.12	.47	4.4	.13
McGovern/Economics	-.35	0.5	-.08	-.14	0.0	.02	-.30	2.5	-.11
Nixon/Economics	.42	1.4	.11	.15	0.4	.09	.35	1.5	.09
Race	.44	1.6	.12	.03	0.0	.00	.34	0.8	.08
Nixon/Warm-Cold	.41	0.0	.03	.17	2.5	.20	.35	0.5	.08
Nixon/Welfare	.25	0.1	-.03	.02	1.8	-.19	.20	0.5	.06
McGovern/Welfare	-.40	0.1	.04	-.11	0.3	.08	-.34	0.5	-.06
Nixon/Safe-Dangerous	.62	1.7	.16	.09	0.0	-.02	.50	0.4	.07
McGovern/War	-.27	0.0	.03	-.23	0.2	-.05	-.28	0.3	-.06
Party	.26	0.5	.05	-.11	0.5	-.11	.21	0.3	.05
Education	-.25	0.1	-.03	.02	1.7	.19	-.19	0.2	-.01
Nixon/Morality	.21	0.0	.01	.04	0.2	-.05	.17	0.2	.04
Income	-.20	0.1	-.04	-.03	0.2	-.06	-.17	0.2	-.04
McGovern/Morality	-.20	0.0	.02	-.07	0.6	.14	-.16	0.1	-.04
McGovern/Effective	-.35	0.4	-.06	.16	0.5	.13	-.24	0.1	-.03
McGovern/Crime	-.07	0.3	-.05	-.01	0.0	.00	-.08	0.1	-.04
Nixon/War	.28	0.0	-.03	.22	0.1	-.05	.26	0.0	.03
McGovern/Smart-Dumb	-.20	0.3	-.05	.08	0.1	-.05	.11	0.0	-.03
McGovern/Trust	-.35	0.5	-.09	.21	3.5	.19	-.21	0.0	-.03
Nixon/Smart-Dumb	.22	0.6	-.06	.14	0.4	.09	.21	0.0	-.02
McGovern/Warm-Cold	-.22	0.0	-.01	.07	0.4	-.09	-.15	0.0	-.02
Occupation	-.22	0.6	-.07	-.08	0.9	-.16	-.19	0.0	-.08
Age	-.05	0.1	-.05	.11	0.2	.07	-.01	0.0	.00
Nixon/Strong-Weak	.40	0.0	.00	.02	0.0	-.03	.32	0.0	.00
Nixon/Crime	.07	0.0	.02	.06	0.6	-.12	.06	0.0	-.01
McGovern/Strong-Weak	-.31	0.1	-.04	.16	0.0	.04	-.19	0.0	-.01
Total variance explained (R²)	68.4% (N=462)			17.0% (N=141)			51.3% (N=618)		

attributes—the political party of the candidate, the personal qualities
of the man, or the stands he took on political issues—was most important in deciding which candidate to vote for.

Well over half of the voters (57 percent) said they took the candidate's stance on issues more into account than either his personal
qualities (30 percent) or his party affiliation (9 percent) (Table 4.15).
Nixon voters were more likely to name both position on issues and
personal qualities, while McGovern voters were much more apt to
name party. Indeed, over 80 percent of those listing party as the
decisive attribute were in the McGovern camp, and it did not seem to
matter whether they had made up their minds before July or later in
the campaign: similarly high proportions of early and late deciders
said they voted for McGovern primarily because he was a Democrat.

Issues, Images, Demographics, Party,
and Vote Decisions

Table 4.16 represents a beginning exploration of the relative
import on the vote decision of issue and image perceptions, demographic characteristics, and political party identification.

It is apparent that among voters in the Summit County panel, the
main predictors of actual vote were perceived image attributes, especially as applied to Richard Nixon. Perceived agreement of voters
with both Nixon's and McGovern's positions on economics closely followed the main image attributes. After these, race entered into the
picture, followed by a lengthy intermixing of images, issue positions,
and demographic indicators. Political party appears relatively low
on the list, and explained considerably less variance in vote than many
of the image and issue position perceptions. Generally, the same
mixed pattern held when early deciders were compared with late
deciders, with differences appearing between the two groups in accord-
ance with results presented in earlier discussions.

A CONCLUDING NOTE

Voters' own positions on issues, their perceptions of McGovern's
and Nixon's positions, and voters' image perceptions of candidates
were critical predictors of their final vote decisions. Voters' perceptions of candidates' images and their perceptions of agreement between
their own positions and those of the candidates were intermixed in
predictive ability, although perception of Nixon as trustworthy was

the prime indicator. However, strong differences were found between early-deciding and late-deciding voters.

Most notably, voters' issue and image perceptions explained only 10 percent of the variance in vote choice among late deciders, but explained 63 percent among early deciders. Indeed, issue and image perceptions, combined with key demographic and political characteristics, explained but 17 percent of variance in vote choice among late deciders, while explaining 69 percent among early deciders. Late deciders, in short, seem highly unpredictable in their vote choices, at least by standard indicators such as those described here.

Late deciders gave a more definite appearance of acting according to either immediate circumstances of the campaign, social pressures, or perhaps, in some cases, whims of the moment. The role of mass media as agents of influence among this group during the campaign obviously needs closer inspection. Certainly, the attributes on which the "rational" voter would be assumed to base his choice of presidential candidate seem to have relatively little bearing among late deciders.

Among early deciders, on the other hand, it is clear that issue and image perceptions are highly related to vote decisions, and that the often-raised argument over whether issue or image perceptions are the more important in vote decisions seems moot. Rather, it appears that the specific issue and image perceptions voters hold vis-a-vis a given candidate are crucial.

Given these data, it is apparent that simplistic models of vote prediction based upon demographic and/or political indicators alone tell only a small part of the story. It is the interactions between those and more subtle variables, such as image and issue perceptions, that seem to lead to more important differences in electoral decision-making.

THE INFLUENCES
OF THE CAMPAIGN
ON VOTER
DECISION-MAKING

5

CAMPAIGN ORIENTATIONS, MASS MEDIA, AND INFLUENCES ON VOTE DECISIONS

Attention now turns from examining which voters chose which candidates in the 1972 presidential election to looking at the processes by which they did so. Emphasized in this chapter will be ways in which voters oriented themselves to the ongoing political campaign, and the influences of that campaign on their decisions. The role of communications media as agents of influence will be particularly scrutinized. The potential impact of mass communications on voters has long fascinated social scientists, as well as journalists, professional campaign managers, social critics and, of course, political candidates.

A review of current thinking about ways in which voters react to campaigns in general will be presented, followed by an examination of influences on voter decision-making within the Summit County panel during the 1972 presidential race. As will be seen, the process is complex; nonetheless, specific uses of the campaign, including mass media, by the voters can be discerned and related to how they made up their minds in choosing a President.

INFLUENCES OF COMMUNICATION ON VOTER DECISION-MAKING: AN OVERVIEW

David Sears (1969) has called voting "the main form of political participation for most Americans," and it is also apparent that "the most dramatic political changes in America usually derive from elections."

Theoretically, potential voters enter campaigns highly involved and knowledgeable, yet nonpartisan, intent on choosing the best

candidate for the country's needs on the basis of information presented
to and evaluated by them during the campaign. However, common
sense, everyday observations, and a catalog of research evidence tell
us that such ideal voter types are rarely found in American society.
It was through the pioneering work of Paul Lazarsfeld and his col-
leagues at Columbia University during the 1940s that the present
understanding of the basic dynamics of the American voter began to
evolve (Lazarsfeld, Berelson, and Gaudet 1948; Berelson, Lazarsfeld,
and McPhee 1954).

Survey studies of voter behavior in the 1940 and 1948 presidential
elections, conducted under Lazarsfeld, dispelled myths of the time
that voter decision-making was primarily a "rational" marketplace
process, that volatile political changes occurred during election campaigns, and that mass media played significant roles in influencing
voter behavior. Rather, Lazarsfeld's research suggested that upward
of 80 to 90 percent of voters in those elections had chosen candidates
well before the formal campaign got under way. These early-deciding
voters seemed to base their choices on party preferences in conjunction
with their socioeconomic characteristics. Those few voters making up
their minds during the campaign appeared the least politically interested, and typically were under cross-pressures from contrasting
reference groups.

Lazarsfeld also offered data strongly disputing the then-popular
"hypodermic" model of media effects, couched in psychological learning
theory, which assumed that exposure to a communication could be
equated with effect from that communication: if only a person could
be exposed enough times to a message, the assumption went, that person would be affected in the direction intended by the message.

Instead, Lazarsfeld found that the contribution of mass communications to whatever voter influence processes took place over the
campaign seemed nil. Voters who had already made a choice appeared
to expose themselves primarily to media content supporting their
existing biases, and undecided voters seemed to pay little attention to
media per se. Thus media were hypothesized to play more of a reinforcing role during campaigns, rather than actively helping voters
make up their minds or converting to another candidate those who
already had decided. Lazarsfeld further suggested that interpersonal
communications were more influential than mass media as agents of
influence on voters, and that a "two-step flow" of political communication took place within communities. That is, more politically adroit
and media-attentive "opinion leaders" were seen to serve as trans-
mitters of campaign information and/or influence to their less involved
acquaintances.

However, precise data justifying the above propositions were
scarce. While mass communications certainly did not seem to be

exerting strong influence on voters one way or another, there was really no direct evidence that voters were being "reinforced" by the media. More seriously, no clear comparisons of media or interpersonal communication behaviors and their possible effects were made among voters who decided upon a candidate prior to the campaign, those who initially decided during the campaign, and those who switched candidates or were "converted" during the campaign. Likewise, the process by which political opinion leaders supposedly informed or influenced their "followers" was never satisfactorily delineated. While arguments offered in these early studies were compelling in their clarity and inherent logic, the evidence was not substantial. Critical reviews of this research and other early attempts at voter assessment are found in P. H. Rossi (1959), D. Sears (1969), and C. A. Sheingold (1973).

Since no data-gathering studies in political communication near the level of the Columbia attempts were repeated for years, Lazarsfeld's findings tended to have the impact of the final word. This impact was not softened by the publication of Joseph Klapper's Effects of Mass Communication (1960), which still stands as the comprehensive, single-volume reference on the subject, despite being in need of extensive updating. The book devoted its opening sections to mass media and political persuasion research, leaning heavily on the Lazarsfeld studies. More important, it summarized those results more tightly and clearly than before. As cautious as Klapper was in warning his readers that he was inferring tentative emerging generalizations in the way of a "phenomenistic" model of communications and was presenting such generalizations mainly to stimulate research, his propositions were taken much at face value; and the "limited effects" model became quite solidly entrenched in communication research, particularly as applied to politics and the mass media.

Research on election campaigns during the 1950s and early 1960s tended to focus on demographic and, especially, psychological factors in voter behavior, at the expense of further study of communication and other social interaction variables. The University of Michigan Survey Research Center, for example, has examined presidential elections since 1952 by interviewing national samples of citizens and has uncovered substantial information about psychological and sociological patterns of voting in the United States. (See, for example, Campbell, Gurin, and Miller 1954; Campbell, Converse, Miller, and Stokes 1960; Converse, Clausen, and Miller 1965; Converse, Miller, Rusk, and Wolfe 1969; Miller, Miller, Raine, and Brown 1973). Unfortunately, that research has virtually ignored communication processes as factors in voter decision-making.

Since the mid-1960s, however, a "new look" in political communication research has emerged, questioning particularly many of

the earlier assumptions about the lack of impact of mass media on
voter decision-making. The need for a reevaluation seemed clear,
especially as the inconclusiveness of the earlier studies became obvi-
ous in the light of contemporary events. Not only had fundamental
changes occurred in the makeup of the mass media marketplace during
the 1950s and 1960s, but the nature of the political system and actions
of voters within it also had altered. Most notably, of course, the
introduction of television, with its seemingly limitless "instant"
audience, had changed the structure and functions of the broadcast and
print media. Television also had become the prime purveyor of political images and events, if not of sheer information. Candidates for
office have grown dependent upon television and other media for exposure, and media enterprises in turn count on sizable portions of
advertising revenue and news content from candidates (Nimmo 1970;
Alexander 1972).

Politically, the country no longer looked as stable as it had
during the earlier decades of this century. The sometimes violent
social unrest of the 1960s reflected crisis in government over both
foreign and domestic policies. Voters' attachments to the Democratic
and Republican parties had been on the downswing for several years,
and many observers suggested that the new political input of television
played a role in the decline of party influence (Mendelsohn and Crespi
1970). Concurrently voter turnout declined, as did expressions of
trust in governmental institutions and officials.

Many of the research projects initiated during the 1960s that
reopened issues related to political communication effects were couched
in terms of a "uses-gratifications" approach to examining communication behavior (Katz, Blumler, and Gurevitch 1974). An outgrowth of
the earlier functionalist model, the uses-gratifications paradigm
essentially asks not what media can do to audiences, but what audiences
can do with media, and with what consequences. The paradigm's appli-
cation to political research was exemplified by J. G. Blumler and
D. McQuail (1969) in their survey investigation of the 1964 British
national elections. They emphasized in their study "the gratifications
that people derive from consumption of media materials, and the uses
to which they put them in the circumstances of their own lives." As
such, they aimed to "determine how (if at all) the persuasiveness of a
political message depends upon an individual's motivation for receiving
it." Among their principal findings was that voters' interest in the
campaign and motivations to use television to follow it were in many
instances related to voters' attitude changes on campaign issues, and
perhaps to candidate preferences, as a function of voters' exposure
and attention to television campaign content.

More recent, smaller-scale attempts have been carried out to
delineate more clearly the functions media may serve during campaigns

and have considerably clarified the uses voters make of political communication materials to fulfill informational and emotional needs.
(See, for example, McCombs and Shaw 1972; Atkin 1973; Katz, Hass
and Gurevitch 1973; McLeod, Becker, and Byrnes 1974; McLeod
and Becker 1974).

Recent studies have turned away from considering persuasion
as the only communication consequence worth examining, and have
begun to look at more subtle but nonetheless important effects. For
instance, the extent to which would-be voters learn new information
from the media has been more closely scrutinized (Becker, McCombs,
and McLeod 1975). There also seems to be some evidence of an
"agenda setting" function of media; that is, audiences of given news
media have been found to perceive the importance of political issues
in the same ranks as the news media to which they are most exposed
(McCombs and Shaw 1972; McLeod, Becker, and Byrnes 1974; Tipton,
Haney, and Baseheart 1975).

Communication behaviors of voters also have been linked to
their level of involvement in campaigns and other political activities.
For example, P. E. Converse (1966) and E. C. Dreyer (1971) have
indicated that voters less exposed to mass media are more apt to
change candidate preferences during campaigns and party identifications between campaigns. W. DeVries and V. L. Tarrance (1972)
found voters who split their ballot choices between parties to have
been more exposed to campaign media. More revealingly, J. G.
Blumler and J. M. McLeod (1974) found communication behaviors of
British citizens to be more predictive of voter turnout than traditional
demographic and political factors. Critical overviews of the past and
current state of research in the political communication area can be
found in H. Mendelsohn and I. Crespi (1970), M. McCombs (1972),
D. Sears and R. Whitney (1973), L. B. Becker, M. E. McCombs,
and J. M. McLeod (1975), and G. O'Keefe (1975).

If there is one conclusion that has been consistently drawn in
the research sketched above, it is that relationships between communication behaviors of voters and how they choose candidates are
not explainable by any one set of factors or circumstances. It is in
fact necessary to consider several levels of conditions under which
different voters act in order to gain a meaningful view of these processes. Recent thinking on this problem, as indicated earlier, has
rested more upon the uses to which voters put communication behaviors during campaigns and the gratifications sought from such behaviors. Moreover, a broader research perspective has been offered by
J. M. McLeod and G. J. O'Keefe (1972) and S. H. Chaffee (1973),
among others, arguing that more attention should be paid, in general,
first to identifying clear patterns of communication behavior among
voters, then to tracing these patterns to their functional antecedents,

and finally to looking for consequences dependent upon both antecedents and communication behaviors. That is, consequences or "effects" of communication, such as influence on vote decisions, rarely seem to derive from communication behaviors alone. More typically, the communication behavior is one necessary condition for the effect to occur, and there are a number of contributory or contingent conditions that heighten the probability of that effect occurring. S. H. Chaffee has suggested that considerably more attention be given to specifying and examining contingent conditions under which communication behaviors are likelier to lead to effects.

The following discussion of communication and decision-making among voters in the Summit County panel is based on such a general perspective. While the limits of the data gathered in 1972 preclude an extensive adaptation of the approach, it was useful in providing guidelines for investigation. In the discussions that follow, major emphasis will be placed on examining voters' perceptions of how their candidate choices were influenced by various media contents and events that took place during the campaign. The contributions of three kinds of factors to such influence will be considered.

The first set of factors includes general demographic and political characteristics of voters, or political dispositions, described in Chapter 2. While these were not good predictors of voters' reporting of influence per se, they were associated with many communication activities of voters and serve as a useful backdrop against which to depict voter influence processes.

A second factor that will be seen as quite indicative of influence has been labeled the decision condition under which voters made their final choice of a presidential candidate. As described in Chapter 2, voters were divided into those who made up their minds on a candidate early and stuck with their choice (early deciders), those who decided early but switched during the campaign (switchers), and those not reaching any decision until late in the campaign (late deciders). Presumably those voters who either switched candidates or decided late were responding to the campaign differently from those who made a final choice early.

A third set of factors intimately tied to the influence process describes how voters were oriented toward the ongoing campaign. Such orientations encompass various communication-related characteristics, including general expectations voters had about the campaign, uses voters made of the campaign, their activities during the campaign, and the consequences of such expectations, uses, and activities. These campaign orientations will be described more fully below. In ensuing sections of this chapter, the orientations and decision conditions will be related to reporting of influence by voters and to their ultimate vote decisions. The political dispositions will serve mainly as background factors against which to discuss ongoing processes over the campaign. In sum, how were different kinds of voters oriented toward the campaign, when did they make up their minds, and what impact resulted in terms of influencing their choices?

ORIENTATIONS OF VOTERS TO POLITICAL CAMPAIGNS

As with seasoned actors in any drama, voters come into the campaign theater with a certain amount of professional skill and experience. They have been through it before, for the most part, in many cases several times. Even first-time voters are likely to have certain anticipations regarding what is expected of them, based upon close observation of adult political models throughout their lives. Not only are most voters apt to have notions about whom they are likely to vote for and why, but they may well also have clear expectations concerning their orientations toward the campaign itself as an event. In particular, voters may have relatively well-defined predispositions concerning their communication behaviors vis-a-vis political campaigns. While the "script" may differ from election to election, the mechanics of campaigning and of voter action and response would seem to remain fairly constant. While campaign content is likely to change from election to election, certain regularities in the patterning of campaign communication and decision-making endure.

At the beginning of a campaign, voters are apt to have some coherent expectations of what they are going to do in terms of reacting to the upcoming sequence of events. Some voters may fully expect to spend abundant quantities of time and energy within the political arena, because of commitment to a particular candidate, felt personal responsibilities of citizenship, enjoyment of a good political game, or for all of these reasons and others. On the other hand, many voters may anticipate devoting little extra time and effort to the campaign, and they enter the arena with an air of relative apathy. They might fully intend to vote, but they have already made their decision or they assume that sooner or later their decisions will be made by or for them.

Voters are likely to act, at least in terms of overall patterns of behavior, much the same in any one campaign as in others. Again, candidates change, issues change, party loyalties may change; but it can be argued that individual voter decision-making processes remain largely the same. Of particular interest here is the nature of communication processes during a campaign. Basic campaign communication strategies and processes may be "learned" and developed in

previous campaigns and through other political experiences. Voters
may have quite clear expectations, for example, as to where they are
going to seek information about the candidates when they need it and
what they are going to do in terms of processing that information.
Voters may well anticipate what kinds of political stimuli they are
going to look for on television versus in the newspapers. They may
know in advance which of their friends and acquaintances are going to
be the most involved in the campaign: they may anticipate whom they
can seek out for specific advice when they need it, and to what extent
that advice will be heeded or ignored. If the voting act can be considered the product of a sometimes easy, sometimes difficult decision-
making process, the voters may also hold anticipations prior to the
campaign regarding to what extent various communications sources
are going to play a role in "helping them decide" or "influencing" them
in their electoral decisions. Such preconceptions on the part of voters
can act to set the style of political communication behaviors, in terms
of both what the behaviors are used for and how the voter may be
affected by the behaviors.

There are a considerable number of indicators that human communication patterns develop over years of different situations into
relatively firm attributes of one's personality. It is assumed that
political communication patterns, while related to the overall communication style of an individual, form a unique set of behaviors that
are relatively seldom called to the surface. For most Americans,
political communication behavior, in terms of its utility in vote
decision-making, becomes functional only once every four years—
during presidential election campaigns. This is not to say that events
occurring between campaigns may not be very significant influences
on voting, as K. Lang and G. E. Lang (1968) pointed out, and to which
the more recent Watergate scandals sharply attest. However, a dis-
tinction must still be made between attitudes that potential voters may
form between campaigns, when their power to act directly is limited,
and the translation of those attitudes into components of a decision
when the time for action, in the form of voting, arrives.

If voters are shown to enter campaigns with particular communication orientations in the form of anticipations or expectations as to
what they are going to get, when these are combined with actual communication behavior patterns they can be considered conditions under
which given communication effects may be obtained. That is, any consequences that may result from given patterns of communication use are
apt to be dependent not only on use and exposure patterns but also on the
perceived motives, needs, and anticipations underlying such use. A
voter who closely follows the political news every evening in the newspaper, with no other anticipation than that he is going to enjoy reading
about it, is more likely to be "affected," or really gratified, by what he

reads in terms of feelings of pleasure than to be affected in terms of having his political viewpoint swayed. Conversely, the voter who anticipates following campaign news because Election Day is near and there is a decision to be made is likelier to be affected in the sense of receiving at least some degree of help in deciding whom to vote for. This would be particularly true if he has always relied on the newspaper for this kind of assistance. Likewise, the voter who anticipates reading the paper to seek justification of a decision already tentatively made is apt to be affected in a different way.

At minimum, then, processes such as these may be considered as broad orientations that voters have toward election campaigns. Generally, these orientations may be divided into presentiments, or beliefs, attitudes, expectations, and motivational dispositions voters may have prior to their communication behavior during a campaign; and the communication behaviors themselves, which may include watching campaign-related television programming, reading political stories in newspapers, discussing the campaign, and so on. Presentiments and communication behaviors are seen as having potential consequences on voter decision-making during a campaign. In the 1972 Summit County study, exploratory use was made of such a schema to guide examination of the impact of the campaign on voters.

Following extensive reduction of the data gathered in the Summit County panel, several such orientations held by voters emerged as paramount in voter decision-making processes. These orientations included the following:

- Anticipatory influence, or expectations voters held prior to the campaign regarding their probable uses of communications as sources of influence in deciding for whom to vote
- Difficulty of decision, or the extent to which voters experienced difficulty in deciding on a candidate
- Voters' interest in the campaign, or the motivational basis for following an ongoing campaign
- Attention paid by voters to the campaign, or the extent to which they did follow it
- Degree of exposure to campaign-related mass media content
- Dependence on newspapers for information gratifications pertinent to the campaign
- Dependence on television as a news medium for information gratifications
- Interpersonal discussion about the campaign
- Interpersonal seeking of guidance on voting, or the extent to which voters asked other persons for information and advice concerning for whom to vote

● The consequence of reported influence, or the extent to which
voters said they were influenced in their decisions by media
campaign coverage or specific events during the campaign.

Each of these orientations will be more fully described below
and related to the political dispositions of voters; then associations
between reported influence and the other orientations will be presented
as they apply to how the voters made up their minds and for whom.

Anticipatory Influence

As has been discussed, consideration has to be taken of voters'
past experience with campaigns, particularly in terms of whether they
generally see themselves as relying on communication sources to help
them decide whom to vote for. Voters who described themselves prior
to a campaign as counting on communications for help may be seen as
anticipating such influence more than other voters. As a result, they
may differ in their approaches toward using mass media and interpersonal communications during a campaign, and may be more prone
to having their decisions influenced by such sources.

For the purposes here, anticipatory influence is a construct
depicting potential voters' overall probable reliance upon various communications as sources of influence or help in decision-making, over
the course of a presidential campaign. It is a reflection of citizens'
pre-campaign orientations, a description of a set of expectations
voters have as to the potential for influence of those communications.
Operationally, an elementary but effective index of anticipatory influence was created by summing voters' responses to five items asked
them in July 1972 concerning the extent to which they would count on
specific media and interpersonal sources to help them decide whom
to vote for in a presidential election. (Items appear in Appendix B.)

Within the 1972 Summit County panel, voters more likely to
anticipate influence seem most readily identified by their relative
youth (Table 5.1). Voters under 50, and particularly 18-24-year-old
first-time voters, clearly tended more to anticipate influence than
did voters 50 and over. Also more likely to anticipate influence were
the more educated voters, especially those who had completed college;
white-collar (as compared with blue-collar) workers; and those living
in higher-income households. Voters higher in anticipatory influence
also appeared less politically cynical. Democrats were slightly less
likely to anticipate influence than Republicans or Independents, women
were slightly more apt to anticipate influence than men, and whites
were likelier to do so than black voters. In sum, it seems the younger

TABLE 5.1

Anticipatory Influence, Difficulty of Decision, and
Campaign Interest, by Key Political Dispositions
(N = 618)

	Anticipatory Influence	Difficulty of Decision	Interest in Campaign
Overall Mean Score	1.82	1.28	2.24
Sex			
Female	1.84	1.31	2.24
Male	1.79	1.23	2.26
Race			
Black	1.69	1.26	2.14
White	1.83	1.29	2.25
Age			
18-24	1.94	1.31	2.11
25-34	1.90	1.21	2.15
35-49	1.91	1.30	2.28
50-64	1.62	1.30	2.43
65+	1.58	1.29	2.08
Education			
1-11 Years	1.60	1.27	2.10
12 Years	1.79	1.33	2.19
Some College	1.92	1.27	2.30
Completed College	2.07	1.21	2.43
Occupation			
Blue-Collar	1.73	1.29	2.15
White-Collar	1.98	1.24	2.32
Union Members	1.82	1.33	2.19
Income			
Less than $10,000	1.70	1.34	2.15
$10,000-$14,999	1.86	1.26	2.22
$15,000 and over	1.91	1.21	2.36
Party Identification			
Democrat	1.79	1.34	2.18
Republican	1.87	1.15	2.53
Independent	1.88	1.27	2.23
Political Cynicism			
Low	1.93	1.31	2.35
High	1.65	1.23	2.06

Note: Scored 1 = low; 2 = moderate; 3 = high.

more educated, and more affluent voters were highest in anticipation of influence. Two dynamics may be operating here, with the more educated and affluent being more anticipatory because of greater interest in and experience with campaign communications in the past, while the young admit their lack of experience and say that they are more open to influence in deciding for whom to vote. Further, past research on propaganda effects and innovation diffusion has demonstrated that it is generally the more sophisticated who are more open to ideas of all sorts and consequently are more likely to seek useful information and to be influenced by the information they encounter.

Difficulty of Decision-Making

Often overlooked in the voting-behavior research literature are the possible associations between psychological decision-making components of voters and their communication behaviors. While some attention has been given to cognitive decisional factors related to information-seeking (Carter 1965; Chaffee, Stamm, Guerrero, and Tipton 1969; Atkin 1973; Edelstein 1973 and 1975), practically no data have been offered applying such thinking to more naturalistic vote decision situations.

One aspect of decision-making—the amount of difficulty voters perceive in choosing a candidate—was found to be a key indicator of reporting of influence by voters in the 1972 Ohio panel. Difficulty of decision, as we have seen, obviously is dependent upon numerous factors and in turn impinges on several others. Components of difficulty of decision include number of alternative candidates, number of attributes discriminating between alternatives (for example, images and issue positions of candidates), lack or excess of information, perceived importance of the decision in light of its consequences, degree of commitment to the decision, and publicity of the decision.

In the 1972 study it seemed appropriate to begin inquiry into difficulty by asking voters after the election how difficult it had been for them to decide to vote for either McGovern or Nixon. To review, 7 percent reported it had been very difficult, 15 percent said somewhat difficult, and 78 percent said it had not been difficult at all. Voters responding that the choice had been very or somewhat difficult were asked why it had been so. Their answers generally implied that while they had formed certain perceptions of the candidates, they lacked the ability to discriminate adequately between the contenders. Fifty-four percent of the voters said their difficulty arose from viewing both candidates in a negative light. A scant 4 percent traced their difficulty to holding positive attitudes toward both men. The remaining voters gave mixed reasons (such as concern over voting against the candidate of their party, confusion over campaign issues, and concern and confusion over such campaign events as the peace talks and the Watergate affair). Fully 65 percent of the reasons given pertained to personality or image attributes of McGovern or Nixon, while only 11 percent dealt exclusively with the stands of the candidates on issues. Twenty-two percent of the reasons included both image- and issue-related components.

Difficulty of decision thus seemed mainly a result of inability to discriminate meaningfully between the contenders, although some voters suggested that they had found differences separating the men but that the candidate of their choice had negative qualities that were hard to overlook (for instance, "I never could vote for that Nixon, so I guess it was McGovern, but I don't trust him.").

Of course, only those who voted are being considered here. Further investigation of the role of difficulty is due among that near-majority of citizens who did not vote at all in 1972.

Given the circumstances of the 1972 presidential campaign, it is not surprising that Democrats and Independents had a more difficult time deciding than did Republicans (Table 5.1). Presumably those Democrats who ended up voting for Nixon had a particularly hard time of it; also, the more politically cynical had less difficulty, and women appeared to have more difficulty than men. Voters earning less than $10,000 per year expressed greater difficulty than those earning more; but no consistent differences in difficulty were found between the more and less educated, between blue-collar and white-collar voters, or between young and old voters.

There seems to be no evidence here of one particular typology of voters who are likelier to have difficulty regardless of the nature of the election. Rather, factors inherent in the 1972 presidential election may be more at the root of why some voters had greater difficulty than others in deciding.

Campaign Interest

Voters' levels of interest in the 1972 presidential campaign were indexed by summing responses to an item included in three waves of interviews, ascertaining whether voters saw themselves as "very interested," "somewhat interested," or "not at all interested" in the campaign.

Studies of voters beginning with The People's Choice have depicted those persons more interested in politics in general as typically being older, more established, higher socioeconomic status members of their communities; voters in the Summit County panel most interested in the campaign followed precisely the same pattern (Table 5.1). Interest in the campaign steadily increased with age, peaking in the 50–64-year-old age bracket, and sharply declining thereafter. It seems a safe assumption that such interest increases with age as a function of persons gaining more experience with the political system and seeing more things personally at stake in the outcome of particular elections. Also, to some extent, generations that entered the political arena during extremely active periods (such as the Roosevelt years for those aged 50–64 in 1972) may remain relatively more politically interested than other generations. One finding that clearly stands out is that 18–24-year-old voters, as a group apart from college students, were not the highly involved partisans many observers either hoped or feared they would be.

Campaign interest also rose consistently with years of education, income level, and occupational status. Black voters tended to be less interested than whites, and Democrats and Independents were less interested than Republicans. One suspects that both of these findings are in large part a result of white voters and Republicans being likelier to be in higher educational and income categories. Virtually no difference in interest was found between men and women. As one might suspect, the less politically cynical a voter was, the more likely he or she was to be more interested in the campaign.

In sum, the voters most interested in the campaign seemed to be those 50–64, college-educated, earning over $15,000 per year, employed in white-collar or professional jobs, Republican in party identification, and rather politically uncynical. Voters least interested tended to be either very young or very old, had a high school education or less, earned less than $10,000 annually in blue-collar occupations, were likely to be black, Democratic in affiliation, and relatively high in political cynicism.

Campaign Attention, Media Exposure, and Discussion

Voters' attentiveness to the campaign indicates the degree to which they kept up with campaign events. If interest in the campaign is a basis for motivation, the attention to the campaign is a product of that motivation. The Summit County voters were asked over three waves of interviews whether they found themselves paying "a great deal of attention, only a little attention, or no attention at all" to what was going on in the presidential election campaign (see Appendix B for items).

Voters' degree of exposure to the wide variety of campaign-related messages emanating from the mass media was indexed by a series of items asked of the respondents over all waves of the study. The index was quite general, covering exposure to such diverse contents as regular print and broadcast news, the national conventions, political advertising, television specials on the campaign, and so on (see Appendix B for items). While more meaningful analysis might be carried out by examining exposure to specific content, this broad index was useful to gain an overview of gross exposure patterns on which voters could be compared.

The extent to which voters discussed the campaign with other people was measured by asking the panelists over three waves whether they had been discussing the campaign "very often, occasionally, or hardly at all" (see Appendix B for item).

One would expect that those voters who were more interested in the campaign should be more attentive and more exposed to campaign media content and to have discussed it more. By and large that is what was found (Table 5.2).

Clearly, voters with more years of education were likelier to orient themselves to the campaign in all of these ways, with a minor exception being that college graduates attended to the campaign slightly less than those voters with only some college training. White-collar workers and those who earned incomes over the median level were likelier than their lower-status counterparts to be more attentive, more exposed, and more talkative vis-a-vis the campaign; blacks, more cynical voters, and Democrats tended to be less oriented to the campaign along these dimensions.

However, two other findings were somewhat out of line with the general proposition that attention, exposure, and discussion are always highly associated with interest. For one thing, the age group in which discussion of the campaign was likeliest to occur was 18-24-year-olds, and amount of discussion decreased with age thereafter. While the younger members of the "television generation" scored decidedly lower than older voters on attention and exposure to the campaign, they seem to have talked about it a good deal more, perhaps indicating less use of the media for political things. This finding is a rather striking anomaly, and it needs further pursuit in later research. Whom were they talking to? With what results? What were their information needs? Will that generation continue to rely less on the media? Why or why not?

Another somewhat curious finding was that while men and women did not differ essentially with regard to interest in or attentiveness to the campaign, women were somewhat likelier than men to be exposed to campaign media content, while men were likelier than women to discuss the campaign. This may be partially accounted for

TABLE 5.2

Campaign Attention, Media Exposure, and Discussion,
by Key Political Dispositions
(N = 618)

	Campaign Attention	Campaign Exposure	Campaign Discussion
Overall Mean Score	2.28	1.98	1.92
Sex			
Female	2.29	2.06	1.90
Male	2.29	1.92	1.96
Race			
Black	2.24	1.93	1.82
White	2.30	2.04	1.94
Age			
18-24	2.23	1.87	2.04
25-34	2.24	1.99	1.97
35-49	2.29	1.99	1.97
50-64	2.47	2.15	1.90
65+	2.22	2.04	1.58
Education			
1-11 Years	2.21	1.95	1.76
12 Years	2.24	2.00	1.90
Some College	2.40	2.06	1.99
Completed College	2.34	2.10	2.15
Occupation			
Blue-Collar	2.25	1.93	1.90
White-Collar	2.30	2.10	2.04
Union Members	2.22	1.90	1.89
Income			
Less than $10,000	2.26	1.94	1.79
$10,000-$14,999	2.29	2.06	1.93
$15,000 and over	2.39	2.04	2.16
Party Identification			
Democrat	2.23	1.99	1.82
Republican	2.41	2.05	2.02
Independent	2.32	2.01	2.02
Political Cynicism			
Low	2.36	2.07	2.02
High	2.17	1.91	1.78

Note: Scored 1 = low; 2 = moderate; 3 = high.

142

by the common finding in much audience research that women spend more time with media in general than men do. However, the greater amount of discussion by men may be a function of role typing dictating what kinds of content are "supposed" to be discussed by men and by women. At any rate, it seems clear that no sex differences exist in the more basic orientations of interest and attention, but only in the more expressive orientations of exposure and discussion.

Within overall campaign media exposure patterns, which media tended to be relied on most for coverage of the campaign? Voters consistently named television as the medium of information most often used in following the campaign, with newspapers ranked a high second (Table 5.3). Television scored highest as the main source of information about the two major national party conventions, and continued to be listed as the most relied-upon medium throughout the post-convention period. Television was ranked as the major source of information by approximately half of the voters during the campaign, with newspapers so ranked by about a third of them. Interpersonal communication was a distant third, being mentioned by less than 5 percent, with radio and magazines close behind.

Among those voters paying "high" attention to the campaign, the pattern of reliance remained much the same as for the whole sample. Greater proportions of high-attention voters than voters in general named television as their primary source of convention coverage.

In October, Summit County voters were asked which of the mass media—magazines, newspapers, radio, or television—was doing the "best job" of giving them information about the campaign. Television was chosen most often (by 40 percent of the sample), closely followed by newspapers (36 percent), and then by magazines (6 percent) and radio (5 percent).

Closely allied with perceptions of media performance are judgments as to how "fair" newspapers and television are in covering political campaigns. Panel voters were asked in July whether newspapers and television were fair in the way they treated political matters. Half of the sample said they thought television was fair, while no more than 34 percent said the same of newspapers. Thirty-one percent labeled newspapers as being unfair, and 20 percent accused television of being biased. The remainder of the voters gave mixed responses.

Dependence on News Media for Information Gratifications

That television is the "most relied upon" and most believed medium for national news, including national political news, has been

TABLE 5.3

Main Campaign Information Sources, by Attention
(percentages)

	Democratic Convention	Republican Convention	September	October	November
Television					
Total	62	58	44	54	51
High Attention	69	67	46	54	52
Newspapers					
Total	22	21	37	34	39
High Attention	19	21	42	36	39
People					
Total	5	3	3	2	5
High Attention	3	4	3	2	4
Radio					
Total	4	4	7	4	3
High Attention	4	3	4	4	3
Magazines					
Total	4	1	4	4	3
High Attention	4	1	4	4	2

Note: Total = percent of total sample (N = 618); High Attention = percent of high-attention respondents (N = 254).

144

fairly well accepted. What is less clear is the nature of the specific information-giving functions television news may serve for voters during a presidential campaign. While newspapers may be statistically relegated to a secondary role in the political news dissemination process, in terms of audience size their potential service to the voter is no less powerful. Television news may be "first" in covering breaking news and stories that accentuate the visual for the largest audience, but under most circumstances newspapers provide the greater depth of content.

Hence, quite apart from amounts of attention to the campaign and exposure to campaign media content, it is important to consider the kinds of campaign information needs voters see the media as serving. Sets of gratifications potentially sought by voters in campaign media have been delineated in earlier studies (Blumler and McQuail 1969; McCombs and Shaw 1972; Katz, Blumler, and Gurevitch 1974; McLeod and Becker 1974). Focus in this study was on four relatively basic information gratifications culled from earlier research, and the extent to which voters counted on newspaper and television news content for them. Voters defined as regular attenders to newspaper (regularly read a daily newspaper) and to television news (watch evening news show at least twice a week) were asked the extent ("a lot," "a little," "not at all") to which they counted on either of the media for the information gratifications of (1) agenda cuing or campaign surveillance, including providing information concerning "what to look for" in the ongoing campaign; (2) agenda-setting, as defined by M. McCombs and D. Shaw, the providing of information as to "what the important issues" of the presidential campaign are; (3) information as to the respective candidates' positions on issues of import; and (4) information as to the candidates' personality attributes, or "images" (see Appendix B for items).

Within the Summit County sample, those voters more dependent on newspapers looked to a great extent like those more involved in the campaign (Table 5.4). They were generally more educated, employed in white-collar jobs, above average in income, likelier to be Republican than Democratic or Independent, and less politically cynical. Young, first-time voters were considerably less likely to depend on newspapers than older, more experienced voters; women were slightly less likely to do so than men; and black voters were slightly less likely than were whites. Those more dependent on television, however, were identified primarily as earning less income, being older, and more likely to be black (Table 5.4). Women tended to be more television-dependent than men. Essentially no differences in television dependence were found among Democrats, Republicans, and Independents, or between voters with high versus low levels of political cynicism.

TABLE 5.4

Newspaper Dependence, Television Dependence, and Interpersonal
Guidance-Seeking, by Key Political Dispositions
(N = 618)

	Newspaper Dependence	Television Dependence	Guidance-Seeking
Overall Mean Score	2.23	1.79	1.91
Sex			
Female	2.22	1.87	1.92
Male	2.28	1.73	1.90
Race			
Black	2.21	1.94	1.87
White	2.24	1.78	1.91
Age			
18-24	2.11	1.65	2.25
25-34	2.28	1.74	2.03
35-49	2.27	1.73	1.89
50-64	2.23	1.96	1.64
65+	2.27	2.01	1.59
Education			
1-11 Years	2.13	1.82	1.72
12 Years	2.24	1.83	1.93
Some College	2.35	1.82	2.00
Completed College	2.27	1.66	1.91
Occupation			
Blue-Collar	2.22	1.70	1.95
White-Collar	2.32	1.78	1.97
Union Members	2.18	1.67	1.95
Income			
Less than $10,000	2.20	1.87	1.85
$10,000-$14,999	2.28	1.81	1.89
$15,000 and over	2.27	1.71	1.96
Party Identification			
Democrat	2.27	1.81	1.95
Republican	2.40	1.82	1.68
Independent	2.12	1.78	2.10
Political Cynicism			
Low	2.29	1.80	2.03
High	2.17	1.79	1.76

Note: Scored 1 = low; 2 = moderate; 3 = high.

Voters also differed in their perceptions of the objectivity of newspaper and television news in their coverage of the candidates; it is useful to digress at this point to consider some of those differences. There is particular concern with evaluating such perceptions in light of the ongoing debates over the appropriateness of the now-classic "selective exposure" hypothesis. In its most elemental form the hypothesis suggests that in their communication behaviors, people are more likely to seek supportive messages and to avoid messages that do not support previous beliefs, attitudes, values, and opinions. Likewise, people are expected to interpret the messages they do receive in line with their predispositions. (For explorations of the selective exposure controversy, see Klapper 1960; Sears and Freedman 1967; Katz 1968; Atkin 1973; and Donohew and Tipton 1973).

Voters who attended regularly to newspaper and television news were asked in September to estimate the relative amounts of attention being paid to McGovern and Nixon by each news medium, and to indicate which candidate they though each medium wanted to win the election. Two out of every five voters counted as regular readers of a daily newspaper in September said they thought the paper they regularly read was balanced in terms of the attention given to the candidates (Table 5.5). Twenty-three percent said more attention was being given to Nixon than to McGovern, and 21 percent indicated McGovern had the edge. Seventeen percent said they were undecided. Among voters who reported in September that McGovern was their choice for President, 38 percent said the paper was giving more attention to Nixon, and 13 percent said more attention was being given to McGovern. Conversely, 28 percent of those preferring Nixon in September said the newspaper was paying more attention to George McGovern, and 12 percent said Nixon was receiving more attention. Among undecideds, 24 percent thought Nixon was getting more play, and 15 percent said McGovern was.

In contrast with the selectivity in perception exhibited by voters as to which candidate the newspaper was paying more attention to, there was high agreement as to which candidate the newspaper "wanted to win the election." Forty-seven percent of all voters, including 52 percent of the McGovern supporters, declared that they thought their newspaper wanted Nixon to win (Table 5.5). Only 9 percent of all voters named McGovern as their newspaper's choice. This finding is rather surprising, since none of the newspapers serving Akron had yet endorsed either candidate. *

---

*Over 80 percent of the sample named the Akron Beacon-Journal, owned by Knight Newspapers, Inc., as the paper they read most regularly. Publisher John Knight, in a widely publicized editorial prior

TABLE 5.5

Perceptions of Relative Newspaper Treatment of Candidates,
by Voters' Candidate Choice
(percentages)

| | Candidate Choice | | | |
	McGovern (N=192	Nixon (N=269)	Undecided (N=82)	Total (N=543)
More Newspaper Atten-tion Given to*				
McGovern	13	28	15	21
Nixon	38	12	24	23
Neither	31	44	40	39
Don't Know	18	16	21	17
Perceived Newspaper Choice†				
McGovern	8	10	9	9
Nixon	52	45	43	47
Neither	14	16	16	15
Don't Know	26	29	32	29

*Item: "As far as you can tell, is the (Newspaper) paying more attention to George McGovern or to Richard Nixon in the 1972 presidential campaign?"

†Item: "Which candidate, Richard Nixon or George McGovern, does the (Newspaper) want to win the election in November?"

Survey research efforts in the area of selectivity generally have upheld the view that a de facto form of selective exposure holds (that is, people are more likely to be exposed to communications, particularly from the mass media, that are compatible with their existing opinions and beliefs than to communications that are incompatible). Laboratory experimental research, on the other hand, has found little conclusive evidence that people are motivated either to seek supportive information or actively to avoid nonsupportive information. Rather, a host of mitigating factors, including utility and availability of infor-

---

to the time these items were asked, declared he was not going to vote for either candidate. Later, days before the election, the Beacon-Journal itself gave a lukewarm endorsement to President Nixon.

mation and confidence of the individual, confound the situation in complex ways.

The nature of the selective exposure phenomenon will be dealt with from different approaches in ensuing chapters, particularly in terms of specific media contents, such as McGovern's major Vietnam policy speech and political commercials. At present, discussion is restricted to selectivity in voter perceptions of campaign news coverage.

Nevertheless, a near majority of the readers had clear perceptions as to whom they thought the papers were supporting. These perceptions may have derived mainly from long-standing feelings that the newspaper was traditionally Republican or subtleties in the presentation of information about the candidates.

The juxtaposition of these results with those found for "attention paid" to candidates is interesting. Readers' perceptions of attention paid followed vote preferences somewhat, yet perceptions of whom the paper was "really" for did not. One explanation may be that the readers saw enough ambiguity in news coverage to allow selective perception to act more strongly, but they shared a sense that deep down the newspaper was behind Nixon. It may be that they felt that even though the newspaper was for one candidate, it was giving relatively equal play to both in the news columns.

The pattern found for perceptions of television news on the above dimensions was somewhat similar, although 23 percent of the voters regularly watching television news said more attention was being paid to McGovern and 15 percent said Nixon received more attention (Table 5.6). The majority (54 percent) saw television news as giving equal attention to both candidates. Again, voters who had decided for McGovern perceived television news as paying more attention to Nixon than to their candidate, and Nixon supporters said television news gave more time to McGovern.

Fourteen percent of the voters indicated that they thought the television news programs wanted McGovern to win, and 19 percent said they thought they wanted Nixon to win. As opposed to the results for newspapers, more McGovern supporters were inclined to think the television news programs wanted Nixon to win (26 percent) than felt the news programs hoped their candidate would be victorious (15 percent). Nixon supporters split rather evenly, with 16 percent naming Nixon as the news programs' favorite and 14 percent naming McGovern.

Again, it is striking that so many voters could name a candidate whom they thought the programs favored. Further research is obviously needed on this issue, perhaps in terms of relating specific newspaper and television news content to audience perceptions.

TABLE 5.6

Perceptions of Television News Treatment of Candidates,
by Voters' Candidate Choice
(percentages)

| | Candidate Choice | | | |
	McGovern (N=131)	Nixon (N=166)	Undecided (N=35)	Total (N=332)
More Television News Attention to[*]				
McGovern	11	33	20	23
Nixon	26	7	9	15
Neither	55	52	60	54
Don't Know	8	8	11	8
Perceived Television News Choice[†]				
McGovern	15	14	6	14
Nixon	26	16	8	19
Neither	37	46	46	43
Don't Know	22	24	40	24

[*]Item: "In your opinion, are the early evening television news programs you watch paying more attention to Richard Nixon or to George McGovern in the 1972 presidential campaign?"

[†]Item: "Which candidate do the early evening television news programs you watch want to win the election in November—George McGovern or Richard Nixon?"

Seeking of Interpersonal Guidance

As a corollary of amount of discussion, respondents were asked over three waves of the study the extent to which they had asked other people for "their opinions or advice about which presidential candidate to vote for" (see Appendix B for item).

The most salient indicator of seeking interpersonal guidance in the Summit County sample was age, with younger voters much likelier to seek guidance than older ones (Table 5.4). Voters aged 18-24 ranked especially high in this regard. Hence, not only did younger voters discuss the campaign more, but they used those discussions to seek guidance in deciding for which presidential candidate to vote.

Less politically cynical voters and those who had completed high school were also more apt to seek guidance from other people, but by and large the other political dispositions were relatively unrelated to the seeking of guidance.

INFLUENCES ON VOTER DECISION-MAKING

The concept of influence is a troublesome one. Too often the word has been used as a catch-all, even more abstract than "persuasion," in discussing interpersonal and mass communication effects. Even in the classic work Personal Influence (1955), it is difficult to tell from E. Katz and P. Lazarsfeld's presentation whether it is "influence" or "information" presumably flowing between opinion leaders and followers. In one sense, influence has served as a rubric for outcomes of social interaction situations where some form of change within individuals occurs. R. A. Dahl (1957) has called influence "a shift in the probability outcome"; W. A. Gamson (1968) suggests that influence occurs when "A is at least partially determining B's behavior, altering it from what it would have been in A's absence"; and D. Easton (1953) has argued that "to give (influence) any differentiated meaning we must view it as a relationship in which one person or group is able to determine the actions of another in the direction of the former's own ends." The term "influence" was chosen here precisely because of its all-encompassing qualities, and at minimum because a label was needed to which voters could readily respond.

Broadly speaking, influence is a consequence or "effect." Or, perhaps more directly, it is an impingement on an individual. When voters said they were "influenced," or even that something "helped them decide," they were admitting that something happened to them. It is entirely another matter as to whether or not they wanted something to happen to them. If a voter is motivated early in the campaign, for any number of reasons, to seek information or advice concerning whom to vote for, if he exposes himself to a political debate for the purpose of making up his mind (even to the possible extent of having someone or something make up his mind for him), and he comes away from the debate decided as to his candidate, it might be said that that voter was influenced. He wanted to be, and the influence may be viewed as gratification that the voter attended the debate to achieve. Likewise, the "already decided" voter, seeking confirmation, seeking ammunition to ward off opposition, seeking one more rationale for voting in a particular way, may attend the same debate and come away more convinced than ever that the first choice was the right one, and more

determined than ever to vote as he had decided. Influence? Yes, in
the sense that the voter utilized a particular situation or message to
achieve a particular gratification. Influence in the sense of an individual turning from being a "weak" supporter of a candidate to being
a "strong" one can certainly be recognized and ascertained.

Then there is the more "classic" case of influence: the already
decided voter goes to the debate, hears something unexpected, and
comes away having decided not to vote for the candidate previously
chosen. This is the traditional set of conversion and is thought, with
some justification, to happen rarely during political campaigns. Conversion is actually very different from the other kinds of behaviors
included under the rubric of influence here. For one thing, conversion
is hard to depict as an expected event. If one "expects" to be converted
from one candidate to another, or from one candidate to a decision not
to vote at all, one probably is really seeking further justification for
a decision already made or, at minimum, "in the works." It is likely
a myth in political decision-making that events such as voting decisions
occur over a few seconds or moments; rather, there is apt to be considerable vacillation spreading over numerous political events to which
the voter is exposed. Undecided voters in particular may role-play
with candidate choices over several situations, sending up trial bal-
loons for friends' reactions, listening to a speech as if the candidate
were the voter's own. Conversion, as applied to political candidates,
is more likely to be a slow-moving event, and the influence process
underlying it is apt to take several forms—from learning of something,
through seeking more information, through the stage where the voter
wavers seriously, perhaps through a "gut feeling" that the original
candidate cannot be voted for, to seeking justification for supporting
the opposition. At some point in the process, an anticipation of influence is likely to be felt.

Voters in the Summit County panel could quite easily tell whether
or not they thought they were "influenced" by a given thing or event.
Furthermore, they could very often describe what they meant by having
been influenced. In this elementary venture, it was decided not to go
much further than that. One of the inherent dangers in any research
aimed, even tangentially, at exploring possible motivations behind
communication behavior and the gratifications expected from such
behavior is the use of predetermined (by the researcher) category
schemes forced upon voters, which may not reflect their concept of
the "reality" of the situation. Of course, the acknowledged danger of
the approach used here is that too ambiguous a conceptualization
yields nothing in comparable data over groups of voters.

It seemed appropriate in the 1972 Ohio study to try, at least, to
ascertain voters' perceived meaning of influence essentially by asking
them whether particular events and contents depicted in the media had

"influenced" their decision regarding whom to vote for, and if so, how and/or why they had been influenced (or not influenced). It did not seem reasonable to prescribe set dimensions of influence from the social interaction literature and impose possibly artificial categories upon the respondents. To the extent that voters said a greater number of events and contents influenced them, they were assigned scores on an additive index of influence.

Eleven items posed across the five waves of panel interviews were keyed to reflect an admission by respondents that they saw themselves as having had their decisions for a presidential candidate "influenced" by media contents and specific events during the campaign. The events referred to included the national conventions, Eagleton's resignation, the selection of Shriver as his replacement, the Watergate break-in and its aftermath, pre-election poll results and predictions, Kissinger's cease-fire statement, political television commercials, Election Eve television specials, and events named by the voters in response to open-ended items.*

Voters' own perceptions of influence took several forms. Some spoke of "reinforcement" or "justification" of decisions already firmly made, not really implying any greater degree of attraction toward the chosen candidate, but more a reaffirmation or hardening of the decision itself. ("Since Eagleton resigned, I'm more sure I made the right decision [for Nixon].")

Another facet of influence described was more akin to the strengthening of commitment to a candidate. As a result of new information, some voters described themselves as feeling more positive toward the chosen candidate and/or more negative toward his opponent. ("The Watergate mess made me surer than ever that Nixon is a crook.")

Yet another component involves crystallizing or finalizing a decision based on earlier biases or preconceptions. Voters may feel that a candidate is the right one, but need to muster evidence to convince themselves. ("I always liked Nixon, but the way the war went just before the election really convinced me he was the one to vote for.")

---

*While the items making up the influence index and the attention, exposure, and discussion indices were all repeated concurrently over the five waves of interviews, it is reasonable to assume that influence reported can be regarded as the dependent variable here on conceptual as well as methodological grounds. Each influence index item was preceded by an item appraising the respondent's awareness of a particular event. Hence, a voter had to be aware of a precipitating event before he was asked whether he was influenced by that event: he had to be exposed to some form of communication in order to be aware of the event and thus be influenced by it.

Closely related to crystallization was a perception of being influenced in the sense of facilitating one's decision, or making it easier to decide. For those relatively few voters in the throes of trying to decide, but honestly having a hard time doing so, influence in many cases meant finding out something that made the choice easier. It meant locating an attribute that could discriminate between the candidates in a meaningful way (Carter 1965). ("I couldn't make up my mind until McGovern fired Eagleton—then I went to Nixon.")

Of course, conversion can happen; but it often occurs through discovery of the unexpected, setting a course of change under way. ("Watergate bothered me all along from the first I heard of it, and finally the more I saw the more I had to cut from Nixon to McGovern.")

Hence it became clear that one sizable segment of these voters interpreted influence in terms of justification, or rationale-building, for decisions already made (similar to the classic but still unspecified "reinforcement" effect). On the other hand, another group of voters reported being influenced in terms of receiving help in making up their minds whom to vote for, or in switching from one candidate to another. This latter group appeared influenced in terms of either changing an earlier decision and/or crystallizing decisions regarding candidates at relatively late times during the campaign.

Within the Summit County panel, younger voters were decidedly more likely to report influence than older voters (Table 5.7). Beyond that and a slight tendency for reported influence to increase with education, demographic factors were not indicative of reported influence. Voters identifying themselves as Independents, however, tended to report influence more than Democrats and especially more than Republicans. It would seem reasonable that those voters with the weakest ties to party organizations would be the most likely to be influenced by campaign events.

The following examples give an indication of responses to open-ended items asking how respondents were influenced by specific events.

- Of the 86 respondents who said they were influenced by the Democratic convention, nearly half indicated they were influenced against the Democratic Party. On the other hand, only 22 percent of the 52 respondents reporting influence from watching the Republican convention indicated negative reactions toward that party.
- Over two-thirds of those who reported being influenced by McGovern's selection of Shriver as a replacement for Eagleton indicated positive response to that action. Over 80 percent of these voters, in discussing why they were influenced, listed personality attributes of Shriver, most notably his link with the Kennedy family, rather than issue positions.

TABLE 5.7

Reported Influence, by Key Demographic Attributes
and Political Dispositions
(N = 618)

	Reported Influence
Overall Mean Score	1.76
Sex	
Female	1.76
Male	1.76
Race	
Black	1.74
White	1.78
Age	
18–24	1.91
25–34	1.83
35–49	1.75
50–64	1.82
65+	1.38
Education	
1–11 Years	1.71
12 Years	1.75
Some College	1.80
Completed College	1.82
Occupation	
Blue-Collar	1.81
White-Collar	1.79
Union Members	1.82
Income	
Less than $10,000	1.75
$10,000–$14,999	1.82
$15,000 and over	1.75
Party Identification	
Democrat	1.76
Republican	1.67
Independent	1.86
Political Cynicism	
Low	1.77
High	1.76

Note: Influence scored 1 = low; 2 = moderate;
3 = high.

TABLE 5.8

Correlations Between Campaign Orientations

	Anticipatory Influence	Difficulty of Decision	Campaign Interest	Campaign Attention	Campaign Exposure	Campaign Discussion	Newspaper Dependence	Television Dependence	Guidance-Seeking	Reported Influence
Anticipatory Influence	1.00									
Difficulty of Decision	-.06[a]	1.00								
Campaign Interest	.16[c]	-.05	1.00							
Campaign Attention	.09[b]	-.03	.61[d]	1.00						
Campaign Exposure	.08[b]	-.05	.36[d]	.32[d]	1.00					
Campaign Discussion	.12[c]	-.07[a]	.43[d]	.46[d]	.28[d]	1.00				
Newspaper Dependence	.19[c]	-.04	.26[d]	.26[d]	.08[b]	.15[c]	1.00			
Television Dependence	.06[a]	.02	.22[d]	.27[d]	.44[d]	.18[c]	.12[c]	1.00		
Guidance-Seeking	.18[c]	.01	.19[c]	.20[d]	.09[b]	.38[d]	.05	.09[b]	1.00	
Reported Influence	.13[c]	.19[c]	.20[d]	.15[c]	.13[c]	.16[c]	.06[a]	.07[a]	.18[c]	1.00

[a] $p < .10$; [b] $p < .05$; [c] $p < .01$; [d] $p < .001$.

- Of the 82 voters who said they had been influenced by charges made against the Nixon administration with respect to the Watergate affair, over one-fourth said their previously held opinions had been strengthened; other voters said it had caused them to change their minds about whom to vote for. Twenty-six indicated they thought the episode was "negative in general" for the nation as a whole, while 20 thought it reflected negatively on Richard Nixon. Fifteen indicated adverse reactions toward the Republican Party. Fifty-eight voters specified in their open-end responses that they believed the Democratic Party's allegations concerning the matter.

- One hundred and nine voters said the report by Henry Kissinger concerning a cease-fire in Vietnam just prior to Election Day had influenced their vote decisions. When asked how it had done so, 20 percent mentioned that it made them feel more favorable toward the Nixon administration's peace efforts, versus 9 percent who said they felt Nixon was using Vietnam as a political tool. The voters who said they were not influenced were asked why they were not; over one-fourth said they were not influenced because they did not believe Kissinger's statement, 22 percent said they already had their minds made up, and 14 percent said they felt Vietnam was being used as a political tool.

Correlations between campaign orientations are shown in Table 5.8. As expected, the communication characteristics of voters were fairly well related: voters likely to score high on any one aspect of communication over the campaign were likely to score high on others. While voters more interested in the campaign were likely to score higher on communication attributes, voters having greater difficulty in deciding whom to vote for were not. Voters having more difficulty did not differ appreciably in communication from those having less difficulty, except that those with greater difficulty tended to anticipate influence more and discuss the campaign less. Although campaign interest and difficulty of decision-making were the two factors most highly associated with reported influence, they were slightly and negatively associated with one another. All the campaign orientations were at least moderately correlated with reported influence. There may have been two subtypes of voters reporting influence: one group appears to have been more interested, more media-attentive, and more talkative about the campaign, while the other was experiencing greater difficulty because they were generally less oriented toward the campaign. A look at differences among voters according to when they made up their minds, and whether they switched candidates during the campaign, will help to clarify the picture.

INFLUENCE, CAMPAIGN ORIENTATIONS, AND
CONDITIONS OF DECISION

Early deciders, switchers, and late deciders were quite different,
not only in their orientations to the campaign but also in the ways in
which their orientations were associated with their reports of influence
during the campaign.

The Early Deciders

Early deciders differed most from switchers and late deciders
in that they

- Had the greatest interest in the campaign
- Were the most attentive to the campaign
- Were the most exposed to campaign media content
- Depended the most upon television for campaign information
- Discussed the campaign the most
- Had the least difficulty deciding whom to vote for
- Reported the fewest instances of influence

Early deciders, then, were indeed the most involved in the campaign, but nonetheless remained the least likely to report having their
choices of candidates influenced as a function of their involvement
(Table 5.9).

How much of a contribution did each of the campaign orientations
make to reported influence among early deciders? Table 5.10 presents
a regression analysis depicting the relative contributions of each of
the campaign orientations to reported influence. The total variance
explained (R^2) in reported influence by all of the orientations combined
is fairly small (10 percent), indicating that among early deciders
influence was likely to depend on other factors.

Among the orientations, voters' interest in the campaign was
the most indicative of influence: the more interested voters were, the
more they reported influence. Following interest, the orientations
most predictive of influence were difficulty of decision, seeking interpersonal vote guidance, and exposure to campaign media content.
Hence the early deciders most influenced were likely to be those
most interested and those having the hardest time deciding on a candidate. They also tended to have sought more guidance from other
people and to have been more exposed to campaign-related media
content.

TABLE 5.9

Mean Levels of Campaign Orientations, by Vote Decision Mode

	All Voters (N=618)	Early Deciders (N=462)	Switchers (N=60)	Late Deciders (N=81)	Significance[*]
Anticipatory Influence	1.82	1.81	1.98	1.72	a, —, b
Difficulty of Decision	1.29	1.17	1.90	1.49	c, b, c
Campaign Interest	2.23	2.27	2.12	2.07	—, a, —
Campaign Attention	2.28	2.31	2.17	2.16	a, a, —
Campaign Exposure	2.01	2.03	1.90	1.84	—, b, —
Campaign Discussion	1.92	1.99	1.80	1.60	a, c, a
Newspaper Dependence	2.24	2.26	2.30	2.02	—, b, b
Television Dependence	1.79	1.83	1.68	1.59	a, b, —
Guidance-Seeking	1.91	1.89	2.00	1.91	—, —, —
Reported Influence	1.77	1.69	2.15	1.90	c, b, b

[*]F-tests respectively for early deciders versus switchers, early deciders versus initially undecideds, and switchers versus initially undecideds.

a, p < .10 ; b, p < .05 ; c, p < .01. Tests of significance are shown only for descriptive, and not for hypothesis testing purposes.

The extent to which early deciders anticipated influence and attended to the campaign was unlikely to make any difference in whether or not they reported influence. Campaign discussion and dependence on news media by early deciders also were essentially unrelated to influence.

At least superficially, this pattern is consistent with psychological dissonance theory. These voters were likelier to regard influence in terms of reinforcement or justification for decisions already reached, and it would follow that those who were more interested and

TABLE 5.10

Regression Analysis of Reported Influence, by
Campaign Orientations, for Early Deciders
(N = 462)

	r	r^2 Added	Beta
Campaign Interest	.22[c]	4.9%	.14
Difficulty of Decision	.13[c]	1.5	.14
Guidance-Seeking	.18[c]	1.1	.12
Campaign Media Exposure	.17[c]	0.8	.11
Campaign Discussion	.19[c]	0.7	.06
Anticipatory Influence	.07[a]	0.5	.01
Campaign Attention	.17[c]	0.2	.01
Television Dependence	.07[a]	0.1	.01
Newspaper Dependence	.01	0.1	.01

Total variance
  explained (R^2) = 10.1%

[a] $p < .10$; [c] $p < .01$.

who had to "work" harder to choose a candidate would desire greater
support for their decision. One expects the guidance-seeking and
media exposure to have been looking for supportive media content and
discussion.

While early deciders were the most attentive and exposed to the
campaign, they were not necessarily more dependent on newspapers
and television for information that presumably might discriminate more
objectively between the candidates. Such information could have been
viewed as potentially threatening to their prior decisions. Likewise,
such information dependence was a weak indicator of reported influence.

Among early deciders, reported influence seems best explained
by noncommunication factors; and where communication did enter in,
it appeared selective in nature.

The Switchers

Voters who switched from one candidate to another during the
campaign were perhaps the most interesting cohort, from both political

and communication behavior standpoints. These are the "converts," the 11 percent who had chosen a candidate by the end of the summer conventions but later changed their minds and voted for the opposing candidate. These voters

- Scored highest in anticipatory influence
- Fell between early deciders and late deciders in that they expressed moderate amounts of campaign interest, attention, media exposure, discussion, and dependence on television
- Were the most dependent on newspapers for political information
- Were highest in interpersonal guidance-seeking
- Had the greatest difficulty in deciding on a candidate
- Scored highest in reported influence. (See Table 5.9.)

While de facto appearing as the most "influenced" group, at least in terms of exhibiting change, and indeed reporting the most instances of influence during the campaign, switchers tended to be moderates in campaign communication behavior. Yet in July they were found to be the potential voters most likely to indicate reliance on communication sources for help in decision-making during the campaign.

Among switchers it was not interest, but anticipation of using communication sources as vehicles of influence, that best indicated reported influence (Table 5.11). Following anticipatory influence, dependence on television, campaign interest, and dependence on newspapers helped most to explain reported influence. While switchers exhibited the greatest difficulty, that difficulty was overridden as a factor in influence by the communication orientations. In short, switchers likeliest to report influence were those who said prior to the campaign that they were more reliant on communication sources to help them to decide, were the most interested during the campaign, and were the most dependent on newspapers and television for political information about the campaign. Campaign orientations were effective indicators of influence among switchers, in all explaining 23.5 percent of the variance.

It may have happened that these voters found themselves in a pattern of dependence on media for information pertinent to election decisions, and the information they found went against their initial decisions. The fact that McGovern defectors were disproportionately represented among switchers supports this view, given that the preponderance of campaign events could be deemed more negative toward McGovern than toward Nixon.

Simple exposure and attention were not indicative of reported influence, nor were the interpersonal components of discussion and guidance-seeking. Both exposure and interpersonal communication

TABLE 5.11

Regression Analysis of Reported Influence,
by Campaign Orientations, for Switchers
(N = 60)

	r	r^2 Added	Beta
Anticipatory Influence	.28[b]	7.7%	.30
Television Dependence	.17[a]	5.1	.24
Campaign Interest	.21[a]	4.7	.25
Newspaper Dependence	.27[b]	3.6	.23
Difficulty of Decision	.12	0.9	.19
Campaign Attention	.02	0.6	-.19
Campaign Discussion	.13	0.4	.09
Campaign Media Exposure	.11	0.3	-.04
Guidance-Seeking	.16	0.0	.01

Total variance
  explained (R^2) = 23.5%

[a] $p < .10$; [b] $p < .05$.

were weak indicators of influence. The power of person-to-person
interaction inferred from the two-step flow model was not apparent in
this critical group of voters who actually converted during the campaign. Instead, it was the degree to which these individuals depended
on the media for wide-ranging information gratification purposes,
coupled with a high interest in doing so, that most clearly pointed to
their reporting of influence in the course of the campaign.

The Late Deciders

Voters undecided as to a presidential candidate at the campaign's
onset were most characterized by their lack of orientation to the campaign. While they surpassed early deciders (though not switchers) in
reported influence, difficulty of decision, and interpersonal guidance-
seeking, they scored lowest on a number of dimensions.
Compared with early deciders and switchers, late deciders

- Least anticipated influence
- Were the least interested in the campaign

- Were the least exposed to campaign media content
- Depended the least on newspapers and television for campaign information
- Discussed the campaign the least. (See Table 5.9.)

The above pattern supports previous hypotheses about voters who enter a campaign undecided. They do not appear as concerned or necessarily rational voters attempting to weigh issues and candidates through the unfolding race. Rather, they seem to include less-involved citizens who, for some reason, feel an inclination to vote.

These voters seem to have unique perceptions of election campaigns and singular attitudes toward candidates and issues. While they report influence with relative ease, the sources of that influence seem obscure.

Late deciders most apt to report influence were those highest in anticipatory influence, campaign interest, difficulty of decision, newspaper dependence, and campaign discussion (Table 5.12). So, as with switchers, their motivational bases for media use appear as better indicators of influence than exposure or attention. Beyond that, influence was more related to newspaper than television dependence among late deciders, and interpersonal communication played more of a role among them than it did among switchers. Perhaps being less adept at and/or experienced with campaign media usage, late deciders tended more toward personal sources for guidance.

In sum, the role of the mass media as agents of influence during the campaign seems in some ways submerged, and in other ways quite dominant. Campaign media exposure alone was only indicative (and weakly at that) of influence among the already-decided, presumably those seeking justification for their decisions. Exposure actually was negatively related, albeit slightly, to influence, after other factors were controlled for among switchers and late deciders. Hence mere exposure to campaign media was not indicative of influence associated either with voters' making up their minds or with their changing them. However, more than exposure obviously needs to be considered here. Primarily, voters most interested in the campaign were more likely to be influenced, whether they were early deciders, switchers, or late deciders. While anticipatory influence was quite nonpredictive of influence among early deciders, it was the most predictive factor among switchers and late deciders.

Switchers and late deciders clearly knew in July, before their final vote decisions were made, that they would be more open to various sources of influence during the campaign. Further, switchers, especially those who tended to report greater influence, claimed more dependence on newspapers and especially on television news for information about the campaign. This dependence on media, independent

TABLE 5.12

Regression Analysis of Reported Influence, by
Campaign Orientations, for Late Deciders
(N = 81)

	r	r^2 Added	Beta
Anticipatory Influence	.24[b]	6.0%	.17
Campaign Interest	.27[b]	4.7	.12
Difficulty of Decision	.14	2.1	.14
Newspaper Dependence	.24[b]	1.8	.13
Campaign Discussion	.24[b]	1.2	.09
Campaign Attention	.23[b]	1.1	.04
Guidance-Seeking	.20[a]	0.5	.07
Television Dependence	.15	0.1	.04
Campaign Media Exposure	.09	0.0	-.03

Total variance
  explained (R^2) = 17.4%

[a] $p < .10$;   [b] $p < .05$.

of degree of exposure or attention, among this critical group of voters
needs much greater elaboration. While media exposure may be unrelated to influence among voters deciding during a campaign, the
dependence on media for certain information gratifications seems to
be a crucial factor in influence. Personal influences sources, reflected
by degree of discussion and guidance-seeking, seem to have very little
impact on reported influence.

INFLUENCE, CAMPAIGN ORIENTATIONS, AND
PRESIDENTIAL VOTING

Those voters deciding for either McGovern or Nixon and staying
with their choices throughout the campaign were very much alike in
their campaign orientations (Table 5.13). Early deciders for McGovern
appeared to have only a slightly more difficult time deciding, and were
somewhat more likely to report having been influenced, than their
counterparts who favored Nixon. In other respects the differences
were minimal. Given the fact that the McGovern and Nixon early
deciders differed greatly in demographic and socioeconomic makeup,

TABLE 5.13

Mean Campaign Orientations for McGovern and Nixon Voters,
by Decision Condition

	Early Deciders		Switchers		Late Deciders	
	McGovern (N=206)	Nixon (N=256)	McGovern (N=28)	Nixon (N=22)	McGovern (N=50)	Nixon (N=31)
Anticipatory Influence	1.80	1.83	2.00	1.96	1.68	1.80
Difficulty of Decision	1.22	1.14	2.01	1.65[b]	1.60	1.40[a]
Campaign Interest	2.27	2.28	2.05	2.25[a]	1.96	2.17[a]
Campaign Attention	2.34	2.29	2.09	2.27	2.03	2.32[a]
Campaign Exposure	2.00	2.05	1.79	1.82	1.63	2.23[c]
Campaign Discussion	1.94	2.03	1.71	1.91[a]	1.54	1.73[a]
Newspaper Dependence	2.25	2.27	2.22	2.62[c]	2.02	2.02
Television Dependence	1.83	1.83	1.70	1.65	1.51	1.76[a]
Guidance-Seeking	1.97	1.85	1.88	2.20[a]	2.01	1.85
Reported Influence	1.78	1.62[a]	1.95	2.48[c]	1.91	1.90

[a] $p < .10$; [b] $p < .05$; [c] $p < .01$.

165

the consistency in their orientations to the campaign was somewhat
surprising. However, the act of deciding early in a campaign, combined with the generally higher political involvement of those who do
decide early, may well strongly affect the ways in which voters behave
vis-a-vis campaigns.

More substantial differences were found among those voters who
switched candidates during the campaign, depending on whether they
switched from McGovern to Nixon or vice versa. Voters changing
from Nixon to McGovern seemed to have the more difficult time; but
those moving over from McGovern to Nixon are seen as having been
more interested, having discussed the campaign more, depending
more on newspapers, and reporting sizably more influence. It could
be that those who chose Nixon early and then switched were primarily
Democrats who had begun with doubts about McGovern, but then decided
that party loyalty dictated they vote for the Senator. They do not seem
to have used the campaign as a vehicle for changing their minds so
much as they perhaps used personal weighing of the situation. On the
other hand, those converting from McGovern to Nixon appear to have
been very much in tune with the campaign, and these voters may well
have included high proportions of Democrats in relatively high social
and economic levels. These voters may have become disenchanted
with their initial choice as the campaign unfolded.

The markedly higher reported influence scores of switchers
from McGovern to Nixon suggest they were definitely responding to
the campaign environment, apparently with substantial reliance on
newspapers. While the low numbers of individuals in each of the
cohorts discussed make generalization hazardous, it is interesting
to note some of the specific campaign events that switchers said influenced them. Six of the 22 McGovern-to-Nixon switchers said they had
been influenced by what they saw of the Republican National Convention
on television. While none of these voters said Thomas Eagleton's
resignation had influenced them, 10 reported influence from the selection of Sargent Shriver as the new Democratic vice-presidential nominee. Seven named political television commercials as an influence.

Even fewer of the 28 initial Nixon supporters who moved over
to McGovern named specific events as influences. For example, only
five of them named Watergate as an influence, and four named political
commercials. A more complete perspective on the impacts of some
of these campaign events will be given in Chapter 6.

Late deciders who chose McGovern tended to have a more difficult time deciding and to be less interested in the campaign, less
attentive to it, and less exposed to campaign media. They also discussed it less than did late-deciding Nixon voters, and counted less on
television news for information gratifications. Thus, the less politically involved "have-nots" among late deciders—almost exclusively

TABLE 5.14

Perceived Sources of Communication Influence on Vote Preferences
(percentages)

| | Early Deciders | | All Late Deciders* | |
	McGovern (N=206)	Nixon (N=256)	McGovern (N=88)	Nixon (N=53)
Pamphlets				
Yes (5%)	10	3	2	0
No (95%)	90	97	98	100
Campaign worker conversations				
Yes (4%)	7	8	1	2
No (96%)	93	92	99	98
Newspapers in general				
Yes (48%)	53	51	28	40
No (52%)	47	49	72	60
Newspaper content, percent "yes" on				
Regular news (38%)	42	41	24	28
Columns (4%)	2	4	5	6
Editorials (6%)	8	6	--	6
General conversation				
Yes (23%)	28	20	21	15
No (77%)	72	80	79	85
Candidates' speeches				
Yes (33%)	48	25	34	17
No (67%)	52	75	66	83
Television in general (excluding speeches)				
Yes (36%)	43	36	23	38
No (64%)	57	64	77	62
Television content, percent "yes" on				
Regular news (23%)	26	22	16	25
Talk shows (6%)	9	4	5	6
Commercials (7%)	7	7	2	9
Campaign specials (15%)	17	15	10	15
Magazines				
Yes (16%)	19	18	5	9
No (84%)	81	82	95	91
Radio				
Yes (18%)	21	18	11	9
No (82%)	79	82	89	91

*Includes switchers.

Note: Category percents are based on all voters.

Democrats—eventually cast their lots with McGovern, while the more aware "haves," although still preponderantly Democrats, went to Nixon. The pattern was not very different from that found among switchers, but campaign events seemingly played an even lesser role in the selection of candidates.

In October, voters who had decided for either McGovern or Nixon were asked a series of questions about which communication sources had helped them in making up their minds about whom to vote for. As Table 5.14 indicates, Newspapers were the source named most frequently overall (by 48 percent of the voters), followed by television (36 percent) and the specific category of candidates' televised speeches (33 percent). Regular news presentations about the campaign were the most mentioned content subset for both newspapers and television. Strong differences were not found between Nixon and McGovern voters, excpet that McGovern voters were considerably more likely to name candidates' speeches as a factor, * and were somewhat more likely to name interpersonal communication sources. McGovern supporters were also more apt to name political pamphlets and other campaign materials.

It was among those who decided for a candidate later in the campaign that more meaningful differences in influence sources, depending upon candidate choice, tended to occur. Late deciders for Nixon who indicated help from newspapers and television substantially outnumbered late deciders for McGovern doing so. Late deciders for Nixon were partial to mass media. Early deciders for McGovern said they were helped more by newspapers and television than did early deciders for Nixon.

There is also much in these data that can be taken as tacit support of a "reinforcement" or justification model of communication during election campaigns. Taken as a whole, the early deciders perceived proportionately greater amounts of assistance across communication sources than did late deciders. It might be argued that those sources "helped" them make up their minds in terms of providing information supportive of decisions already formulated; on the other hand, the late deciders—supposedly those in greater need—appear to have been "helped" less.

---

* During the campaign President Nixon made relatively few speeches, particularly over television, while McGovern was conducting a series of well-publicized half-hour televised specials.

MASS MEDIA AND INFLUENCE ON VOTING

In sum, a good number of voters did see their choosing of a presidential candidate as having been influenced by what happened during the campaign. Voters arriving at their final choices early in the campaign were the least likely to report influence but the most apt to have been interested in and attentive to the campaign, to have been exposed to campaign media content, and to have discussed the campaign. Voters deciding later in the campaign, on the other hand, were likelier to report influence but tended to be less oriented to campaign communications processes and less interested in the campaign in general; however, these later deciders did have a harder time making up their minds.

Influence as defined here seems rather weakly predicted by voters' communication behaviors over the campaign. Instead, across all voters, those more influenced were likelier to be either those more interested in the campaign or those who had a harder time making a decision. Among voters deciding later in the campaign, those who anticipated more influence tended to report influence more during the campaign. While interest, difficulty, and anticipation seem to be more important factors than communication behavior per se in predicting influence, this does not mean that communication behavior has no impact on influence. Rather, influence seems more clearly explained as a consequence both of such factors as decision condition, anticipation, difficulty, and interest, and of campaign attention, media exposure, news media dependence, and so forth.

Voters who decided early looked fairly homogeneous in terms of their orientations to the campaign, regardless of whether they voted for McGovern or Nixon. However, voters deciding late for Nixon (including those who switched to him from McGovern) seemed more communicative and more attuned to the campaign in general. Those deciding late for Nixon were likelier to name media as sources of influence, while late deciders for McGovern tended to name interpersonal sources.

6

THE INFLUENCE OF TELEVISED POLITICAL COMMERCIALS ON VOTE DECISIONS

In recent years paid political commercials on radio and television have become integral elements of election campaigns in the United States. The presidential campaign of 1972 offered no exceptions. Most recently, paid political commercials themselves have become issues in campaigning, touching off an ongoing debate regarding their effiacy and the possible need for controlling them (Mendelsohn and Crespi 1970). The concern about televised political advertising stems from the possibility that vote decisions may be unduly affected by exposure to it. The assertion of "undue influence" implies that televised advertising for political candidates may cause voters who are exposed to it to vote for candidates they had previously not intended to support. The findings from the Summit County study offer little basis for such concern. Rather than "converting" large numbers of voters, exposure to televised political commercials appears to be used primarily as support for choices previously made, as a means for easing the difficulty involved in making a vote choice, and as a vehicle for crystallizing vote choices where none had been made early in the campaign. In short, the specific influences wrought by exposure to televised political advertising in Summit County in 1972 were of the same order as the general influences on vote decisions that have been discussed in Chapter 5. Other recent perspectives on potential influences of political advertising can be found in C. L. Atkin, L. Bowen, and K. G. Shein-kopf (1973) and T. Patterson and R. McClure (1974).

Three-fourths of the Summit County voter panel claimed to have seen paid political commercials on television during the 1972 presidential campaign. In light of traditional research findings on the absence of substantial media influences on voting decisions, it is extremely important to note the finding that a full fourth of the voter panel as a whole claimed that their final vote decisions in 1972 had been influenced by exposure to televised political commercials. From these two observations alone, it seems evident that television advertising plays a rather substantial role in contemporary vote decision-making.

As a subset, the 121 voter-viewers in the panel (27 percent totally) who claimed that the televised campaign commercials they had seen had influenced their choice of a presidential candidate in 1972 were most often distributed among

- Young, first-time voters (33 percent)
- High school graduates (32 percent)
- Catholics (34 percent)
- Voters in the $10,000-$14,999 annual income bracket and those undergoing a moderate degree of economic stress (33 percent)
- Democrats (33 percent)
- Voters exhibiting a relatively low level of political knowledge (34 percent)
- Political guidance-seekers (34 percent).

Modally, it appears that voters who most often reported influence on their vote decision by the televised commercials they had seen generally exhibited characteristics that were more closely linked to McGovern supporters than to Nixon partisans.

In point of fact, by a margin of 31 percent to 20 percent, McGovern voters in the Summit County panel were more likely than Nixon backers to have had their vote decisions affected by exposure to political commercials of either candidate (Table 6.1). This was particularly true among early deciders. At the beginning of the 1972 campaign, 28 percent of those who had registered commitment to McGovern (compared with 21 percent of those who had chosen Nixon) later claimed that the political commercials they witnessed had influenced their vote decisions.

A reverse tendency took place with regard to late deciders and switchers. Both late deciders for Nixon and voters who switched to him were more likely to have stated that their decisions had been affected by commercials than was the case for McGovern's late deciders and switchers.

It seems apparent that for the early deciders who were exposed to televised commercials and claimed to have been influenced by them, "influence" occurred in the form of support for decisions already reached. For late deciders, exposure to campaign commercials undoubtedly helped crystallize a final vote decision.

TABLE 6.1

Claims That Vote Decisions Were Influenced by Political
Commercials, by Votes for Nixon and McGovern
(percentages)

	Claimed Vote Decisions Were Influenced by Political Commercials
Early Deciders for	
Nixon (N = 192)	21
McGovern (N = 150)	28
Late Deciders for	
Nixon (N = 20)	40
McGovern (N = 33)	36
Switched to	
Nixon (N = 14)	43
McGovern (N = 29)	38
Voted for	
Nixon (N = 228)	20
McGovern (N = 220)	31
Total* (N = 448)	27

*Total of panel voters who saw political commercials

For the switchers, exposure to political commercials helped
convert their allegiance from one candidate to another. However, it
must be kept in mind that the absolute number of cases in this latter
subset is relatively small: 43 individuals out of a total of 448 (10 percent) who had been exposed to televised paid political commercials.
Still, projecting this proportion to the national electorate during a
close race, the figure takes on a more than statistical significance.

Overall, in considering the possible effects of political commercials on voters, whether anything is "learned" from them and whether
they can "change" attitudes or opinions regarding candidates seem to
be equally of secondary importance. Of primary concern from the
voters' perspective is how helpful televised political commercials are
in either supporting or crystallizing their choices. Additionally, helpfulness in vote decision-making must be examined in the light of the
difficulty voters experienced in reaching a decision.

In comparison with all voter-viewers in the panel who claimed
political commercials had affected their voting choices (27 percent),

those who were undergoing stress in trying to reach a vote decision (37 percent) were considerably more likely to report that the political commercials they had seen had influenced their final choices. This was particularly pertinent with regard to the disproportionately high numbers who experienced difficulty in deciding, reported influence of commercials on their vote decision, and eventually cast their ballots for George McGovern (23 percent, as compared with 15 percent of all voters in this particular subset).

In brief, one important influence of exposure to political commercials was the easing, somehow, of the development of commitment or the undergirding of commitments already made to a candidate of relatively limited appeal, a candidate whose campaign had foundered from its very inception: George McGovern.

EXPOSURE TO POLITICAL COMMERCIALS

In ascertaining whether and to what extent exposure to paid televised political commercials may have influenced the vote choices of significant numbers of voters, it is important to examine two quite independent sets of antecedents to such influence. One relates directly to exposure as a necessary condition for influence to occur; the other relates to the overall campaign orientation components of influence, discussed in Chapter 5.

Who Watched Whose Commercials

Selective exposure hypotheses suggest that partisanship influences exposure to messages, to the degree that one tends to seek messages with which one is in agreement and to avoid messages that run counter to one's point of view. Thus, it would be expected that Nixon voters would address themselves almost exclusively to Nixon commercials on television, and that McGovern voters would have acted similarly vis-a-vis McGovern's televised advertisements. Contemporary television programming makes it almost impossible to avoid being exposed at one time or another to messages that are incongruent with one's political point of view. In all, 72 percent of the 618 voters in the Summit County panel claimed to have seen paid televised commercials for either candidate during the 1972 campaign. Of the 448 voters who claimed such exposure, 88 percent reported they had seen pro-McGovern commercials and 83 percent mentioned encounters with pro-Nixon advertisements. At the very least, then, three-fourths of

TABLE 6.2

Paid Televised Political Commercials for Both Candidates
(percentages)
(N = 448)

	For Nixon	For McGovern
Commercials Seen		
None	17	12
1-6	57	49
7 or more	26	39

TABLE 6.3

Frequency of Exposure to Televised Political Commercials,
by Vote
(percentages)

	Voted for Nixon	Voted for McGovern
Number of Commercials for Nixon Seen		
None (N = 76)	49	51
1-6 (N = 254)	55	45
7 or more (N = 118)	51	49
Number of Commercials for McGovern Seen		
None (N = 54)	48	52
1-6 (N = 218)	49	51
7 or more (N = 176)	55	45
Total Viewers of Campaign Commercials	51	49

the Summit County voters who saw any televised political commercials during the 1972 campaign were exposed to both pro-Nixon and pro-McGovern commercials. Modern television provides no place to hide from the opposition's campaign propaganda.

One might expect that the more time Summit County voters spent watching television in general, the more apt they were to see political commercials. Regardless of how much television viewing of a general nature took place, a large majority of Summit County voters from all walks of life encountered televised paid political advertisements during the campaign. Nonetheless, voter predispositions, combined with frequency of television viewing, often resulted in an enhanced likelihood of coming upon televised political commercials among various specific voter subsets.

On a proportionate basis, not only were greater numbers of voters more likely to have seen pro-McGovern commercials but, as Table 6.2 shows, they were considerably more likely to have seen more of them, or at least more repeat showings of McGovern spots, compared with televised Nixon advertisements.

That contemporary television viewing plays hob with selective exposure processes as they relate to witnessing paid political commercials is amply illustrated by the data on viewership in Table 6.3. Overall, frequency of exposure to partisan commercials for both Nixon and McGovern was directly related to the amount of general daily viewing of television. As general television viewing increased, so did frequency of encounters with both Nixon's and McGovern's paid political announcements (Figure 6.1).

Heavy television viewers (those who watched four or more hours daily, representing 26 percent of all voters) were more apt to see more commercials for either candidate than were either moderate or light viewers. Additionally, heavy viewers were more likely to see greater numbers of commercial presentations on behalf of McGovern than on behalf of Nixon. It is interesting to note that despite their routinely heavy encounters with television, fully 15 percent of the heavy viewers could not recall having seen any pro-Nixon commercials at all in 1972.

Moderate television viewers (two to fewer than four hours daily, representing 36 percent of all voters) were far more likely to have seen greater numbers of pro-McGovern televised advertisements than pro-Nixon commercials.

Light viewers (fewer than two hours daily, representing 34 percent of all voters) were more likely to have seen commercials for Nixon than those favoring McGovern. On the other hand, light viewers were more apt to have seen the highest numbers of McGovern presentations as compared with the number of Nixon advertisements seen. No matter how much general television viewing voters were accustomed to engage in, they were bound to encounter the highest frequencies

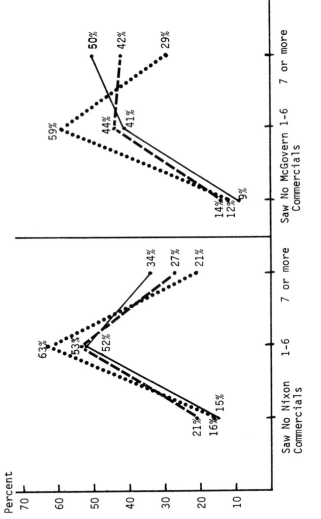

FIGURE 6.1

Frequency of Exposure to Nixon and McGovern Commercials,
by Time Spent Viewing Television Daily

——— Heavy Viewers (N=128)   ▬ ▬ Moderate Viewers (N=128)   •••• Light Viewers (N=153)

(seven or more) of McGovern's, rather than Nixon's, political commercials. Two factors seem to have operated in this regard: first, the McGovern commercial presentations to Summit County voters outnumbered those on behalf of Nixon; and second, the saturation placement of McGovern spots within the general television programming spectrum was better able, apparently, to catch the attention of voters of varying viewing habits than was the placement of Nixon's commercials.

To sum up, light viewers of television were less likely to encounter any pro-Nixon commercials, and they were most apt to have seen moderate numbers of presentations on behalf of both candidates. Moderate viewers most often encountered one to six commercials, particularly Nixon's. In the high range of seven or more presentations, moderate viewers were far more apt to have seen McGovern commercials than Nixon ones. Heavy viewers were most likely to have witnessed the most McGovern commercial announcements.

These data on the relationship between general television viewing habits and exposure to paid political commercials suggest that "selective exposure" to such "propaganda" may not be so much a function of partisanship as it is a function of customary media habits. The data from the Summit County panel show that partisanship, as measured by party identification, did not affect either exposure or frequency of exposure to paid political commercials.

Attitudes and Interest as Influences on Exposure

Although partisanship failed to affect exposure to political commercials in Summit County, interest in the 1972 campaign and voters' attitudes regarding the usefulness of political commercials did influence exposure to some extent.

Overall as interest in the 1972 presidential campaign increased, so did reported exposure to paid political television commercials (Table 6.4). The Summit County data underline the general mass communications principle that exposure to media content is a function of prior interest: the greater the prior interest, the more likely is exposure. This is not to say that lack of strong prior interest is necessarily followed by nonexposure. After all, six in every ten voters in the Summit County panel reported having seen campaign commercials, even though they admitted to being relatively disinterested in the 1972 campaign.

Interest in the 1972 campaign affected nonviewing of Nixon and McGovern commercials as well as high frequency of exposure to them

TABLE 6.4

Exposure to Paid Political Commercials, by Interest
in the 1972 Presidential Campaign
(percentages)

	Watched Televised Campaign Commercials		
	Yes	No	Can't Recall
Interest in 1972 Presidential Campaign			
High (N = 269)	77	20	4
Moderate (N = 224)	70	26	4
Low (N = 125)	60	38	3
Total (N = 618)	72	24	4

TABLE 6.5

Number of Nixon and McGovern Commercial
Presentations Seen, by Interest in Campaign
(percentages)

	Nixon Commercials Seen			McGovern Commercials Seen		
	None	1–6	7+	None	1–6	7+
Interested in Campaign						
Not Much (N = 44)	28	55	17	19	62	19
Somewhat (N = 143)	16	62	22	10	53	37
Very Much (N = 261)	14	53	33	10	41	49
Total (All viewers of campaign commercials) (N = 448)	17	57	26	12	49	39

(Table 6.5). Voters who were generally disinterested in the campaign were least likely to see any commercials for either candidate, and were least apt to see many televised advertising presentations for either Nixon or McGovern as well. Voters who were interested in the campaign were more likely to have been exposed to McGovern's commercials than to Nixon's in both the high and moderate frequency categories. In general, as interest in the campaign increased, so did high-frequency exposure to either Nixon or McGovern commercials; on the other hand, as interest in the campaign waned, nonattendance to either candidate's televised advertising increased.

Table 6.6 shows that voter attitudes regarding the helpfulness of television commercials in generating vote decisions was most frequently a determinant of whether or not they could recall having seen such advertisements. Thus voters who thought commercials useless were most apt to report not having seen any commercials at all. Otherwise, attitudes regarding helpfulness were, on the whole, relatively ineffectual in influencing frequency of exposure to either candidate's televised commercials. In similar fashion, whether or not voters believed they depended on commercials for voting guidance was most likely to determine either exposure or nonexposure to either candidate's televised propaganda, but not frequency of exposure.

Data on exposure to partisan televised commercials present no clear-cut picture of the precise role frequent exposure played in final vote decision-making (Table 6.3). While there was a tendency for voters who were exposed to moderately frequent (one to six) presentations of pro-Nixon commercials to vote for the incumbent President, a similar pro-Nixon vote tendency was discernible among voters who had been exposed most often to pro-McGovern commercials. Put another way, it appears on the surface that the more pro-McGovern commercials voters were likely to see, the more apt they were to vote for Nixon. These findings suggest either that Nixon supporters, compared with McGovern partisans, were more likely to be exposed to more commercials overall, or that frequent exposure to McGovern commercials in some way resulted in sufficient audience disaffection (particularly among viewers leaning to Nixon, regardless of party affiliation) to warrant withholding support from the Democratic nominee.

Summit County voters who saw paid political television commercials for both candidates during the 1972 campaign generally were more likely to estimate greater numbers of television presentations on behalf of George McGovern (48 percent) compared with Nixon (15 percent). A fourth of the viewers (27 percent) believed the number of television advertising presentations for both candidates was about equal.

Actually, McGovern's televised commercial presentations in Summit County were considerably more numerous than Nixon's, yet

TABLE 6.6

Attitudes Toward and Reliance on Televised Political
Commercials, by Frequency of Exposure to
Nixon and McGovern Commercials
(percentages)

	Nixon Commercials Seen			
	None (N=76)	1-6 (N=254)	7+ (N=118)	Total (N=448)
Believed Campaign Commercials Are Helpful in Making Vote Decisions	20	38	39	35
Are Not Helpful in Making Vote Decisions	72	56	52	57
Relied on Television Campaign Commercials	12	21	15	17
Did Not Rely on Campaign Commercials	87	76	79	79

	McGovern Commercials Seen			
	None (N=54)	1-6 (N=218)	7+ (N=176)	Total (N=448)
Believed Campaign Commercials Are Helpful in Making Vote Decisions	17	39	36	35
Are Not Helpful in Making Vote Decisions	71	56	48	57
Relied on Television Campaign Commercials	11	19	17	17
Did Not Rely on Campaign Commercials	87	78	77	79

180

voters' estimates of the numbers of ads presented were based primarily on their choices of candidates. Thus two-thirds of the voters who supported Nixon (65 percent) perceived the number of McGovern's televised commercials to be excessive. At the same time, the same proportion of backers of McGovern (68 percent) perceived the number of pro-Nixon commercials to exceed the number of ads presented on behalf of their candidate. By a ratio of 61 percent to 39 percent, a greater proportion of McGovern supporters than Nixon voters considered the number of television advertisements for the two presidential candidates about equal.

THE INFLUENCE OF POLITICAL COMMERCIALS
ON VOTE DECISIONS

Frequency of Exposure to Commercials and Influence

Chapter 5 discussed the concept that exposure by itself is not a powerful predictor of influence: it is clear that with regard to influencing vote decisions, exposure to the media may be a necessary condition in many instances, but by no means can it be considered a sufficient one in most cases.

Across the board, general frequency of television viewing did not affect the likelihood of being influenced by political commercials. Of both light and heavy television viewers in the panel who were exposed to political commercials, no more than 8 percent of each reported that their vote decisions had been influenced by the advertisements they had seen. Ten percent of the moderate television viewers reported a similar experience.

Among the heavy viewers who claimed their vote decisions had been influenced by exposure to political commercials, the following modal profile emerges. Persons most likely to have been influenced were

- Aged 25–34 years (12 percent)
- Educationally nonmobile (12 percent)
- Low in socioeconomic status (12 percent)
- Lacking in political knowledge (13 percent)
- High in campaign–related media exposure (13 percent) but with relatively low dependence on newspapers for political information (14 percent)
- Greatly dependent on television for political information (14 percent)

TABLE 6.7

Influence of Political Commercials, by Vote and Frequency
of Exposure to Nixon and McGovern Commercials
(percentages)

	All Voters Who Claim to Have Been Influenced by Political Commercials	Voters Claiming Influence from Political Commercials and Voting for	
		Nixon	McGovern
Number of Television Political Commercial Presentations Seen			
None for Nixon (N=76)	18	5	13
None for McGovern (N=54)	15	7	7
1-6 for Nixon (N=254)	30	12	17
1-6 for McGovern (N=218)	28	11	17
7 or more for Nixon (N=118)	28	17	11
7 for more for McGovern (N=176)	30	15	14
Total (All viewers of campaign commercials) (N=448)	27	12	15

• Political guidance-seekers (13 percent)
• Those who claimed the highest degree of influence on their
  vote decisions by the mass media in general (19 percent).

If, from the data thus far presented, one were to develop an
ideal typology of Summit County voters whose vote decisions in the
1972 campaign had been influenced by political commercials, the most
likely prospects for persuasion would be younger, politically unsophisticated voters who, when they encountered difficulties in coming to a
decision (particularly on behalf of George McGovern), found guidance
in the one medium with which they customarily came into high contact
for news and information—television.

It has already been pointed out that the more hours a voter spent
in general television viewing, the more commercial presentations on

behalf of either Nixon or McGovern (but particularly on behalf of
McGovern) he or she was likely to encounter. Did the number of commercials seen affect the degree of influence on viewers' vote decision-
making?

Frequency of exposure to candidates' television advertising did
not affect vote decisions across the board; however, frequency of
commercials seen did affect vote decision-making in one specific
instance. Compared with all Nixon voters who claimed their vote
decision had been influenced by political commercials, voters who
saw the most pro-Nixon advertising presentations were most apt to
have cast their ballots for him (Table 6.7). However, whether exposure served as an independent or dependent variable here cannot be
ascertained from the data in hand, and no causal relationship can be
inferred.

Otherwise, relative differences in vote behavior were noted only
within frequency-of-exposure subsets. For example, voters who saw
no Nixon commercials at all were more likely to have voted for
McGovern and to claim that commercials (obviously those of McGovern)
affected their decision to do so. Similarly, voters who witnessed
moderate numbers of either pro-Nixon or pro-McGovern commercials
were more likely to have favored the Democratic nominee, and simultaneously to have reported influence on their choice by the political
commercials they had seen.

Attention to Commercials and Influence

Although television viewer-voters of whatever political inclination
are in no position to avoid being exposed to televised commercial
presentations of opposition candidates, it is quite possible to avoid
paying close attention to them.

Overall nearly four in every ten Summit County voters in the
panel reported having followed the 1972 televised campaign commercials
with more than casual interest. Proportionately fewer Nixon voters
(36 percent) than McGovern voters (40 percent) stated that they had
followed the 1972 campaign commercials attentively. This is not to
say, however, that voters in either candidate's camp closed their
minds to televised advertising messages on behalf of the opposition.
On the contrary, while well over half of all the voters who viewed
either Nixon's or McGovern's commercials and then voted for one of
them claimed to have followed their own candidate's televised messages
with considerable attention, more than four in ten individuals in this
subset reported having paid very close attention to the commercials
of the candidate for whom they did not vote.

The data on party affiliation show a similar relationship. Among both Democrats and Republicans, 55 percent in each camp claimed high attentiveness to McGovern commercials in the first instance and to Nixon commercials in the second. At the same time, 46 percent of the Democrats claimed they paid close attention to Nixon's commercials, and 52 percent of the Republicans reported a high degree of attentiveness to those of McGovern.

The relationship between attentiveness to political commercials and their subsequent influence on vote decisions was relatively weak among Summit County voters, suggesting that the latter is not necessarily dependent on the former.

Totally, 19 percent of the Summit County panel members who had seen televised political commercials in 1972 reported that they had paid close attention to McGovern's commercials and had been influenced by them in their vote decision-making. The figure for voters who were attentive to Nixon commercials and had their vote decisions affected by them was 16 percent. In other words, the great majority of voters who claimed they were attentive to either candidate's televised commercials did not necessarily believe that they had been influenced by them, at least as far as vote decision-making was concerned.

The data appear to support contemporary theories with regard to "noninvolvement" in television advertising; that is, one does not necessarily have to be involved with advertising in order to be influenced by it (Krugman 1965).

Assessments of Commercials and Influence

It is clear that voters who saw paid political television commercials during the 1972 campaign not only viewed them attentively, but also most often took them to be serious sources of candidate information. In this regard, substantial majorities of the 448 voters who were exposed to televised political advertisements of either candidate considered them to have done a good to excellent job of informing voters of the candidates' stands on important issues (72 percent), and of informing voters of candidates' qualifications (61 percent).

Contrary to many hypotheses regarding the alleged power of political commercials to project candidate imagery, the voter-viewers in Ohio judged the performance of televised commercials in presenting candidates' postures on issues in a more favorable light than they assessed their performance in projecting candidate qualifications.

Partisans of McGovern (49 percent) and of Nixon (51 percent) did not differ in their "good to excellent" appraisals of television commercials' efforts to present candidate stands on issues, but their evalu-

ations vis-a-vis projecting candidate qualifications did differ. Here
53 percent of the McGovern voters, compared with 47 percent of the
Nixon partisans, rated the commercials as having done a good to
excellent job of presenting the candidates' qualifications.

Because most voters in the Summit County panel were exposed
to both Nixon and McGovern commercials, it is possible to determine
their reactions on a comparative rather than absolute basis. Voters
who claimed to have seen the televised campaign commercials of both
presidential candidates were asked to compare them on six attributes:
good taste, interest appeal, annoyance, informativeness, credibility,
and conviction appeal. Table 6.8 indicates that overall, voter-viewers
tended to rank Nixon commercials relatively high on conviction and
credibility; moderately high on informativeness, good taste, and
interest appeal; and proportionately low on annoyance. In other words,
viewers of Nixon commercials were most likely to consider them to
be convincing and least likely to evaluate them as annoying.

In contrast, the general reactions to McGovern commercials
tended to be proportionately high with regard to their informativeness,
interest, conviction appeal, and annoyance, and relatively low in
credibility and good taste.

Where evaluations of Nixon's commercials tended to be generally
positive, assessments of McGovern's presentations were quite ambivalent overall. In comparative terms, voter-viewers were more apt
to favor Nixon commercials over McGovern messages, totally on the
positive attributes of good taste, credibility, and conviction. At the
same time, McGovern commercials were more likely to be considered
annoying. Relatively insignificant differences appeared between
assessments of the two candidates' commercials with regard to their
interest appeal and informativeness, although there were slight tendencies to favor McGovern's materials over Nixon's.

Although self-selection had relatively small influence on exposure
to paid political television advertising in Summit County, it operated
fully in affecting the perceptions of commercials with regard to their
attributes. Whether voters reacted favorably to paid political spots
during the 1972 campaign was almost exclusively associated with those
whom they eventually chose to vote for. Overall, nearly nine in ten
voters who claimed to have witnessed paid political commercials on
behalf of either Nixon or McGovern were most likely to perceive their
favorite's commercials, rather than those of the opposition, as being
more tasteful, less annoying, more believable, and more convincing.

Upon submission to a regression analysis of all six evaluative
attributes—relative tastefulness, interest, annoyance, informativeness,
conviction, and credibility—of the political commercials seen by panel
members, only credibility and conviction stand out as predictors of
influence on vote decision. Table 6.9 shows that, overall, voters who

TABLE 6.8

Comparative Evaluations of Nixon's and McGovern's
Television Commercials
(percentages)
(N=448)

| | Television Campaign Commercials for | | |
	Nixon	McGovern	Neither
Viewer Evaluations:			
Commercials Were More			
Tasteful	30	24	19
Interesting	28	31	15
Annoying	22	30	27
Informative	31	33	11
Believable	33	27	15
Convincing	36	31	13

TABLE 6.9

Regression Analysis of Influence of Political Commercials,
by Commercial Attributes

	r	r^2 Added	Beta
More Interesting	.00	0.0%	.02
More Good Taste	.00	0.0	.01
More Informative	.01	0.0	.03
More Believable	.02	0.2	.19
More Convincing	-.05	1.1	.18
More Annoying	.05	0.2	.08

Total variance explained (R^2) = 1.0%

Note: "Commercials helped" scored 1; "did not help" scored 3.
In all cases Nixon = 1; McGovern = 3.

TABLE 6.10

Regression Analysis of Influence of Political Commercials,
by Commercial Attributes and Voter Preference

	r	r^2 Added	Beta
McGovern Voters			
Interesting	-.07	0.5%	-.06
Good Taste	-.06	0.1	.01
Informative	-.08	0.1	-.03
Believable	.00	0.7	.20
Convincing	-.14	2.1	-.19
Annoying	.10	0.8	.10
Nixon Voters			
Interesting	.10	1.0%	.05
Good Taste	.08	0.2	-.06
Informative	.12	0.6	.06
Believable	.20	2.8	.22
Convincing	.10	0.1	-.04
Annoying	-.02	0.0	-.02
Total variance explained (R^2) = 4.8%			

Note: "Commercials helped" scored 1; "did not help" scored 3.
In all cases Nixon = 1; McGovern = 3.

saw the political commercials presented on television during the 1972
campaign and found them relatively credible or convincing were more
likely to claim their vote decisions for either candidate had been
affected by the advertisements. Moreover, the data in Table 6.10 show
that credibility alone, when applied to Nixon commercials, was most
predictive of influence on voters' decisions for Nixon, whereas credibility plus conviction were most predictive of decision influence for
McGovern.

Believing Nixon's commercials was a highly powerful influence
on the viewers who chose the incumbent President; on the other hand,
before McGovern's commercials could influence viewers' votes on his
behalf, they not only had to be believable but, it would appear, they
had to convince viewers as well. In other words, McGovern's commercials had to perform two complex persuasive tasks in order to
become effective, whereas Nixon's had to perform only one.

Attitudes Toward Commercials, Difficulty of Decision,
and Influence

Compared with all Summit County voters who claimed their vote
choices had been influenced by the political commercials they had
seen, voters expressing negative attitudes toward televised political
commercials in general manifested neither more nor less advertising
influence on their presidential choice-making (Table 6.11). In other
words, on a relative basis, negative attitudes toward televised commercials generally did not inhibit their reported influence on vote
decisions. Voters might express negative feelings regarding political
commercials and still be influenced by them, particularly if they
favored McGovern.

TABLE 6.11

Influence by Political Commercials, by Vote and
Negative Attitudes Toward Paid Political
Television Commercials
(percentages)

	All Voters Who Claim to Have Been Influenced by Political Commercials	Voters Claiming Influence from Political Commercials and Voting for	
		Nixon	McGovern
Believe Political Commercials Do Not Help Voters to Decide on a Candidate (N=253)	27	12	15
Believe Political Commercials Should Not Be Allowed on Television (N=143)	27	9	18
Claim Not to Depend on Political Commercials for Help in Deciding for Whom to Vote (N=352)	26	13	13
Total (N=448)	27	12	15

TABLE 6.12

Influence of Political Commercials, by Vote and by Making
Purchases as Result of Exposure to Consumer Commercials
During Three Months Prior to Inverview
(percentages)

| | Made Purchase as Result of Seeing Consumer Commercials | | | |
	Yes (N=76)	No (N=350)	Can't Recall (N=22)	Total (N=448)
All Voters Who Saw Political Commercials	17	78	5	100
All Voters Who Claim to Have Been Influenced by Political Commercials	36	27	9	27
Voters Who Claim to Have Been Influenced by Political Commercials and Voted for				
Nixon	17	12	5	12
McGovern	18	15	5	15

That political commercials may either help overcome the difficulties many voters encounter in the vote decision process (or perhaps
exacerbate them in some instances) is illustrated by the following
findings. Whereas, in all, 27 percent of the Summit County voters
who viewed paid political commercials claimed to have been influenced
by them, 37 percent of the voters who experienced difficulty in vote
decision-making claimed that the political commercials they had seen
had influenced their final decisions. Further, whereas totally 15 percent of the voters in the panel had reported advertising influence on
their decision to vote for McGovern, 23 percent of the voters who
encountered difficulty in making their final choices indicated that
exposure to political commercials had affected their decision to vote
for the Democratic nominee. It is evident that McGovern voters who
were encountering difficulty in deciding for him were most likely to
have been influenced by the political commercials they saw. It is

possible the commercials these voters were exposed to may have either initiated or increased their difficulty; but knowing this subset's propensity toward the media for political guidance, it is more likely that exposure to political commercials served to resolve some of the stress these voters were experiencing.

Also examined in the Summit County study was whether influence by televised political commercials may be related to habitual reactions to consumer advertising on television.

Voters in the study were asked, "Regarding television commercials in general during the past three months or so, have you looked into or tried a product or service just because you happened to see it on television?" Only 17 percent of all voters in the panel who reported having seen political commercials also made purchases as a result of witnessing consumer commercials, but fully twice that proportion (36 percent) of those who claimed political advertisements actually influenced their voting decisions stated that they had also tried a product or service after seeing it in a television commercial (Table 6.12). Clearly, the habit of responding to television advertising generally spilled over into the area of response to political advertising. Although viewers who were habituated to reacting to televised consumer advertising were most likely to be influenced by political commercials, they were not unduly influenced to vote for either presidential candidate.

Campaign Orientations, Commercials, and Influence

Nine campaign orientation factors were associated with the mix of overall reported influence on vote decisions among the Summit County voters in the panel: campaign interest, campaign attention, campaign exposure, dependence on newspapers for campaign news and information, political guidance-seeking, campaign discussion, difficulty in vote decision-making, and anticipation of influence on vote decisions. Whether and how these factors interacted with influence depended to a significant extent on when voters made up their minds. The nine factors were far more powerful predictors of overall influence among switchers than they were among the early deciders.

To what extent did the nine factors predict a more concise influence, such as that produced by televised commercials? It has been noted that early deciders were the least likely to claim influence from political commercials on their choices. Further, all nine campaign orientation factors combined explained no more than 6 percent of the total variation in reported television advertising influence among early deciders (Table 6.13). What emerges here is that for a relatively small number of early deciders, paid political commercials

TABLE 6.13

Regression Analysis of Influence of Political Commercials,
by Campaign Orientations: Early Deciders[*]
(N = 342)

	r	r^2 Added	Beta
Campaign Interest	.12[c]	1.5%	.16
Guidance-Seeking	.10[b]	1.4	.13
Difficulty of Decision	.09[b]	1.0	.09
Campaign Discussion	-.03	0.7	-.14
Newspaper Dependence	.07	0.5	.05
Anticipatory Influence	.10[b]	0.4	.05
Television Dependence	.08[b]	0.2	.04
Campaign Attention	.04	0.1	.03
Campaign Exposure	.03	0.0	.01

Total variance explained (R^2) = 6.2%

[b] $p < .05$; [c] $p < .01$.
[*]Only voters who saw political commercials.

served to satisfy an interest in the 1972 campaign, particularly among those who seemed to have arrived at their early decisions with some misgivings and sought either support for that decision or reasons for changing their minds. However, the media played minor roles as sources of news and information in this quest, as did interpersonal conversations.

Early deciders appeared to reflect a rather passive orientation to the campaign per se, and their encounters with televised political advertisements appear to have been both casual and haphazard, occurring more as by-products of using television for entertainment than for political knowledge.

The profile for late deciders offers quite a different set of characteristics. Table 6.14 shows that late deciders who reported being influenced by television commercials tended to seek more interpersonal guidance, had a more difficult time deciding on a candidate, had more interest in the campaign, and were less dependent on television news for information. The regression analysis indicates that the factors that most explained advertising influence were guidance-seeking, television dependence, and difficulty of decision. Whether of not these voters were interested in the campaign becomes less

TABLE 6.14

Regression Analysis of Influence of Political Commercials,
by Campaign Orientations: Late Deciders[*]
(N=53)

	r	r^2 Added	Beta
Guidance-Seeking	.38[c]	4.2%	.47
Television Dependence	-.18[a]	6.2	-.18
Difficulty of Decision	.23[b]	4.0	.17
Anticipatory Influence	-.04	3.2	.19
Campaign Attention	-.06	3.0	.19
Campaign Interest	.14	2.8	.19
Campaign Exposure	-.08	0.9	.11
Campaign Discussion	.08	0.5	.08
Newspaper Dependence	-.03	0.1	.01

Total variance explained (R^2) = 35.1%

[a] $p < .10$; [b] $p < .05$; [c] $p < .01$.
[*]Only voters who saw political commercials.

TABLE 6.15

Regression Analysis of Influence of Political Commercials,
by Campaign Orientations: Switchers[*]
(N = 43)

	r	r^2 Added	Beta
Difficulty of Decision	-.33[b]	11.0%	-.28
Television Dependence	.33[b]	10.2	.21
Campaign Interest	-.23[a]	5.6	-.28
Guidance-Seeking	.14	3.9	.24
Campaign Exposure	.21[a]	3.6	.21
Campaign Discussion	-.23[a]	2.6	-.27
Newspaper Dependence	.04	1.6	.16
Anticipatory Influence	.08	0.9	-.10
Campaign Attention	-.20[a]	0.1	-.01

Total variance explained (R^2) = 39.2%

[a] $p < .10$; [b] $p < .05$.
[*]Only voters who saw political commercials.

indicative of influence than anticipatory influence and campaign attention when other factors are controlled for.

Here a subset of guidance-seeking voters emerges: voters who entered the 1972 campaign with no particular candidate in mind because they were meeting difficulty in coming to a decision. They did not, however, turn to the serious aspects of the media for help; instead, in their routine use of television for entertainment, they encountered political advertising that served as an aid to crystallizing a final choice. These late deciders appear not to have been skilled information-seekers as such, but welcomed guidance-giving information from whatever "noneffort" source it might come, including televised political commercials.

While several factors were well correlated with reports of influence of commercials among switchers, it is clear that such influence was most apt to occur among switchers who had a less difficult time deciding, were less interested in the campaign, sought more interpersonal guidance, and were more exposed to campaign-related media content. Being less interested, they paid less attention to the campaign and discussed it less (Table 6.15).

In determining whether switchers would be influenced by political commercials, two factors stand out. The less difficulty switchers had in shifting their votes, the more likely they were to be influenced by commercials. Similarly, the more use they made of the media (particularly television) for political news and information, the more apt their vote decisions were to have been influenced by political commercials.

Whereas the influence of paid political commercials on late deciders occurred as a rather randomized consequence of voters' lack of information-gathering skills, television advertising influence on switchers seems to have resulted mainly from their conscientious utilization of television as a major source of political news, information, and guidance.

CHAPTER
7
INFLUENCE OF CAMPAIGN EVENTS ON VOTE DECISIONS

As is the case with drama, a political campaign is composed of a series of events that influence the characters in different ways—some on a short-term, temporary basis, others in consequential fashion. Just as the same events portrayed in a stage play may affect different audiences in different ways, so we can expect voters to react to campaign events in variable ways. Some may be aware of certain events, while others remain ignorant of their occurrence. For some voters a given event may be highly salient, while others may be quite disinterested. Some voters' prior choices as candidates may be strengthened by a given campaign event, while the decisions of others may be weakened, or even changed.

Attention now turns to studying three such specific events that took place during the 1972 presidential campaign: Senator Eagleton's resignation as the Democratic vice-presidential candidate; the Watergate break-in disclosures; and the major Vietnam policy speech that George McGovern delivered over national television on the evening of October 10, 1972. In each instances three factors will be analyzed: awareness of the event, reactions to the event, and the influence on voting decisions that each event may have produced.

Let us begin with the "Eagleton affair" and its potential effects on the voters of Summit County, Ohio, in 1972.

THE INFLUENCE OF THE EAGLETON RESIGNATION ON VOTE DECISIONS

The disclosures concerning George McGovern's 1972 vice-presidential running mate Thomas Eagleton's alleged mental health problems touched off an unprecedented swirl of publicity and political reaction early in the 1972 campaign, resulting in the Missourian's withdrawal from the Democratic ticket. Since that time, speculations regarding the effects of the "Eagleton affair" on the electorate and on McGovern's subsequent defeat have proliferated. Data gathered from the Ohio panel can serve to shed some light on reactions among at least one American political cohort: the voters of Summit County, Ohio.

Awareness of the Event

Fieldwork on the initial July phase of the Summit County voting study was already in progress when the Eagleton story broke. As a consequence, interviews regarding voters' reactions to the event were completed with only 278 of the 618 voters in the panel. In all, 96 percent of the voters queried had heard about the event immediately after it occurred.

Newspapers (cited by 45 percent of the voters who were aware of the occurrence) and television (cited by 43 percent) served equally as primary information sources regarding the Eagleton disclosures. Radio was named as a major source by 9 percent, and magazines by an additional 3 percent.

At the time voters were generally value about the details relating to the entire Eagleton matter. As a consequence, among the voters who had heard of the event

- 23 percent referred to Eagleton's resignation and alluded to his alleged health problems in general
- 23 percent referred to his resignation and specifically mentioned alleged mental health problems (excluding possibilities relating to alcoholism); an additional 4 percent mentioned both his resignation and his alleged alcoholism, but did not refer to general health problems
- 12 percent referred only to Senator Eagleton's withdrawal from the vice-presidential race and did not allude to allegations of either general or mental health difficulties
- 6 percent referred to alleged mental health problems (excluding references to alcoholism) but did not mention withdrawal from the race
- 5 percent mentioned general health problems relative to Senator Eagleton, but did not allude to his resignation as Democratic vice-presidential candidate

- 4 percent made general comments about Eagleton as the Democratic vice-presidential candidate, but made no references either to allegations of his general or mental health difficulties or to his resignation
- 1 percent alluded to allegations of alcoholism related to Senator Eagleton, but made no reference to his resignation as the Democratic candidate for Vice-President
- 20 percent made miscellaneous comments that referred neither to Eagleton's alleged health difficulties nor to his withdrawal as a candidate.

Two facts are worth noting from these data. Despite the considerable publicity regarding charges that the Democratic candidate may have been an alcoholic, this allegation was mentioned by only a minority of voters in the Summit County panel who were aware of the Eagleton matter (5 percent). A full third of the voters who were aware of the Eagleton affair apparently remained uninformed of his withdrawal from the vice-presidential race, despite the substantial attention the media gave to the event.

Reactions to the Eagleton Resignation

As noted, 62 percent (166 voters) who were cognizant of the Eagleton disclosures were aware that Senator Eagleton had resigned as the vice-presidential nominee for the Democrats. When these voters were asked their opinions about the propriety of the resignation, a majority (52 percent) said it was the right thing to do; 30 percent thought it was wrong; 7 percent believed it was neither right nor wrong; and 10 percent had no opinion.

In particular, four variables appeared to have strongly influenced voters' reactions to the Eagleton resignation: party affiliation, age, interest in politics generally, and attentiveness to the 1972 campaign.

Democrats for Nixon (65 percent) and nondefecting Democrats (58 percent) were most frequently supportive of the resignation. The Independents in the panel (41 percent) most often opposed the resolution of the Eagleton affair, claiming it was wrong for him to have withdrawn. It is interesting that as age of voters increased, support for Eagleton's resignation increased: a low of 23 percent of the first-time voters in the panel endorsed it, but fully seven in ten voters aged 50 and over approved of his withdrawal. On the other hand, 59 percent of the youngest voters, in contrast with 23 percent of those aged 50 and 8 percent 65 and over, voiced opposition to the withdrawal.

In short, the older the voter, the more likely he or she was to approve of McGovern's handling of the Eagleton matter. And the

younger the voter, the more apt he or she was to experience frustration
and disappointment over the entire affair and McGovern's role in it.

As interest in general politics increased, Summit County voters
were more likely to endorse Eagleton's resignation (64 percent among
the very interested, 49 percent among the moderately interested, and
42 percent among the relatively disinterested). On the other hand, it
was the voter with a moderate interest in politics (40 percent) who
was most likely to oppose the Eagleton withdrawal from the Democratic ticket.

Voters who were moderately attentive to the 1972 campaign (63
percent) were most often in favor of the Eagleton resignation; those
who were relatively inattentive were most likely to oppose it (53 percent).

Panel members who endorsed Senator Eagleton's withdrawal
supported George McGovern by a margin of 52 percent, as compared
with 48 percent who favored Nixon in the presidential race. Those
who believed the Senator's action was incorrect supported Richard
Nixon by a margin of 54 percent versus 46 percent for McGovern.

No matter whether they supported or opposed the Eagleton
decision to resign, voters encountered considerably more difficulty
in coming to an ultimate decision for George McGovern than they did
for Richard Nixon. Whereas 8 percent of those who believed resignation was the right thing to do had met with difficulty in reaching a
decision to vote for Nixon, 18 percent had found arriving at a decision
for McGovern to be arduous. Similarly, 6 percent of those who were
in disagreement with the Eagleton withdrawal experienced travail in
voting for Nixon, compared with 16 percent who found themselves
troubled in deciding for McGovern.

Whatever other impact the Eagleton affair may have had on voters
in the Summit County panel, one thing is certain: the withdrawal of
the Senator from the vice-presidential contest made deciding for
McGovern more difficult.

Overall, Summit County voters who were aware of the Eagleton
withdrawal were considerably more likely to perceive the resignation
as doing more harm (46 percent) than good (25 percent) to the candidacy of George McGovern.

Nixon voters were most apt to think the Eagleton matter would
hurt McGovern's chances (60 percent), while McGovern voters were
most likely to believe the affair would help the South Dakotan's cause
(66 percent).

Influence of the Eagleton Resignation on Vote Decisions

According to the testimony of the voters who were aware of the
Eagleton withdrawal, 10 percent (16 cases) declared that the affair
had influenced their vote decisions at the time. Precisely half of this
subset ultimately voted for President Nixon; the remaining 50 percent
cast their ballots for Senator McGovern. Among Summit County voters,
then, the overall effect of the Eagleton affair on voters whose choices
were directly affected by it was a standoff (Table 7.1).
    Although the subset of 16 affected voters divided their votes
equally between Nixon and McGovern, the effect of the withdrawal on
early deciders for Nixon (50 percent, versus 19 percent for McGovern
voters) was marked. The possibility that the Eagleton resignation may
have turned McGovern supporters in Summit County toward Nixon is
not borne out by the findings. In no instance among panel members

TABLE 7.1

Claimed Influence of Eagleton Resignation
on Vote Decision
(percentages)

	All Voters Who Were Aware of Resignation (N = 166)	Voters Who Claimed Decision Influenced by Resignation (N = 16)
Voted for		
Nixon	49	50
McGovern	51	50
Early Deciders for		
Nixon	39	50
McGovern	35	19
Late Deciders for		
Nixon	5	—
McGovern	7	25
Switched to Nixon		
from McGovern	4	—
Switched to McGovern		
from Nixon	6	6
Democrats Who		
Voted for Nixon	16	6

did the Eagleton matter cause voters to switch from McGovern to Nixon, as far as final vote choice was concerned. Actually, one voter who averred that the Eagleton action had influenced his vote choice ultimately switched from Nixon to McGovern.

Where the data give some basis for speculation that the Eagleton resignation may have helped very small numbers of voters to come to an early decision for Nixon rather than for McGovern, they further show that the Eagleton affair also affected late deciders for McGovern slightly, but had no effect on late deciders for Nixon.

Overall, the minuscule numbers of voters who claimed that their vote decisions had been affected by the withdrawal of Senator Eagleton had most often reacted negatively to it, either by considering the resignation to have been a mistake (20 percent) or by believing that the action would hurt McGovern's chances in the election (18 percent).

Influence of Selection of Sargent Shriver on Vote Decisions

In all, 85 percent of all 618 voters in the Summit County panel were aware of McGovern's selection of Sargent Shriver as his running mate following Eagleton's removal from the Democratic ticket.

When voters who were cognizant of Shriver's selection were asked if the choice had influenced their vote decision at the time, 19 percent replied in the affirmative.

Overall, on a proportionate basis, members of unions that had endorsed the Democratic nominee (25 percent) and Catholics (24 percent) were most apt to report that the selection of Shriver had influenced their vote decision. Among those who claimed the selection of Shriver had influenced their choices, 57 percent ultimately voted for McGovern and 47 percent for Nixon. In short, the subsequent appointment of Shriver served primarily as reassurance to numerous McGovern supporters who earlier had been somewhat shaken by the Eagleton affair. Again we find that for the majority of voters, "influence" is equated with finding support for previously reached choices, rather than with finding bases for reaching new decisions.

THE INFLUENCE OF THE WATERGATE DISCLOSURES ON VOTE DECISIONS

The full import of the June 1972 break-in at the Democratic National Headquarters in the Watergate complex in Washington, D.C.,

TABLE 7.2

Awareness of Watergate Break-in, by Political Attributes
(percentages)

	Aware of Break-in	Unaware of Break-in
Party Identification		
Democrat (N = 311)	85	15
Republican (N = 130)	95	5
Independent (N = 177)	85	15
Democrats for Nixon (N = 83)	88	12
Interest in Politics Generally		
High (N = 210)	91	9
Moderate (N = 323)	85	15
Low (N = 81)	86	14
Self-Ascribed Political Knowledge		
High (N = 246)	91	9
Moderate (N = 154)	87	13
Low (N = 218)	82	18
Actual Political Knowledge		
High (N = 116)	99	1
Moderate (N = 259)	98	2
Low (N = 243)	69	31
Campaign Interest		
High (N = 269)	92	8
Moderate (N = 224)	88	13
Low (N = 125)	75	25
Campaign Attention		
High (N = 254)	93	7
Moderate (N = 286)	85	15
Low (N = 78)	77	23
Campaign Participation		
High (N = 195)	90	10
Moderate (N = 217)	91	9
Low (N = 206)	81	19
Total (N = 618)	87	13

was not felt until well into 1973. While subsequent research has documented the impact on the public of that wide-ranging scandal (O'Keefe
and Mendelsohn 1974; Holm, Kraus, and Bochner 1974; Robinson
1974; Edelstein and Tefft 1974; White 1975; Mendelsohn, O'Keefe, and
Liu 1975), it is helpful to reexamine voter reaction to the emerging
crisis during the 1972 campaign.

Awareness of the Watergate Disclosures

Nearly nine in ten (87 percent) voters in the Summit County panel
were aware of the Watergate break-in by October 1972. Republicans
(95 percent) were more often aware of the Watergate burglary and
wiretapping attempts than were all Democrats (85 percent), Democrats
who voted for Nixon (88 percent), or Independents (85 percent). Nixon
voters (51 percent) and McGovern voters (49 percent) were about
equally aware of the illegal entry (Table 7.2).

As Tables 7.2 and 7.3 indicate, awareness of the Watergate
break-in was intimately tied to involvement in politics and in the media
among voters in the Summit County panel. With regard to political
involvement, as political knowledge increased among voters, so did
the level of their awareness. The same holds true for increases in
interest in the 1972 campaign, as well as for active participation in it:
as interest and active participation in the campaign climbed, awareness
of the Watergate break-in increased.

The more likely voters were to attend to both general and
campaign-related news media, and the more they depended on television
and (especially) newspapers for political information, the more likely
they were to be aware of the Watergate break-in. Similarly, the more
voters expected that the media might influence their vote choices, the
more apt they were to be aware of the Watergate burglary.

Reactions to the Watergate Disclosures

Voters who were aware of the break-in were asked, "The Democrats claim that highly placed persons in the Nixon administration are
responsible for the Watergate break-in and spying. The Republicans
claim that no one highly placed in the Nixon administration is responsible for the matter. Whom do you tend to believe—the Democrats or
the Republicans?"

The responses yielded the following profile of the panel members
who were aware of the break-in:

TABLE 7.3

Awareness of Watergate Break-in, by Media Attributes
(percentages)

	Aware of Break-in	Unaware of Break-in
General News Media Exposure		
High (N = 214)	92	8
Moderate (N = 192)	89	11
Low (N = 212)	81	19
Campaign Media Exposure		
High (N = 209)	92	8
Moderate (N = 203)	87	13
Low (N = 206)	83	17
Dependence on Newspapers for Political Information		
High (N = 258)	91	9
Moderate (N = 250)	86	14
Low (N = 110)	79	21
Dependence on Television for Political Information		
High (N = 164)	88	12
Moderate (N = 163)	89	11
Low (N = 291)	86	14
Anticipatory Influence		
High (N = 112)	92	8
Moderate (N = 281)	89	11
Low (N = 225)	82	18
Reported Influence		
High (N = 110)	85	15
Moderate (N = 255)	89	11
Low (N = 253)	86	14
Total (N = 618)	87	13

- 38 percent said they believed the Democrats' assertions
- 12 percent replied that the Republicans' version was acceptable to them
- 8 percent found both versions equally plausible
- 24 percent could not bring themselves to accept either version of who was to blame
- 17 percent had no opinion about the matter.

By no means, then, as late as October 1972, was there a consensus among Summit County's voters regarding who was responsible for the Watergate break-in. At most it was evident that there was willingness among at least four in ten voters to entertain the possibility of the Nixon White House having some involvement in the illegal entry. For many voters, confusion regarding whom to blame for the Watergate break-in was the principal reaction.

Primarily, voters' acceptance of either the Democrats' or the Republicans' version of who was responsible for the Watergate entry and bugging was almost exclusively dependent on vote choices (Table 7.4). Of the voters who believed the Democrats' version, three-fourths were McGovern supporters; in contrast, eight of ten voters who accepted the Republican version voted for Nixon.

Early deciders for Nixon were most likely to accept the Republicans' version, by a margin of 72 percent over the 18 percent who went along with the version put forth by the Democrats.

Of early deciders for McGovern, 57 percent believed the Democrats' version, while 11 percent gave credence to the Republicans' side of the story. Late deciders for McGovern were five times as likely to accept the Democrats' interpretation, while Nixon late deciders were two and a half times more likely to believe the Republican version of White House involvement in the Watergate case than were McGovern late deciders. Voters who switched to McGovern from Nixon were equally likely to accept either version of who was to blame, as were switchers to Nixon from McGovern.

Whether or not voters believed the Democrats' assertions regarding Nixon's responsibility for the Watergate break-in depended primarily on partisanship and political and media involvement. Voters making up the McGovern cohort (the least well-educated, 48 percent; blacks, 63 percent; members of unions supporting McGovern, 67 percent; and Democrats, 52 percent) were most likely to believe the Democrats' version. Additionally, voters who were generally very interested in politics (50 percent), those who considered themselves well-informed politically (49 percent), and those who actually were quite politically knowledgeable (46 percent) most often placed the blame on the Nixon White House. Finally, the voters who were most likely to agree with the Democrats' accusations were those having high

TABLE 7.4

Votes for Nixon and McGovern, by Opinions Regarding
Responsibility for Watergate Break-in
(percentages)

	Early Deciders for		Late Deciders for	
	Nixon	McGovern	Nixon	McGovern
Believed Democrats' Version: Nixon Administration Was Responsible (N = 212)	18	57	2	11
Believed Republicans' Version: Nixon Administration Was Not Responsible (N = 64)	72	11	5	2
Believed Neither Version (N = 127)	55	14	7	6
Believed Both Versions (N = 43)	72	7	9	2
No Opinion (N = 92)	50	25	8	13

	Switched to		Voted for	
	Nixon	McGovern	Nixon	McGovern
Believed Democrats' Version: Nixon Administration Was Responsible (N = 212)	2	6	23	77
Believed Republicans' Version: Nixon Administration Was Not Responsible (N = 64)	3	6	80	20
Believed Neither Version (N = 127)	6	7	69	31
Believed Both Versions (N = 43)	2	7	84	16
No Opinion (N = 92)	1	3	59	41

exposure to the media (50 percent) and those who both anticipated (49 percent) and later reported (53 percent) relatively high amounts of media influence on their vote choices. In short, 1972 voters who believed the accusations of Nixon White House complicity in the Watergate break-in were politically involved McGovernites who followed media coverage of the matter.

Two attributes affected voters' acceptance of the Nixon administration's denial of involvement in Watergate: on a proportionate basis, Republicans were most likely to be receptive to the official Nixon denial (20 percent), followed by political guidance-seekers (17 percent).

Influence of the Watergate Disclosures
on Vote Decisions

The insignificant role played by Watergate in influencing voters' choices in the 1972 presidential campaign is evidenced by the fact that no more than 15 percent of the voters who had heard about the illegal entry into the Democratic Party's Washington headquarters reported that the event had influenced their vote decisions. Overall, the Watergate disclosures were most likely to affect vote choices for McGovern: 82 percent of those who claimed to have been affected by the case supported the South Dakota Senator. A majority of these voters (60 percent of all those claiming Watergate influence) had made up their minds for McGovern early in the campaign, probably well before Watergate became a full-blown issue. Consequently, the influence that Watergate wielded was primarily a lending of support to the choices for McGovern that had already been registered in July 1972. Additionally, it appears that Watergate helped late deciders to settle more frequently on McGovern (13 percent) than on Nixon (2 percent). That the influence of Watergate on vote decision-making was of a more supportive than converting nature is highlighted by the data on switching. Here a mere 7 percent of the voters who claimed that Watergate had affected their vote decisions switched their votes to McGovern from Nixon, and only 6 percent made a change in the opposite direction.

Belief of White House involvement in the Watergate break-in was critical in determining its influence on vote decisions, particularly on decisions in favor of McGovern. Altogether, 78 percent of the voters who accepted the Democrats' interpretation of the matter reported that their vote choices were influenced by the early break-in disclosures (Table 7.5): 28 percent of the voters in this subset voted for George McGovern, compared with 2 percent who chose Nixon. In

TABLE 7.5

Influence of Watergate Break-in Disclosure and Vote,
by Opinions Regarding Responsibility for Break-in
(percentages)

	All Voters Aware of Watergate Break-in	All Voters Claiming Influence by Watergate Break-in Disclosures
Believed Democrats' Version: Nixon Administration Was Responsible (N = 212)	39	78
Believed Republicans' Version: Nixon Administration Was Not Responsible (N = 64)	12	8
Believed Neither Version (N = 127)	24	1
Believed Both Versions (N = 43)	8	6
No Opinion (N = 92)	17	6

	All Voters Claiming Influence by Watergate Break-in Disclosures and Voting for	
	Nixon	McGovern
Believed Democrats' Version: Nixon Administration Was Responsible (N = 212)	2	28
Believed Republicans' Version: Nixon Administration Was Not Responsible (N = 64)	9	2
Believed Neither Version (N = 127)	—	1
Believed Both Versions (N = 43)	7	5
No Opinion (N = 92)	1	4

sharp contrast, no more than 8 percent of the voters who accepted the
administration's denial of complicity in the Watergate break-in admitted to having been influenced by the affair; of these, 9 percent
voted for Nixon and 2 percent for McGovern.

As might be expected, political attributes and mass media behavioral patterns determined the relative impacts of the early Watergate
disclosures on voters' choices (Tables 7.6 and 7.7). Both Republicans
and Democrats who voted for Nixon were highly unlikely to report that
the news concerning the break-in had affected their presidential
choices, while Independents and all Democrats were as likely as not
to do so.

The more interested voters were, either in general politics or
in the 1972 campaign specifically, the more apt they were to claim
that news about the Watergate break-in had affected their vote choices.
Similarly, as self-ascribed and actual political knowledge increased
among Summit County voters, so did the likelihood that their voting
decisions would be affected by the 1972 Watergate disclosures. The
same cumulative process pertained to voters' attention to and active
participation in the campaign: the higher the score in each instance,
the greater the likelihood of influence. Whether the news about
Watergate influenced voter decisions or not, then, rested significantly
on the degree of political involvement or detachment that Summit
County voters exhibited. The greater the degree of political involvement, the greater was the likelihood of influence; and, the more
politically detached voters tended to be, the less likely they were to
be affected by early news concerning the Watergate break-in.

Three media attributes affected the early Watergate disclosures'
influence on vote decisions. Voters who claimed high dependence on
newspapers for political information were proportionately more likely
to mention the influence that the Watergate matter had on their vote
choices; panel members who anticipated high media influence on their
vote decisions were more apt to report that the news about the break-
in had affected their vote choices; the same held true for those
reporting high media influence on their final vote decisions.

In sum, voters who were highly involved with both politics and
the media (particularly newspapers) appear to have been more aware
of the early 1972 disclosures regarding Watergate, to have accepted
the possibility that the Nixon White House was responsible for the
affair, and to have their early commitments to McGovern strengthened
by disclosure of the event.

The findings offer no support for speculation that the early
Watergate disclosures either substantially undermined support for
Nixon or caused substantial defections from the incumbent President
to his challenger. At most, they seem to have served a crystallization

TABLE 7.6

Influence of Watergate Break-in on Vote Decision,
by Political Attributes
(percentages)

	All Voters Aware of Watergate Break-in	All Voters Claiming Influence by Watergate Break-in Disclosures
Party Identification		
Democrat (N = 311)	85	16
Republican (N = 130)	95	5
Independent (N = 177)	85	15
Democrats for Nixon (N = 83)	88	5
Interest in Politics Generally		
High (N = 210)	91	21
Moderate (N = 323)	85	11
Low (N = 81)	86	5
Self-Ascribed Political Knowledge		
High (N = 246)	91	20
Moderate (N = 154)	87	6
Low (N = 218)	82	11
Actual Political Knowledge		
High (N = 116)	99	23
Moderate (N = 259)	98	14
Low (N = 243)	69	9
Campaign Interest		
High (N = 269)	92	20
Moderate (N = 224)	88	11
Low (N = 125)	75	5
Campaign Attention		
High (N = 254)	93	18
Moderate (N = 286)	85	11
Low (N = 78)	77	8
Campaign Participation		
High (N = 195)	90	23
Moderate (N = 217)	91	11
Low (N = 206)	81	7
Total (N = 618)	87	13

TABLE 7.7

Influence of Watergate Break-in on Vote Decision,
by Media Attributes
(percentages)

	All Voters Aware of Watergate Break-in	All Voters Claiming Influence by Watergate Break-in Disclosures
General News Media Exposure		
High (N = 214)	92	16
Moderate (N = 192)	89	15
Low (N = 212)	81	9
Campaign Media Exposure		
High (N = 209)	92	15
Moderate (N = 203)	87	13
Low (N = 206)	83	12
Dependence on Newspapers for Political Information		
High (N = 258)	91	18
Moderate (N = 250)	86	10
Low (N = 110)	79	10
Dependence on Television for Political Information		
High (N = 164)	88	15
Moderate (N = 163)	89	16
Low (N = 291)	86	11
Anticipatory Influence		
High (N = 112)	92	20
Moderate (N = 281)	89	14
Low (N = 225)	82	9
Reported Influence		
High (N = 110)	85	38
Moderate (N = 255)	89	16
Low (N = 253)	86	—
Total (N = 618)	87	13

function for relatively small numbers of late deciders who ultimately favored McGovern.

THE INFLUENCE OF McGOVERN'S VIETNAM POLICY SPEECH ON VOTE DECISIONS

On the evening of October 10, 1972, Senator McGovern made a televised speech to the nation on the war in Vietnam. In a campaign that was not characterized by significant oratory by either candidate, McGovern's televised talk promised to be somewhat of a high point in what had been a rather lackluster contest. Although the Summit County study was set up to trace voter reactions to significant events via the panel method, the timing of the McGovern talk did not allow for investigating viewer reactions to it during the day immediately following its airing. In order to garner near-immediate reactions to the telecast, a supplemental sample of 252 randomly selected eligible voters residing in Summit County was interviewed by telephone during several days immediately following the McGovern speech.

Awareness of the Televised Speech

In all, 35 percent of the 252 voters in the special supplemental Summit County sample said they had viewed McGovern's televised speech on Vietnam. When respondents who did not recall having viewed the presentation were asked whether they were previously aware that the Democratic challenger was going to speak on national television on October 10, 54 percent replied in the affirmative. In other words, although eight out of ten Summit County eligible voters had prior knowledge that Senator McGovern would address the nation on the major issue of Vietnam, less than four in ten elected to tune in.

Three-fourths of the eligible voters who chose not to tune in gave as their reason "busy doing other things," 16 percent said they simply were not interested, and 9 percent cited miscellaneous reasons.

Twenty-eight percent of the eligible voters who did not view the Vietnam speech claimed to have read about it in newspaper reports and commentary the following day, indicating a supplemental function of the print media in reaching sizable audiences not reached by the original telecast.

The selective exposure hypothesis would lead one to expect that a major televised policy discussion on Vietnam by the Democratic candidate would have attracted disproportionate numbers of McGovern supporters. In point of fact, the reverse was true: 54 percent of the audience was made up of Nixon voters and 46 percent were McGovern partisans. Neither did party affiliation affect exposure to McGovern's televised Vietnam talk: roughly a third each of Republicans, Democrats, and Independents tuned in.

The figures below show that weak rather than intense partisan commitment to either candidate (in particular to Nixon) affected exposure to the McGovern Vietnam telecast. Curiously, strong supporters of Nixon were considerably more likely than were strong McGovern partisans to have tuned in the Democrat's policy statement.

	Indicated Relatively Strong Support for		Indicated Relatively Weak Support for	
	Nixon (N=78)	McGovern (N=50)	Nixon (N=23)	McGovern (N=36)
Viewed McGovern's Vietnam Speech	39%	30%	52%	42%

Several equally plausible interpretations are possible here:

1. Strong Nixon supporters may have been seeking justification for their commitments to the Nixon Vietnam posture.
2. Weak Nixon partisans may have sought "ammunition" for use in strengthening their own commitments.
3. Nixon supporters of either stripe may simply have been curious about what the opposition had to say on the issue.
4. Proportionately more weak than strong McGovern supporters may have tuned in, seeking "ammunition" for use in strengthening their own commitments to the Senator.
5. McGovern voters of either strength may have thought themselves sufficiently familiar with his Vietnam stand to warrant ignoring yet another discussion of the matter.

Reactions to the Televised Speech

Congruency theory suggests that audiences ordinarily seek messages consistent with their personal points of view while avoiding those that are not. Moreover, a keystone principle of cognitive dissonance theory asserts that individuals ordinarily do not consciously go out of their way to seek messages of known opposing viewpoints. The Summit County supplemental sample data offer considerable challenge to the universality of this principle. For example, no more than four in ten viewers (39 percent) of the McGovern televised

Vietnam presentation found themselves mostly in agreement with the stand he expressed; a fifth (22 percent) reported that they were mostly in disagreement; and a third (36 percent) could agree or disagree only with parts of the presentation.

Adding these data to the fact that proportionately more Nixon than McGovern partisans tuned in the talk, it is evident that sheer curiosity about the opposition played as important a part in the determination of exposure to McGovern's statement of his Vietnam position as did the strain toward homophily.

More than half of the supplemental sample (54 percent) reported a relatively high degree of interest in the 1972 campaign, a third (35 percent) claimed a lukewarm interest, and 11 percent reported relative disinterest. Additionally, at the time the supplemental interviews were conducted in mid-October 1972, 50 percent of the voters stated that their interest in the campaign was increasing, 10 percent claimed their interest was lagging, and 39 percent averred that their interest was remaining constant.

Interest in the 1972 campaign affected attendance to McGovern's talk far more powerfully than did either partisanship or demographic characteristics. The greater the voters' interest in the campaign, the more likely they were to tune in the telecast. As a consequence, whereas 35 percent of the entire sample tuned in the talk, 43 percent of the highly interested eligible voters queried did so. Conversely, 65 percent of the total supplemental sample did not tune in the McGovern Vietnam policy discussion, and 86 percent of the relatively disinterested voters contacted chose not to do so. Among eligible voters who did not watch, the relatively disinterested were most apt to have been unaware of McGovern's plans for a major telecast on Vietnam (58 percent). Moreover, for those who missed the televised talk, the more interested they were in the campaign, the more apt they were to read about it in the newspapers the following day. Of those who read about the speech, 52 percent were very much interested in the campaign, 26 percent were somewhat interested, and 21 percent reported relative disinterest.

We have seen that by mid-October, at the height of the 1972 presidential campaign, one in ten eligible voters in the supplemental sample reported a decrease of interest in the contest. Yet compared with all individuals who tuned in the Vietnam telecast (35 percent), voters who reported a waning of campaign interest (50 percent) were, on a proportionate basis, more likely to have viewed the talk. Perhaps for those who were becoming surfeited with the long-running campaign, the McGovern speech represented an exciting new "happening" that promised at least temporary reflief from the tedium of ordinary campaign events.

Influence of the Televised Speech on Vote Decisions

Voters who saw McGovern's Vietnam presentation were asked
(1) whether they used the speech in discussing the 1972 contest with
friends, relatives and others; (2) whether they learned things previously unknown to them from the talk; (3) whether the telecast left them
with favorable or unfavorable impressions of George McGovern's qualifications to be President; and (4) whether exposure to McGovern's
Vietnam telecast had influenced their presidential choice in any way.

For four out of ten viewers of the Vietnam telecast (13 percent
of all eligible voters sampled), the talk served as a vehicle for political
discussions that took place in the days following the broadcast:

- 47 percent of these discussions were with family members
- 41 percent were with co-workers
- 32 percent were with friends
- no more than 3 percent were with neighbors.

Strong McGovern partisans and weak Nixon supporters were
most apt to discuss the McGovern Vietnam telecast, as the figures
below indicate; strong adherents to the Nixon candidacy were likely to
talk about the speech with secondary frequency; weak McGovern supporters were least apt to discuss the telecast. In all, it appears that
McGovern's Vietnam talk served as a vehicle for discussion in both
partisan camps; by no means did it satisfy the needs of McGovern
partisans exclusively.

| | Indicated Relatively Strong Support for | | Indicated Relatively Weak Support for | |
	Nixon (N=30)	McGovern (N=15)	Nixon (N=11)	McGovern (N=11)
Discussed McGovern's Vietnam Speech With Others	40%	53%	63%	18%

Totally, 31 percent of the viewers in the supplemental sample
(11 percent of all the eligible voters contacted) claimed they gained
new information from McGovern's telecast on Vietnam. The following
data show that strong McGovern supporters (ostensibly already familiar with the Democratic candidate's Vietnam position) were most likely
to claim to have learned new information from the telecast. Of interest
is the fact that two or more of every ten Nixon supporters who saw the
presentation claimed to have learned something new from it. The

lowest new information gain was claimed by weak McGovern partisans.

	Indicated Relatively Strong Support for		Indicated Relatively Weak Support for	
	Nixon (N=30)	McGovern (N=15)	Nixon (N=11)	McGovern (N=11)
Claimed to Have Learned Something New from McGovern's Vietnam Telecast	27%	47%	20%	9%

In responding to the question "From watching McGovern speak on television last night, did you get the impression that if he is elected, Senator McGovern might be an excellent President, a fairly good President, or a poor President?"

- 18 percent said "excellent"
- 35 percent said "fairly good"
- 24 percent said "poor"
- 23 percent remained uncertain.

For the most part, it appears that McGovern's major television effort to explain his position on Vietnam left Summit County viewers with either a relatively unflattering or an ambiguous image of the candidate's qualifications for the presidency. Only a minority of his viewers came away with a highly favorable impression, suggesting that if the speech had been designed to infuse viewers with confidence in the South Dakotan's presidential qualifications, it failed to do so in any substantive way.

Moreover, it appears from the data that follow that the Vietnam speech was most effective in convincing strong McGovern partisans of his excellent qualifications, and it was least effective in doing so for weak McGovern supporters. It is interesting to note the favorable response that was manifested among weak Nixon supporters; although the number of cases involved is minuscule, it appears the McGovern televised talk may have been better able to project attributes of the candidate's excellence among a few weak Nixon supporters than it did among weak McGovern backers.

	Indicated Relatively Strong Support for		Indicated Relatively Weak Support for	
	Nixon (N=30)	McGovern (N=15)	Nixon (N=23)	McGovern (N=11)
Vietnam Talk Left Viewers with Impression that McGovern Would Be an Excellent President	20%	80%	54%	—

Twenty-seven percent of the viewers who tuned in McGovern's Vietnam speech (9 percent of all eligible voters sampled) claimed the speech had influenced their decision to vote for the candidate they had previously chosen. In no instance did a viewer report a change of mind regarding prior choice of a candidate as a consequence of the speech.

To sum up the findings of this chapter, despite the journalistic play given to dramatic campaign events and the subsequent speculations regarding their allegedly dramatic impacts on voters' changes of decision, the data from Summit County suggest that no more than 10-15 percent of the electorate as a whole may be affected in any way by any one event during a campaign. This seems to hold true no matter how significant the event may be or how great a proportion of voters may be aware of it. Moreover, the data show that "conversion" as a consequence of voter exposure to a single event occurs so rarely as to render it practically nonexistent; this type of conversion, when it does occur, seems equally capable of running in either direction.

Again we see that exposure is not equated with effect. If anything, it seems to be equated more with confusion: the one substantive across-the-board "influence" that seemed to have been produced by news and commentary about both the Eagleton and Watergate affairs was a relatively high state of confusion regarding the nature of each event. Otherwise singular events, as is the case with the campaign as a whole, seem either to lend support to previously determined vote choices or to help crystallize a subconscious or tentative decision.

Whether campaign events will influence a final choice of candidate in terms of either support or crystallization depends in large measure on how politically partisan and involved a voter may be, as well as on his use of the mass media to keep up with an election contest.

APPENDIXES

DESIGN OF THE STUDY

The overall design of the study called for initial personal interviews to be conducted with a sample of 2,000 potential voters aged 18 and older in Summit County, Ohio, during late July 1972. A panel was drawn from this respondent pool for successive repeated interviews by telephone during August, September, October, and following the November election. A small subgroup of the initial pool was chosen to act as a "control" group, these respondents being interviewed in person only once, following the November election.

SAMPLING AND INTERVIEWING

A "multi-stage area" sample design was used to selec the 2,000 potential voter respondents in the first wave of interviews.* The sample selection utilized 1970 U.S. Census Bureau statistics for Summit County and included proportional designation, so that persons living in areas of higher population density had a relatively greater chance of being chosen. The 18 years of age and older population totals were accumulated by city blocks from census data, then stratified by census tracts. Using the accumulated population figures, interviewing blocks were selected by random number designation.

A total of 400 blocks were chosen as sampling points. Complete random selection of blocks was deviated from to allow a conceptually important oversampling of black respondents. Specifically, the 8 percent black population of Summit County (nearly all accounted for by urban Akron) was oversampled to aim at a 15 percent representation within the sample. This was accomplished by specifying that 60 of the

---

*Technical sampling, interviewing, and preparation of the data for computer analysis were carried out under the on-site supervision of the project directors by Marketing Research of Cleveland, Inc., a professional survey research firm with direct access to the Summit County area.

400 blocks chosen be randomly drawn from predominantly black neighborhoods.

Five households were designated within each block for personal interviews. Interviewers were instructed to begin at the second house from a specified intersection and, working clockwise around the block, attempt to secure an interview from every fifth household. In the case of city blocks with too few households to attain five interview attempts, interviewers continued onto the next block in the same pattern. Special accommodations were made for blocks containing apartment complexes, trailer parks, and so on. An adequate representation of the approximately 50-50 ratio of males to females in the county was aimed for by specifying that only females and only males be interviewed on alternate blocks. In order to assure adequate representation of the nearly 20 percent of the county residents aged 18 to 24, the first person designated to be interviewed within each block was to be within that age group. A maximum of five callbacks were made at each household, after which the adjoining household immediately to the left was chosen for interviewing. Ten percent of all completed interviews were validated in this and succeeding interviewing waves.

Wave 1 interviews were conducted between July 28 and August 13, following the Democratic National Convention. In all, 3,208 interviews were attempted and 1,965 were completed, yielding a response rate of 61 percent. Thirteen percent of the potential respondents were unable to be contacted, while 25 percent of those contacted refused to be interviewed for various reasons. Table A.1 summarizes interviewing and completion rates for this and succeeding waves.

Of the respondents interviewed in Wave 1, 1,465 were selected to compose the panel for repeated interviews. They were chosen by random draw of proportional numbers from each block. The remaining 500 respondents made up the control group.

The second wave of interviews, this time with the selected panel, was conducted by telephone between August 26 and September 4, immediately following the Republican National Convention. Completed interviews numbered 1,148 out of 1,465 initial attempts.

The third wave was carried out between September 23 and October 2, during the opening stages of active campaigning. Out of the 1,148 interviews attempted, 959 were accomplished.

The deadline for registration in Ohio fell just prior to the beginning of the fourth wave of interviews, which ran from October 21 through October 30. Those respondents who had not registered by these dates were ineligible to vote, and consequently were dropped from the panel. Of the 959 attempts made in Wave 4, 898 resulted in completed interviews, of which 110 were terminated because of nonregistration by the respondent. The final wave of interviewing was done during the 11 days following the November 7 election. A total

TABLE A.1

Summary of Interviewing and Completion Rates

	Wave 1 July 28– August 13	Wave 2 August 26– September 4	Wave 3 September 23– October 2
Total Interviews			
Attempted	3208	1465	1148
Interviews Completed	1965	1148	959
Reasons for Noncompletion			
Unable to Contact			
Respondent	430	195	87
Refusal	812	122	102

	Wave 4 October 21– October 30	Wave 5 November 8– November 19	Control November 8– November 19
Total Interviews			
Attempted	959	788[*]	500
Interviews Completed	898	653	385
Reasons for Noncompletion			
Unable to Contact			
Respondent	10	73	46
Refusal	51	62	69

[*]Out of the 898 respondents interviewed in Wave 4, 788 were registered to vote. Those not registered were dropped from the panel.

of 653 respondents were interviewed and formed the complete listing of the panel. Of these, 628 had voted for a presidential candidate.

Personal interviews with the 500 respondents composing the control group were likewise attempted between November 8 and November 19, resulting in 385 completions.

In sum, initial pre-election data were gathered for 1,966 respondents in late July and early August; 653 of these respondents, including 628 voters, were reinterviewed in four successive waves through November and another 385 in the control group were reinterviewed once in November.[*]

Looking at the panel subsample in terms of response rates, 365 persons (25 percent out of the initial sample of 1,465) were lost because they were unavailable for further interviews (having moved, disconnected telephones, and so on), 337 (23 percent) refused further interviews at some point, and 110 (8 percent) were dropped because they had not registered to vote. Out of the initial control subsample of 500, 46 (9 percent) were lost, being unavailable, and 69 (14 percent) refused to allow the second interview.

SAMPLE COMPARABILITY

The selection of the sample was not intended to be rigorously generalizable to Summit County adults in toto, nor to any other population group. Rather, Summit County was chosen on the basis of its ability to reflect key variables of concern to this study of vote decision behavior centering upon communications processes. Nonetheless, it is of methodological interest to compare the respondents interviewed with certain demographic attributes of the county. More importantly, a comparison among attributes of the 1,966 Wave 1 respondents, the 385 control group respondents, and the 653 panel members is very much in order.

The subsamples were compared on the key demographic attributes of age, sex, race, education, income, and occupation, and on the politically relevant variables of party identification, political interest, and voting disposition in the 1972 presidential election. Where feasible, 1970 census statistics for Summit County are listed for population comparison purposes.

---

[*]Of the 628 respondents who voted for a presidential candidate, 618 voted for McGovern or Nixon; the 10 respondents who voted for other candidates were dropped from the analysis presented in this report.

Sex

The Wave 1 sample underestimated females in the population by 2 percent, but a relatively greater respondent loss rate among males during the course of the study led to a 4 percent overrepresentation of females in the panel, compared with Wave 1 (Table A.2).

Race

Black adults were intentionally oversampled to achieve a 15 percent representation in Wave 1 (Table A.2). Blacks made up 13 percent of the panel and control samples.

Age

The age distributions of the subsamples compare rather closely with one another and with the total population (Table A.2). A relative disparity was found between Wave 1 and the population universe among 25-34-year-olds, in that 18 percent of the population fell into this age bracket while 22 percent of Wave 1 did so. Additionally, the panel overrepresented by 5 percent the Wave 1 proportion of persons in the 35-49-year-old category while underrepresenting by 4 percent the 65-and-older proportion in Wave 1.

Education

The Wave 1 sample very closely matched available Census Bureau population estimates in terms of proportions of high school and college graduates (Table A.3). The panel respondents tended to be somewhat higher in educational attainment, with 15 percent completing college, versus 11 percent of Wave 1 respondents who had done so.

Income

Again the Wave 1 sample closely matched Summit County population statistics on income, while the panel was higher in the middle

TABLE A.2

Comparison Among Samples by Sex, Race, and Age
(percentages)

	Population	Wave 1 (N=1,965)	Panel (N=653)	Control (N=385)
Sex				
Male	47	49	45	44
Female	53	51	55	56
Race				
White	92	85	87	87
Black	8	15	13	13
Age				
18–24	17	18	15	17
25–34	18	22	24	23
35–49	28	25	30	23
50–64	23	21	21	22
65+	14	14	10	14

TABLE A.3

Comparison Among Samples by Education, Income, and Occupation
(percentages)

	Population	Wave 1 (N=1,965)	Panel (N=653)	Control (N=385)
Education				
1–11 Years	—	33	23	36
12 Years	—	36	40	35
Some College	55	19	23	20
Completed College	11	11	15	10
Income				
Less than $10,000	47	48	38	52
$10,000–$14,999	33	31	38	30
$15,000 and over	20	21	25	18
Occupation				
Blue–Collar	52	60	53	64
White–Collar	48	40	47	36

TABLE A.4

Comparison Among Samples by Party, Political Interest,
and Presidential Vote
(percentages)

	Population	Wave 1 (N=1,965)	Panel (N=653)	Control (N=385)
Party Identification				
Democrat	44	50	50	50
Republican	20	20	21	19
Independent	37	30	29	31
Political Interest				
High		29	33	26
Moderate		48	53	41
Low		23	14	33
Presidential Vote				
McGovern	48.3		48.7	
Nixon	49.9		49.7	
Other	1.8		1.6	

income range (by 7 percent) and upper income range (by 4 percent)
(Table A.3).

Occupation

A greater proportion of blue-collar workers was found in the
Wave 1 sample than in the population as a whole (Table A.3). This may
have been a side effect of the oversampling of blacks. Blue-collar
workers were also more likely to be lost during the stages of panel
interviewing.

Party Identification

While a clear comparison cannot be made between respondents'
perception of party identification and party of record on registration
rolls, the data suggest no strong differences along these lines (Table
A.4). The apparent oversampling of Democrats and undersampling of

Independents is no doubt in part a result of purposeful oversampling
of blacks. More important, the percentage of respondents identifying
with the two major parties was highly consistent over the three subsamples.

Political Interest

    As expected, respondents indicating that they were "hardly inter-
ested" in politics were less represented in the panel sample than in
Wave 1 or the control sample (Table A.4). The less interested were
individuals typically located in the lower socioeconomic strata who,
per se, are usually less available for social survey interviewing.
These respondents normally could be expected to be even less willing
to continue participating in interviews concerning subject matter of
low relevance to them. On the more optimistic side, these low interest
persons can also be assumed to be among the least likely to vote, and
therefore of less substantive import to the study at hand. To be sure,
a complete examination of the relationships between political interest,
voting, and response rate will be conducted at a later date, relying
upon the control sample as a data base.

Presidential Vote

    The presidential vote choices reported by the panel were within
0.5 percent of the actual vote recorded in Summit County (Table A.4).
    In sum, the main sample chosen for this study and the subsequent
subsamples present a somewhat biased view of the adult population of
Summit County. This bias is in part a reflection of design, as in the
oversampling of black potential voters and the elimination of citizens
not registered to vote in the later stages of the panel interviews. The
bias is also a reflection of self-selection of respondents in the sample,
particularly over five waves of interviews. Undoubtedly the panel respondents are "special" in some ways, particularly in terms of political
interest and, presumably, propensity to vote.
    They tend to be more from upper social status strata and some-
what more concerned about the political world, as one might assume
most voters are when compared against the populace at large. The
major goal of the research reported to date was the examination of a
sample of voters holding a multitude of characteristics having potential
bearing on the voting act, and it becomes difficult to discuss biases
in the voting sample in this respect.

Indeed, the panel voters match those Summit County residents who voted in the 1972 presidential election almost exactly on the crucial attribute of candidate choice and closely on the highly salient characteristic of party preference.

SUMMARY OF KEY MEASUREMENT ITEMS
AND INDICES

Presented below are descriptions, in alphabetical order, of individual survey items and various indices utilized in this study.

ANTICIPATORY INFLUENCE

Sum of responses to the following items, divided into low, moderate, and high levels:

"Now I'd like to ask you some questions about television in general, newspapers, magazines, radio, and so on. How much do you count on television in general to help you make up your mind about whom to vote for in a presidential election: a lot, somewhat, or not at all?" (July)

"How much do you count on newspapers to help you make up your mind about whom to vote for in a presidential election: a lot, somewhat, or not at all?" (July)

"How much do you count on radio to help you make up your mind about whom to vote for in a presidential election: a lot, somewhat, or not at all?" (July)

"How much do you count on magazines to help you make up your mind about whom to vote for in a presidential election: a lot, somewhat, or not at all?" (July)

"What about friends, relatives, neighbors, and co-workers—how much do you count on people you can talk with to help you make up your mind about whom to vote for in a presidential election: would you say you count on them a lot, somewhat, or not at all?" (July)

CAMPAIGN ATTENTION

Sum of responses to the following item, divided into low, moderate, and high levels:

"In keeping up with the news these days, do you find you are paying a great deal of attention to what is going on in the presidential

election campaign, only a little attention, or no attention at all?"
(August, September, October)

CAMPAIGN DISCUSSION

Sum of responses to the following items, divided into low, moderate, and high levels:
"In the past six months would you say that you have discussed this year's presidential campaign with family, friends, and others very often, occasionally, or hardly at all?" (July)
"Thinking back over the past four or five weeks, have you been discussing this year's presidential election a lot, somewhat, or hardly at all?" (August, September)

CAMPAIGN INTEREST

Sum of responses to the following item, divided into low, moderate, and high levels:
"Some people are quite interested, while others are not too interested in presidential campaigns. How about you? Would you say that you have been very interested, somewhat interested, or not much interested in the presidential campaign so far this year?" (July, September, October)

CAMPAIGN MEDIA EXPOSURE

Weighted sum of responses to the following items, divided into low, moderate, and high levels:
"Ordinarily, do you listen to the radio mostly for music or mostly for news and information?" (July)
"Thinking back to yesterday, how many newscasts did you hear on the radio altogether?" (July)
"Altogether, how many newscasts did you watch on television yesterday?" (If interviewing on Sunday or Monday, ask "Altogether, how many newscasts did you watch on television this past Friday?") (July)
"During an average week, how many times, if at all, do you usually watch one of the early evening network newscasts, such as

Walter Cronkite on CBS, Howard K. Smith and Harry Reasoner on ABC, John Chancellor and David Brinkley on NBC?" (July)

"During an average week, how many times, if at all, do you usually watch one of the late night TV newscasts presented by local stations at around 11 p.m.?" (July)

"Which daily local or out-of-town newspapers do you get to see more or less regularly?" (July)

"Newspapers include entertainment sections, like sports and comics, and also news sections, like regular news and editorials. When you read the newspaper, do you mostly read the entertainment sections or mostly the news sections?" (July)

"What magazines do you get to see more or less regularly?" (News magazines coded) (July)

"Which daily newspaper do you read more often than any others?" (September)

"Do you watch any early evening news programs on TV at least twice a week?" (September)

"About how many hours altogether did you spend watching the proceedings of the Democratic convention on TV?" (July)

"About how many hours altogether did you spend watching the proceedings of the Republican convention on TV?" (August)

"In the week that just passed, approximately how many television commercials for McGovern for President did you see?" (October)

"Approximately how many television commercials for Nixon for President did you see in the week that just passed?" (October)

"As you may recall, on the Monday night before the election Richard Nixon appeared on one paid political TV program and George McGovern appeared on another paid political program. Did you happen to watch either or both of those programs?" (November)

"Did you see any political commercials for the presidential candidates on TV during the last week before Election Day?" (November)

"On Election Day, before you went out to vote, do you remember having seen or heard any television or radio reports that reported how the election was going?" (November)

CAMPAIGN PARTICIPATION

Sum of responses to the following items, divided into low, moderate, and high levels:

"During the presidential election campaign this year, did you do any of the following things in support of a presidential candidate?" (November)

a. Wear a campaign button?
b. Display a bumper sticker or poster?
c. Try and talk someone into registering to vote?
d. Try and talk someone into voting?
e. Try and talk someone into voting your way?
f. Attend meetings, coffees, luncheons, dinners, or rallies?
g. Make phone calls or hand out leaflets?
h. Donate money?
i. Ask other people to donate money?
j. Work in an office for a political party?
k. Make telephone calls on Election Day?
l. Anything else? (Specify)

CONCERN OVER PRESIDENTIAL VICTOR

"Generally speaking, would you say that you personally care a great deal which candidate wins the presidential election this fall, care somewhat, or don't care very much which candidate wins?" (July)

CONCERN OVER VOTING

"How do you feel about voting in the upcoming presidential election in November? Would you say that you care a great deal about whether or not you will vote, care somewhat, or don't care too much at this time?" (July)

DEMOGRAPHIC INDICES

Standard census-type demographic items were used to assess sex, race, age, religious preference, education, occupation, income, and union membership. (July)

DEPENDENCE ON NEWSPAPERS FOR POLITICAL INFORMATION

Sum of responses to the following items, divided into low, moderate, and high levels:

"How much do you count on the (Newspaper) to help you to find out what the important issues of this year's presidential campaign are? Do you count on it a lot, a little, or not at all?" (September)

"How much do you count on the (Newspaper) to help you to find out where Richard Nixon and George McGovern stand on the important issues in this election year? Do you count on it a lot, a little, or not at all?" (September)

"How much do you cound on the (Newspaper) to help you to find out what Richard Nixon and George McGovern are really like as people? Do you count on it a lot, a little, or not at all?" (September)

"How much do you count on the (Newspaper) to give you hints about things to look for as the presidential campaign moves on toward Election Day in November? Do you count on it a lot, a little, or not at all?" (September)

DEPENDENCE ON TELEVISION FOR POLITICAL INFORMATION

Sum of responses to the following items, divided into low, moderate, and high levels:

"How much do you count on early evening TV news programs you watch to help you find out what the important issues of this year's presidential campaign are? Do you count on them a lot, a little, or not at all?" (September)

"How much do you count on the early evening TV news programs you watch to help you to find out what Richard Nixon and George McGovern are really like as people? Do you count on them a lot, a little, or not at all?" (September)

"How much do you count on the early evening TV news programs you watch to give you hints about things to look for as the presidential campaign moves on toward Election Day in November? Do you count on them a lot, a little, or not at all?" (September)

DIFFICULTY OF DECISION

"How difficult was it for you to decide to vote for Nixon (McGoverr (Schmitz)? Was it very difficult, somewhat difficult, nor not at all difficult?" (If "very difficult" or "somewhat difficult") "What particular things made it difficult for you?" "Anything else?" (November)

EAGLETON RESIGNATION, ATTITUDES TOWARD

"In your opinion, was it right or wrong for Senator Eagleton to resign as the Democratic vice-presidential candidate?" (July)

"Regardless of who you want to win, do you think Senator Eagleton's resignation from the Democratic ticket will help or hurt George McGovern's chances to win the presidential election this fall?" (July)

EAGLETON RESIGNATION, AWARENESS OF

"The name of Senator Thomas Eagleton has been in the news recently. Have you heard or seen any news concerning Senator Eagleton in the past week or two?" (If "yes") "What, specifically, did you hear or see?" (July)

"Which source—radio, newspapers, magazines, television, people you know, or what—helped you the most to keep up with news about Senator Eagleton during these past two weeks?" (July)

EAGLETON RESIGNATION, INFLUENCE OF

"Did the news about Senator Eagleton in any way influence you in deciding whom to vote for for President in November?" (If "yes") "In what specific way did this news influence your decision?" (July)

ECONOMIC STRESS

Weighted index incorporating respondent's annual household income, number of persons living in household, and whether the household had received any financial help from a public welfare agency. (July)

EDUCATIONAL MOBILITY

Comparison of years of education completed by respondent with years of education completed by respondent's father. (July)

ELECTION OUTCOME REACTION

"How do you feel about the outcome of the 1972 presidential election? Are you very pleased, somewhat pleased, not at all pleased, or don't you care one way or the other?" (November)

IMAGES OF CANDIDATES

"Here is a card with pairs of words and phrases people have used to describe persons in political office. (Hand respondent card.) Please tell me the words or phrases in each pair which most closely describe how you feel about President Nixon."

"Now please tell me the words or phrases in each pair which best describe how you feel about Senator George McGovern."

Warm, Friendly	. Cold, Unfriendly
Strong	. Weak
Smart	. Dumb
Can Be Trusted . . .	. Cannot Be Trusted
Safe	. Dangerous
Effective.	. Not Effective
	(July-November)

INFLUENCE SOURCES

"In making up your mind to vote for (Candidate), did any political pamphlets or materials you may have received in the mail or from campaign workers help you in your decision?" (November)

"Did any conversations with campaign workers you may have had in person or over the phone help you in your decision?" (November)

"Did you read anything in the newspapers which helped you in your decision?" (November) (If "yes") "Was what you read regular news, columns signed by specific writers, editorials, or what?" (November)

"Did you have any political conversations with people whose opinions you respect which helped you to make your choice for President?" (November)

"In making up your mind to vote for (Candidate), did any of his campaign speeches help you in your decision?" (November)

"Other than his speeches, did you see anything on television which helped you in your decision?" (November) (If "yes") "Was what you saw a regular news program, talk show, special program about the campaign, commercial for the candidate, or what?" (November)

"Did you read anything in magazines which helped you decide to vote for (Candidate)?" (November)

"Other than his speeches, did you hear anything on radio which helped you in your decision?" (November) (If "yes") "Was what you heard regular news, talk shows, special programs about the campaign, commercials for the candidates, or what?" (November)

INTERPERSONAL CROSS-PRESSURE

Sum of responses to the following items, divided into low, moderate, and high levels:

"Do any of your closest relatives whose opinions you respect disagree strongly with your choice for President in the election this year?" (July)

"Do any of your very closest friends disagree strongly with your choice for President in the election this year?" (July)

"Did people you know and respect put pressure on you to vote for someone other than your own choice for President?" (November)

"Do most of the people you know plan to vote the same way you do or not?" (August, September, October)

"Did most of the people you know vote the same way you did or not?" (November)

ISSUE POSITIONS

"On these cards are some political and social issues people have told us they are concerned about. Would you run through these cards and, as you do, break them into three groups. On your right, please put the cards which have statements you agree with; on the left, please put those you disagree with; and in the middle (in between), please put those you aren't sure about. To make sure you understand what I'm asking you to do, let me repeat. If you agree with a statement, put the card on your right. If you disagree, put the card on your left. And if you can't decide whether you agree or disagree with a particular statement, put the card in the middle, between those you either agree or disagree with."

1. The U.S. should immediately withdraw all armed forces from Vietnam.
2. The government should be spending more money on welfare.
3. More legal controls are needed on guns.
4. There should be stricter legal controls on rising prices of food, clothing, and other family needs.

5. The Supreme Court should have done away with the death penalty.
6. The government should be paying more attention to the needs of the average working man.
7. Marijuana should be legalized for adult use.
8. Children should be bused to schools outside their own neighborhood for the sake of racial balance.
9. The government should cut down on our military spending.
10. The government should be doing more about jobs and unemployment.
11. The government is too concerned about protecting the rights of lawbreakers.
12. Abortion should be legalized.
13. The government should guarantee a minimum income to every American who is not making a decent wage.
14. More tax money should be spent to clean up the environment.
15. The government should make low-cost housing for the poor available in middle-class neighborhoods.
16. America should be less concerned with what's going on in other countries.
17. The government should be doing more to make neighborhoods safer to live in.

"Now, I'd like you to do exactly the same thing again, only do it as you think President Nixon would react to each of these statements. That is, put the cards you think President Nixon would agree with on your right, the ones you think President Nixon would disagree with on your left, and the others in between."

"Now I'd like you to do the same thing one last time, only do it the way you think Senator George McGovern would. That is, put the statements you think Senator McGovern would agree with on your right, the ones you think Senator McGovern would disagree with on your left, and the others in between. (July, November)

MEDIA SOURCE RELIANCE

"As you may know, the Democratic Party convention recently ended in Florida. Many people found out about what happened at the convention from talking to people, from magazines, from television, from newspapers, and from radio. From which of the sources did you find out about what happened at the Democratic convention? Name all the sources from which you heard things about the convention."
(July)

"From what one source did you become best acquainted with what went on at the convention—from newspapers, or radio, or television, or magazines, or talking to people, or where?" (July)

"As you may know, the Republican Party convention recently ended in Florida. Many people found out about what happened at the convention from talking to people, from magazines, from television, from newspapers, and from radio. From which of the sources I mentioned—people, magazines, TV, newspapers, radio, or where, did you find out about what happened at the Republican convention? Please give me all the sources from which you heard things about the convention." (August)

"From what one source did you become best acquainted with what went on at the Republican convention—from newspapers, or radio, or television, or magazines, or talking to people, or where?" (August)

Many people have been following this year's presidential campaign by talking to other people, or from magazines, or from television, or from newspapers, or from radio. From which of the sources I mentioned—people, magazines, TV, newspapers, radio, or where—have you been following the 1972 presidential campaign? Please give me all the sources from which you have been following the campaign." (September, October, November)

"From what one source have you been becoming best acquainted with what is going on in the 1972 presidential campaign so far: from newspapers, radio, television, magazines, talking to people, or where?" (September, October, November)

NEWS MEDIA EXPOSURE

Weighted sum of responses to the following items, divided into low, moderate, and high levels:

"Ordinarily, do you listen to the radio mostly for music or mostly for news and information?" (July)

"Thinking back to yesterday, how many newscasts did you hear on the radio altogether?" (July)

"Altogether, how many newscasts did you watch on television yesterday?" (If interviewing on Sunday or Monday, ask, "Altogether, how many newscasts did you watch on television this past Friday?") (July)

"During an average week, how many times, if at all, do you usually watch one of the early evening network newscasts, such as Walter Cronkite on CBS; Howard K. Smith and Harry Reasoner on ABC; John Chancellor and David Brinkley on NBC?" (July)

"During an average week, how many times, if at all, do you usually watch one of the late night TV newscasts presented by local stations at around 11 p.m. ?" (July)

"Which daily local or out-of-town newspapers do you get to see more or less regularly?" (July)

"Newspapers include entertainment sections, like sports and comics, and also news sections, like regular news and editorials. When you read the newspaper, do you mostly read the entertainment sections, or mostly the news sections?" (July)

"What magazines do you get to see more or less regularly?" (News magazines coded) (July)

"Which daily newspaper do you read more often than any others?" (September)

"Do you watch any early evening news program on TV at least twice a week?" (September)

NEWS MEDIA FAIRNESS

"In your opinion, is television usually fair or not fair in the way it treats political matters?" (July)

"How about newspapers—are they usually fair or not fair in the way they treat political matters?" (July)

PARTY IDENTIFICATION

"Generally speaking, do you usually think of yourself as a Democrat, a Republican, an Independent, or what?"

A seven-point scale of strength of party identification was derived by adding the following two items: (If Democrat or Republican) "Would you call yourself a strong (Democrat/Republican) or not a very strong (Democrat/Republican)?" (If Independent) "Do you think of yourself as closer to the Democratic or Republican party?"

PERCEIVED SOCIAL CLASS

"There's quite a bit of talk these days about different social classes. Most people say they belong to either the upper class, the middle class, the working class, or the lower class. If you had to make a choice, would you call yourself upper-class, middle-class, working-class, or lower-class?" (July)

POLITICAL COMMERCIALS, ATTENTION TO

"When you see television commercials supporting McGovern, do you generally follow them closely or not very closely?" (October)

"What about the TV commercials supporting Nixon—do you generally follow them closely or not very closely?" (October)

POLITICAL COMMERCIALS, ATTITUDES TOWARD

"How do you feel about the short paid-for television commercials that are put on the air by political candidates during election campaigns? Do you think such political commercials on TV help voters to decide which candidate is the best, or not?" (July)

"It has been suggested that paid-for political commercials should not be allowed on TV during election campaigns. Do you think that they should be allowed or that they should not be allowed?" (July)

"Have the presidential campaign commercials you've seen on TV been doing an excellent job, a pretty good job, or a poor job of informing voters about where the candidates stand on the important issues in this year's election?" (October)

"What about informing voters of the presidential qualifications of each of the candidates? Have the TV campaign commercials you've seen been doing an excellent job, a pretty good job, or a poor job of presenting the qualifications of the candidates?" (October)

POLITICAL COMMERCIALS, EVALUATION ATTRIBUTES

"Which TV commercials have been more interesting: those for Nixon or those for McGovern?" (October)

"Which TV commercials have shown more good taste: those for McGovern or those for Nixon?" (October)

"Which have been more informative: those for McGovern or those for Nixon?" (October)

"Which TV commercials have been more believable: those for Nixon or those for McGovern?" (October)

"Which of the campaign TV commercials you've seen have been more convincing: those for McGovern or those for Nixon?" (October)

"Which TV commercials have been more annoying: those for Nixon or those for McGovern?" (October)

POLITICAL COMMERCIALS, EXPOSURE TO

"In the week that just passed, have you seen any television commercials supporting either Richard Nixon or George McGovern?" (October)

"In the week that just passed, approximately how many television commercials for McGovern for President have you seen?" (October)

"Approximately how many television commercials for Nixon for President have you seen in the week that just passed?" (October)

POLITICAL COMMERCIALS, GENERAL
COMMERCIAL INFLUENCE

"Regarding television commercials in general, during the past three months or so have you looked into or tried a product or service just because you happened to see it advertised on TV?" (October)

POLITICAL COMMERCIALS, INFLUENCE OF

"Has watching this year's presidential campaign commercials on TV helped you in any way to decide whom to vote for in the election?" (If "yes") "In what way did they help you decide?" (July)

POLITICAL COMMERCIALS, RELIANCE ON

"Generally speaking, how much do you personally count on political commercials on television to help you make up your mind about whom to vote for in a presidential election? Would you say you count of them a lot, somewhat, or not at all?" (July)

POLITICAL CYNICISM

Sum of responses to the following items, divided into low and high levels:

"People like me don't have any say about what the government does. (Agree/Disagree)" (July)

"Politicians never tell us what they really think. (Agree/Disagree)" (July)

"I don't think public officials care much what people like me think. (Agree/Disagree)" (July)

"Sometimes politics and government seem so complicated that a person like me can't really understand what's going on. (Agree/Disagree)" (July)

POLITICAL GUIDANCE-SEEKING

Sum of responses to the following items, divided into low, moderate, and high levels:

"Compared with other people you know, are you more or less likely than any of them to ask other people for factual information about political matters?" (July)

"Compared with other people you know, are you more or less likely than any of them to ask other people about their views on political matters?" (July)

"In the past four or five weeks have you personally asked anyone for their opinions or advice about which presidential candidate to vote for?" (August, September, October, November)

POLITICAL INTEREST

"How interested are you in politics in general? Are you very interested, somewhat interested, or hardly interested at all?" (July)

POLITICAL KNOWLEDGE (ACTUAL)

Sum of responses to the following items, divided into low, moderate, and high levels:

"As you may have heard, George McGovern named a new running mate a few weeks ago. What is his name?" (August)

"Do you happen to know who is the Democratic candidate for the U.S. Congress (U.S. House of Representatives) from this district? What is his name?" (October)

"Do you happen to know who is the Republican candidate for the U.S. Congress (U.S. House of Representatives) from this district? What is his name?" (October)

"As you may know, results from pre-election public opinion polls have been in the news lately. Which presidential candidate appears to be running ahead: George McGovern or Richard Nixon?" (October)

"By approximately how many percentage points is Richard Nixon leading George McGovern nationally in the poll results you have heard lately?" (October)

"Several weeks ago some people were accused of breaking in and spying at the Democratic headquarters in the Watergate building in Washington, D.C. Have you heard anything in the news about this?" (October)

"Do you happen to know the name of the winner of the U.S. Congressional seat (in the House of Representatives) from your district?" (If "yes") "What is the name?" (November)

"Do you know the name of the winner of the Ohio State Senate seat from your district?" (If "yes") "What is the name?" (November)

"Do you know the name of the winner of the Ohio State House of Representatives seat from your district?" (If "yes") "What is the name?" (November)

POLITICAL KNOWLEDGE (SELF-ASCRIBED)

Sum of responses to the following items, divided into low, moderate, and high levels:

"Compared with other people you know, are you more informed or less informed about what is going on in politics in general?" (July)

"Compared with most people you know, are you more informed or less informed about what is going on in the 1972 presidential election campaign?" (September)

REPORTED INFLUENCE

Sum of responses to the following items, divided into low, moderate, and high levels:

"Did watching the Democratic National Convention on TV influence you in any way toward deciding who you will vote for in November?" (July)

"Did the news about Senator Eagleton in any way influence you in deciding who to vote for for President in November?" (July)

"Did watching the Republican National Convention on TV influence you in any way toward deciding who you will vote for in November?" (August)

"Has the selection of Sargent Shriver as George McGovern's running mate in any way influenced you in deciding who to vote for for President in November?" (August)

"Regardless of the source, has anything else you've learned during the campaign in the past four or five weeks influenced you in any way in deciding who you will vote for for President in November?" (September)

"Have these poll results influenced you in any way in deciding who to vote for?" (October)

"Has what you have heard about the Watergate story influenced you in any way in deciding who to vote for for President?" (October)

"Did watching either of these (Election Eve specials) programs influence your decision on whom to vote for for President?" (November)

"Did seeing these political commercials influence you in deciding which presidential candidate to vote for?" (November)

"Did knowing how the election was going before you actually went out to vote on November 7 influence you in any way in deciding which presidential candidate to vote for?" (November)

"Toward the end of the campaign there was a good deal of talk about a cease-fire in Vietnam. Did the report about Henry Kissinger's and President Nixon's peace efforts in Vietnam influence your vote for a presidential candidate a great deal, somewhat, or not at all?" (November)

SOCIAL CLASS MOBILITY

Comparison of respondent's education, occupation, and perceived social class with respondent's father's education, occupation, and perceived social class. (July)

SOCIOECONOMIC STATUS

Weighted index incorporating respondent's education, annual household income, and occupation. (July)

SHRIVER SELECTION, AWARENESS OF

"As you may have heard, George McGovern named a new running mate a few weeks ago. What is his name?" (August)

SHRIVER SELECTION, INFLUENCE OF

"Has the selection of Sargent Shriver as George McGovern's running mate in any way influenced you in deciding who to vote for for President in November?" (If "yes") "In what specific way did this influence your decision?" (August)

VOTE, VOTE PREFERENCE, AND STRENGTH OF COMMITMENT

"If you were to vote in November, which presidential candidate would you most likely vote for?" (July, August, September, October) (If preference named) "Right now, how strongly do you feel about your choice: very strongly, fairly strongly, or not very strongly?" (July, August, September, October)

(If respondent voted) "Which presidential candidate did you vote for—the Republican, Nixon; the Democrat, McGovern; the American Independent Party candidate, Schmitz; or who?" (November)

WATERGATE BREAK-IN, AWARENESS OF

"Several weeks ago some people were accused of breaking in and spying at the Democratic National Headquarters at the Watergate building in Washington, D.C. Have you heard anything in the news about this?" (October)

WATERGATE BREAK-IN, INFLUENCE OF

"Has what you have heard about the Watergate story influenced you in any way in deciding who to vote for for President?" (If "yes") "How has it influenced you?" (October)

WATERGATE BREAK-IN, RESPONSIBILITY FOR

"The Democrats claim that highly placed persons in the Nixon administration are responsible for the Watergate break-in and spying. The Republicans claim that no one highly placed in the Nixon administration is responsible for the Watergate break-in and spying. Who do you tend to believe: the Democrats or the Republicans?" (October)

BIBLIOGRAPHY

Alexander, H. E. 1972. "Broadcasting and Politics." In The Electoral Process, ed. M. K. Jennings and L. H. Ziegler. Englewood Cliffs: Prentice-Hall.

Atkin, C. K. 1973. "Instrumental Utilities and Information Seeking." In New Models for Mass Communication Research, ed. P. Clarke. Beverly Hills: Sage.

————, L. Bowen, and K. G. Sheinkopf. 1973. "Quality Versus Quantity in Televised Political Ads." Public Opinion Quarterly 37: 209-24.

Becker, L. B., M. E. McCombs, and J. M. McLeod. 1975. "The Development of Political Cognitions." In Political Communication, ed. S. H. Chaffee. Beverly Hills: Sage.

Berelson, B., P. Lazarsfeld, and W. McPhee. 1954. Voting. Chicago: University of Chicago Press.

Blumler, J. G., and D. McQuail. 1969. Television in Politics: Its Uses and Influence. Chicago: University of Chicago Press.

————, and J. M. McLeod. 1974. "Communication and Voter Turnout in Britain." In Sociological Theory and Survey Research, ed. T. Leggatt. Beverly Hills: Sage.

Campbell, A., G. Gurin, and W. E. Miller. 1954. The Voter Decides. Evanston: Row, Peterson.

————, P. E. Converse, W. E. Miller, and D. E. Stokes. 1960. The American Voter. New York: John Wiley.

Carter, R. F. 1962. "Some Effects of the Debates." In The Great Debates, ed. S. Kraus. Bloomington: Indiana University Press.

————. 1965. "Communication and Affective Relations." Journalism Quarterly 42: 203-12.

Chaffee, S. H. 1972. "The Interpersonal Context of Mass Communication." In Current Perspectives in Mass Communication Research, ed. F. G. Kline and P. J. Tichenor. Beverly Hills: Sage.

———. 1973. "Contingent Orientations and the Effects of Political Communication." Presented to the Speech Communication Association, New York City.

———, K. R. Stamm, J. L. Guerrero, and L. P. Tipton. 1969. Experiments on Cognitive Discrepancies and Communication. Journalism Monographs no. 14.

———, L. S. Ward, and L. P. Tipton. 1970. "Mass Communication and Political Socialization." Journalism Quarterly 47: 647-59.

———, J. M. McLeod, and D. Wackman. 1972. "Family Communication Patterns and Political Socialization." In Socialization to Politics, ed. J. Dennis. New York: Wiley.

Converse, P. E. 1966. "Information Flow and the Stability of Partisan Attitudes." In Public Opinion and Electoral Behavior, ed. E. Dreyer and W. Rosenbaum. Belmont, Calif.: Wadsworth.

———, A. Clausen, and W. Miller. 1965. "Electoral Myth and Reality: The 1964 Election." American Political Science Review 59: 321-36.

———, W. Miller, J. Rusk, and A. Wolfe. 1969. "Continuity and Change in American Politics: Parties and Issues in the 1968 Election." American Political Science Review 63: 1083-1105.

Dahl, R. A. 1957. "The Concept of Power." Behavioral Science 2: 201-18.

DeVries, W., and V. L. Tarrance. 1972. The Ticket Splitters. Grand Rapids, Mich.: W. B. Eerdmans.

Donohew, L., and L. Tipton. 1973. "A Conceptual Model of Information Seeking, Avoiding and Processing." In New Models for Mass Communication Research, ed. P. Clarke. Beverly Hills: Sage.

Dreyer, E. C. 1971. "Media Use and Electoral Choices: Some Political Consequences of Information Exposure." Public Opinion Quarterly 35: 544-53.

Easton, D. 1953. The Political System. New York: Knopf.

————, and J. Dennis. 1969. Children in the Political System: Origins
    of Political Legitimacy. New York: McGraw-Hill.

Edelstein, A. S. 1973. "Decision-Making and Mass Communication:
    A Conceptual and Methodological Approach to Public Opinion."
    In New Models for Mass Communication Research, ed. P.
    Clarke. Beverly Hills: Sage.

————, and D. P. Tefft. 1974. "Mass Credibility and Respondent
    Credulity with Respect to Watergate." Communication Research
    1: 426-48.

————. 1975. The Uses of Communication in Decision-Making. New
    York: Praeger.

Flanigan, W. H. 1972. The Political Behavior of the American
    Electorate. Boston: Allyn and Bacon.

Gamson, W. A. 1968. Power and Discontent. Homewood, Ill.:
    Dorsey.

Glenn, N. D. 1973. "Class and Party Support in the United States:
    Recent and Emerging Trends." Public Opinion Quarterly
    37: 1-20.

————, and T. Hefner. 1972. "Further Evidence on Aging and Party
    Identification." Public Opinion Quarterly 36: 176-87.

Hiebert, R. E., R. Jones, E. Lotto, and J. Lorenz, eds. 1971.
    Political Image Merchants: Strategy in New Politics.
    Washington, D.C.: Acropolis.

Holm, J., S. Kraus, and A. P. Bochner. 1974. "Communication and
    Opinion Formation: Issues Generated by the Watergate Hear-
    ings." Communication Research 1: 368-90.

Hovland, C. I., and W. Weiss. 1951. "The Influence of Source Credi-
    bility on Communication Effectiveness." Public Opinion
    Quarterly 15: 635-50.

Jennings, M. K., and R. G. Niemi. 1968. "The Transmission of
    Political Values from Parent to Child." American Political
    Science Review 62: 169-84.

Katz, E. 1968. "On Reopening the Question of Selectivity in Exposure
   to Mass Communications." In Theories of Cognitive Consistency: A Sourcebook, ed. R. P. Abelson, E. Aronson, W. J.
   McGuire, T. M. Newcomb, M. J. Rosenberg, and P. H.
   Tannenbaum. Chicago: Rand McNally.

————, and P. Lazarsfeld. 1955. Personal Influence. Chicago:
   University of Chicago Press.

————, J. G. Blumer, and M. Gurevitch. 1974. "Utilization of Mass
   Communication by the Individual." In The Uses of Mass Com-
   munication, ed. J. G. Blumer and E. Katz. Beverly Hills:
   Sage.

————, H. Hass, and M. Gurevitch. 1973. "On the Use of the Mass
   Media for Important Things." American Sociological Review
   38: 164-81.

Key, V. O. 1966. The Responsible Electorate. Cambridge, Mass.:
   Harvard University Press.

Klapper, J. T. 1960. The Effects of Mass Communications. New
   York: Free Press.

Krugman, H. E. 1965. "The Impact of Television Advertising:
   Learning Without Involvement." Public Opinion Quarterly
   29: 349-56.

Lang, K., and G. E. Lang. 1968. Politics and Television. Chicago:
   Quadrangle Books.

Langton, K. P. 1969. Political Socialization. New York: Oxford.

Lazarsfeld, P., B. Berelson, and H. Gaudet. 1948. The People's
   Choice. New York: Columbia University Press.

————, and R. K. Merton. 1948. "Mass Communication, Popular
   Taste and Organized Social Action." In The Communication of
   Ideas, ed. L. Bryson. New York: Harper.

Lippman, W. 1922. Public Opinion. New York: Macmillan.

McCombs, M. 1972. "Mass Communication in Political Campaigns:
   Information, Gratification and Persuasion." In Current Perspectives in Mass Communications Research, ed. F. G. Kline
   and P. J. Tichenor. Beverly Hills: Sage.

McCombs, M., and D. Shaw. 1972. "The Agenda-Setting Function of the Mass Media." Public Opinion Quarterly 36: 176-87.

McGinness, J. 1969. The Selling of the President, 1968. New York: Trident.

McLeod, J. M., and G. J. O'Keefe. 1972. "The Socialization Perspective and Communication Behavior." In Current Perspectives in Mass Communications Research, ed. F. G. Kline and P. J. Tichenor. Beverly Hills: Sage.

———, and L. B. Becker. 1974. "Testing the Validity of Gratification Measures Through Political Effects Analysis." In The Uses of Mass Communications, ed. J. G. Blumler and E. Katz. Beverly Hills: Sage.

———, L. B. Becker, and J. E. Byrnes. 1974. "Another Look at the Agenda Setting Function of the Press." Communication Research 1: 131-66.

Mendelsohn, H., and I. Crespi. 1970. Polls, Television and the New Politics. Scranton: Chandler.

———, G. J. O'Keefe, and J. Liu. 1975. "Mass Communications and Difficulty of Voter Decision Making: A Longitudinal Analysis of Two Elections." Department of Mass Communications, University of Denver.

Milbrath, L. W. 1965. Political Participation. Chicago: Rand McNally.

Miller, A., W. Miller, A. Raine, and T. Brown. 1973. "A Majority Party in Disarray: Policy Polarization in the 1972 Election." Ann Arbor: University of Michigan Center for Political Studies.

Nimmo, D. 1970. The Political Persuaders. Englewood Cliffs: Prentice-Hall.

O'Keefe, G. 1975. "Political Campaigns and Mass Communication Research." In Political Communication, ed. S. H. Chaffee. Beverly Hills: Sage.

———, and H. Mendelsohn. 1974. "Voter Selectivity, Partisanship and the Challenge of Watergate." Communication Research 1: 345-67.

Patterson, T., and R. McClure. 1974. "Political Advertising: Voter
    Reaction to Televised Political Commercials." Study no. 23,
    Citizens' Research Foundation, Princeton.

Robinson, J. P. 1974. "Public Opinion During the Watergate Crisis."
    Communication Research 1: 391-405.

Rossi, P. H. 1959. "Four Landmarks in Voting Research." In Amer-
    ican Voting Behavior, ed. E. Burdick and A. J. Brodbeck.
    Glencoe, Ill.: Free Press.

Sears, D. 1969. "Political Behavior." In Handbook of Social Psy-
    chology, ed. G. Lindsey and E. Aronson. Vol. 5. Readin,
    Mass.: Addison-Wesley.

——, and J. L. Freedman. 1967. "Selective Exposure to Information:
    A Critical Review." Public Opinion Quarterly 31: 194-213.

——, and R. Whitney. 1973. "Political Persuasion." In I. Pool
    et al., Handbook of Communication. Chicago: Rand McNally.

Sheingold, C. A. 1973. "Social Networks and Voting: The Resurrec-
    tion of a Research Agenda." American Sociological Review
    38: 712-21.

Shulman, M., and G. Pomper. 1975. "Variability in Election Behav-
    ior: Longitudinal Perspective from Causal Modeling." Amer-
    ican Journal of Political Science 19: 1-18.

Stewart, J. G. 1974. One Last Chance: The Democratic Party,
    1974-76. New York: Praeger.

Tannenbaum, P., B. Greenberg, and F. Silverman. 1962. "Candidate
    Images." In The Great Debates, ed. S. Kraus. Bloomington:
    University of Indiana Press.

Tipton, L., R. D. Haney, and J. R. Baseheart. 1975. "Media Agenda-
    Setting in City and State Election Campaigns." Journalism
    Quarterly 52: 15-22.

White, T. H. 1973. The Making of the President, 1972. New York:
    Atheneum.

——. 1975. Breach of Faith. New York: Atheneum.

ABOUT THE AUTHORS

HAROLD MENDELSOHN is Professor and Chairman in the Department of Mass Communications at the University of Denver where he has been a faculty member since 1962. Prior to joining the University of Denver, he served in a variety of research posts with the Psychological Corporation, the Bureau of Social Science Research, and the U.S. Department of State. During 1973-74, Dr. Mendelsohn served as President of the American Association for Public Opinion Research. He was elected a Fellow of the American Sociological Asso-ciation in 1961, and in 1975 he was elected a Fellow of the American Psychological Association.

Dr. Mendelsohn was a member of the U.S. Surgeon General's Scientific Advisory Committee on Television and Social Behavior, and he is a coauthor of the Committee's monograph-report, Television and Growing Up: The Impact of Televised Violence. Additionally, he is the author of Mass Entertainment, and is the coauthor with David Bayley of Minorities and the Police and with Irving Crespi of Polls, Television, and the New Politics.

Dr. Mendelsohn received his Ph.D. in Sociology from the New School for Social Research, his M.A. from Columbia University, and his B.S. from the City College of New York.

GARRETT J. O'KEEFE is an Associate Professor in the Department of Mass Communications at the University of Denver. He is an active member of the Association for Education in Journalism, the American Association for Public Opinion Research, and the American Psychological Association.

Dr. O'Keefe has contributed numerous pieces to scholarly journals and books in the communications field, and has worked on a variety of of research projects focusing on political communication behavior and political socialization.

Dr. O'Keefe received his Ph.D. from the University of Wisconsin-Madison in 1970, and has a background in professional journalism as well as political communication research and theory.

THE CONSTITUTION AND THE CONDUCT OF
FOREIGN POLICY

> Francis O. Wilcox
> Richard A. Frank

LEGISLATIVE POLITICS IN NEW YORK STATE:
A Comparitive Analysis

> Alan G. Hevesi

POLITICAL CLUBS IN NEW YORK

> Norman M. Adler
> Blanche Davis Blank
> Foreword by Roy V. Peel

STATE CONSTITUTIONAL CONVENTIONS: The
Politics of the Revision Process in Seven States

> Elmer E. Cornwell, Jr.
> Jay S. Goodman
> Wayne R. Swanson

COMMUNICATIONS AND PUBLIC OPINION: A
Public Opinion Quarterly Reader

> edited by Robert O. Carlson